RSAC

OCT   2008

The Entrepreneur's Guide to Managing Information Technology

Recent Titles in
The Entrepreneur's Guide

The Entrepreneur's Guide to Managing Growth and Handling Crises
Theo J. van Dijk

The Entrepreneur's Guide to Writing Business Plans and Proposals
K. Dennis Chambers

The Entrepreneur's Guide to Hiring and Building the Team
Ken Tanner

The Entrepreneur's Guide to Managing Information Technology

CJ Rhoads

PRAEGER

Westport, Connecticut
London

Library of Congress Cataloging-in-Publication Data

Rhoads, CJ
    The entrepreneur's guide to managing information technology / CJ Rhoads.
       p. cm.—(The entrepreneur's guide, ISSN 1939–2478)
    Includes bibliographical references and index.
    ISBN 978–0–275–99545–4 (alk. paper)
    1. Information technology—Management. 2. Management information systems.
    3. Business—Computer programs. I. Title.
    HD30.2.R525 2008
    004.068—dc22   2007048615

British Library Cataloguing in Publication Data is available.

Library of Congress Catalog Card Number: 2007048615
ISBN: 978–0–275–99545–4

First published in 2008

Praeger Publishers, 88 Post Road West, Westport, CT 06881
An imprint of Greenwood Publishing Group, Inc.
www.praeger.com

Printed in the United States of America

The paper used in this book complies with the
Permanent Paper Standard issued by the National
Information Standards Organization (Z39.48–1984).

10 9 8 7 6 5 4 3 2 1

Contents

Illustrations	vii
Acknowledgments	ix
Introduction	xiii
1. What Information Technology Is and Why We Need to Map It	1
2. Pounce Like a Panther	17
3. Why Non-IT People Find IT So Difficult	39
4. Why IT People Are So Difficult	52
5. The Essential Balance: Matching the Process	66
6. Why IT Vendors Are So Difficult	85
7. The Inside Secrets of Software and Hardware Vendors	104
8. Getting the Most from Networking	130
Appendices	157
A: Technology Map Examples	157
B: Common Technology Issues Most Business Leaders Experience	173
C: Basic IT Ability and Experience Sample Assessment	175
References	177
Index	179

Illustrations

TABLES

1.1 Calculating the Risk/Cost Benefit of IT Knowledge   5

1.2 PC Hardware Inventory Sample   14

FIGURES

I.1 Information Technology Investment in the United States   xvi

1.1 Partial Technology Map   11

3.1 Experience/Ability Chart   40

5.1 Euwish Insurance Company Internal Claim Process   74

5.2 Roles of the Information Technology Decision Maker   78

5.3 Internet Utilization by Decision Maker   79

5.4 Formula for Productivity   80

6.1 Length of Product Life   99

Acknowledgments

As those who have their names on the cover of a book know, no book is written solely by the author. A good book cannot exist without an entire team of people, and it is only by convention and convenience (not to mention space) that not all of those names appear on the cover. They are no less responsible for its birth than I.

If this book is a success, it will be due to the determined and intelligent assistance of many people, many of them my students, partners, and employees, who helped me with the hard labor of viewing, reviewing, discussing, arguing, revising, and redoing all of the work embedded within these pages. Those who specifically helped me by supplementing my knowledge with their expertise: Jack Bradt, Vanessa DiMauro, Francois Dumas, Pamela Gockley, Scott Herman, Brenda Moretti, Joe Puglisi, and Patrick Schmid. My graduate students also helped a great deal; they are: Anil Aras, Michael Axman, Robert Gourley, Julie Gower, Brett Harbach, Tammy Hein, Brian Meares, Susan Miller, Dave Musante, Mariya Papazova, Bryan Rathman, Andrew Sims, and Todd Dierksheide.

Additionally, tops in my book would be Jeff Olson, initially my agent, and then my series editor, and then my acquisitions editor, who worked tirelessly to make this series possible and had the judgment (whether good or not has yet to be seen) to ask me to step in as series editor when he moved up. I would also like to thank Nicholas Philipson, the original acquisition editor at Praeger, for his faith in this project. Furthermore, Andrea Clemente kept things on track and Marcia Goldstein ensured we had the right permissions from the right people.

The following people did the difficult task of reviewing various chapters of the book as it was being written: Bill Bauerle, Fred Beste, Polly Beste, David Bonner, Jack Bradt, Jeff Benzel, Joel Cardis, Greig Clark, Laura Donovan, Roger Ganser, Roger Hibbs, Con Karlson, Jan Lipper, George Lipper, John McNamara, Skip Torresson, and Molly Tremblay. The following people offered to review various chapters: Reuel Launey, Thomas Penn, Sandra Walker, David Freschman, Steve Meng, Lila Bellando, Dan Conley, Leigh Wood, Jay Coen Gilbert, Robert Clemens, Doug A. Bloom, Dan

McKinney, Sean Mallon, Laura Lorber, Anne Marie Smith, Michael Reddy, Fred Hafer, Jenn Mossholder, Maria Koba, John Moore, John R. Moore, Jon Reed, Anne Marie Smith, Gergely Tapolyai, and Carol Tunnessen.

Many of my clients appear in these pages, though few with their real names. In any case, my own knowledge is always expanded greatly by those for whom I serve, for I learn much from them in the course of our activities together. I'd especially like to extend my heartfelt thanks to Lee Baker, Peter Baker, David Bosler, David Dries, Bob Goodman, Michael Guido, Joanne Just, Conrad Karlson, Andy Klee, Pat Krick, Harriet Layton, Jane Palmer, Samantha Reimert, LuAnn Seyler, Patrick Sullivan, Anthony Triano, and Linda Wade.

Additionally, many CEOs and senior executives have taken time out of their busy schedules to appear on panels or speak on the topics presented here. I learned from each of them as well: Bill Alberte, Sandy Becker, Ed Barrett, Steve Bobick, Tom Baumann, Greg Baxter, Larry Bergman, Terry Carpenter, Dennis Cichelli, Andrew Downer, Don Gould, Dennis Hague, Keith Hill, John Kruglinski, Bob Lewis, Rob McCord, Ray Melcher, Brenda Moretti, Sean Moretti, Michael Mullen, Dianah Neff, Chris Miller, Jayashree Raman, Kevin Raudenbush, Edie Ritter, Harry Roberts, Bill Ruhl, Laura Scott, Shawn Shirk, Charles Sullivan, Rick Sutton, Brian Von Stetten, Phil Theis, Chet Winters, and John Weidenhammer.

Furthermore, even more CEOs and business owners took time to answer survey questions and speak with me at length about the challenges they face as they manage their information technology: James Adams, Vernon Babilon, Ed Barrett, Carolyn Bazik, Christopher Bernard, Chand Bhutra, Steve Bobick, Dale Bolger, Larry Bonfante, Ann Borza, Michael Boylan, William Buckholz, John Bungert, Rick Burkey, James Chan, Chris Del Valle, Joseph DiAngelo, Mark Dillon, Ann Earon, Jill Edwards, Bob Ehlinger, Suzanne Fairlie, William Flippin, Diane Galbraith, John Gantz, Paul Gentile, Matthew Gilbert, John Glaser, Lisa Guzzardo, David Haas, Scott Hafer, Robert Harrop, Michael Hund, Fidel Ikem, Werner John, Paul Jones, Charles Kelly, Andy Klee, Chris Kraras, Ginger Kunkel, Michael Lawrence, George Lipper, Daniel Little, Timothy Mack, Donald Martin, Laura Matrisciano, Terry Maurer, Dave Meckley, Charles Miller, Tom Murphy, Joseph Narieka, Stephanie Olexa, Steve Olshevski, Joe Ostraner, Robert Page, Melvin Pankuch, Gregory Payne, Michael Pellegrino, William Peterson, Susan Phillips Speece, Rick Principato, Joseph Puglisi, Ronald Rhode, Mark Rimler, Peter Rittenhouse, Jeff Salvino, Joseph Schaeffer, Lisa Scheller, Robin Schroeder, Grace Schuler, Anne Searle, Michael Shea, Ryan Smith, Helane Stein, Richard Stichter, Tom Stine, Camille Stock, Steven Talarico, Barry Unger, Jody Wagner, Peter Webster, Steve Willems, Charles Willis, Stacey Zbyszinski.

I would also like to thank the faculty and staff of the College of Business (in alphabetical order): Okan Akcay, Dan Benson, Pat Blatt, Henry Check, Donna DeLong, Arifeen Daneshyar, Mark Dinger, Ken Ehrensal, Tom Grant, Keshav Gupta, David Haas, John Hamrick, Ray Heimbach, Roger

Hibbs, Eileen Hogan, Fidel Ikem, Jonathan Kramer, John Kruglinski, James "Doc" Ogden, Patricia Patrick, Elisabeth Rogol, Paul Sable, Norman Sigmond, David Wagaman, and John Walker. Their encouragement and support enabled me to focus on writing two summers in a row. Additionally, I thank the employees of my business: Elle Hargrave, Stella Deeble, George Deeble, and Bonnie Taylor, who all had to put up with my split focus while I was writing.

Furthermore, several people picked up the slack for me in the Pacem In Vita program I developed—a leadership program for kids based on Taijiquan. I must thank Jack Solchurch, Judy Butler, Vicky Lee Levy, Luke Jih, Heidi Markwalder, Victoria Mehl, Judd Meinhart, Sandy Wise, and Bill Wheeler.

Of course none of this would be possible without my many mentors over the years (in alphabetical order): Fred Beste, Mike Bolton, David Bosler, Jack Bradt, Tom Casey, Betsy Chapman, Martin Cheatle, Jim Collins, Vanessa DiMauro, Jonathan Dreazen, Francois Dumas, Marsha Egan, Dale Falcinelli, John Lucht, John MacNamara, Nancy Magee, Ray Melcher, Pete Musser, Maggie Newman, Josephine Painter, Joe Puglisi, Leo Robb, Robert Rubin, Lee Scheele, Steve Sperling, Alan Weiss, and Kevin Wren. Though the amount of time I spent with each varied, each one has given me a gift that has turned out to be of extreme value in my never-ending quest to improve myself.

No list would be complete without my fabulous family: my mother, Judith Liffick, and my father, Martin Devlin, and his wife, Jeri, along with my brothers and sisters, Jeffrey Devlin (and his wife Melissa), T. Max Devlin, Eileen Piccolo, and Denise Rankin. I also received a great deal of help and advice from several of my accomplished aunts and uncles, most of whom are authors in their own right: Tom and Barb Liffick, Blaise and Alana Liffick, Kathy Liffick, Mike Lillich, Charles and Elsie Jane Lorber, and Anita and Gary Young. I wish to thank Marianne Pawlikowski as well—who provided the LBI getaway that formed the backdrop of many hours of my writing.

For anyone who I have inadvertently left off this list, I am heartily sorry. My own feeble-minded brain does the best that it can, but it is far from perfect.

Most important of all, of course, is my patient and loving husband Bob. He is my life and my world, and I am so lucky to have found my soul mate and true love so early in my life. To have spent the past 26 years with a man of his incredible talents would have been a treat to anyone, but to have loved him, and been loved by him, all that time is a pleasure of epic proportion.

Introduction

WHY YOU SHOULD READ THIS BOOK

As an entrepreneur and/or business owner, do you ever make decisions that involve information technology? (Throughout this book, I will use the terms *technology, information technology,* and *IT* interchangeably. The definition will be explored in detail in a later chapter, but keep in mind that I do not limit technology to hardware and software. *Information technology* includes the people and processes as well.)

Have you ever made a technology decision that, in retrospect, turned out to be a mistake? You're not alone. The information in this book will improve your track record in making decisions involving information technology. The information described here will help you assess past decisions and will provide guidelines as you make decisions in the future. This information will enable your organization to experience smooth computing, the holy grail of effective organizations and profitable businesses.

Some guidelines you may recognize immediately as functional. You might find that you've been using them without realizing it. Others may strike you as counterintuitive, or will go against what others have told you. But you will find that, in practice, following these guidelines will work, for you and your organization.

Few Know the Secrets or Understand Their Importance

Making the right information technology decision is actually relatively rare. The Standish Group published the "CHAOS" report in 1995, noting that only 9 percent of the technology projects in large companies were successful. That same study reported that even successful technology projects fulfilled only an average of 42 percent of their original requirements. Even the Gartner Group reported that 70 percent of technology projects did not deliver the expected benefits—and the Gartner Group relies upon the vendor community for income and would prefer to report that most technology projects are successful.

My experience mirrors these grim statistics. Most technology projects end up achieving no more than a mere shadow of their original goals— even, or especially, the ones that are paraded as successes by those who initiated or paid for the projects. People who worked on the project know the truth—the project was actually a failure by all objective standards of measure.

The fact is, there are many more technology losers (leaders who make the wrong decision) than technology winners (leaders who make the right decision). The difference between the two is not whether they make mistakes—they all make mistakes. The difference is whether they learn from their mistakes or keep making the same mistakes over and over and over again. This book will set you on the path to becoming a technology winner—someone who makes the right decisions and understands how to get the best value for your money.

Examples abound. A failed baggage-handling project at the new Denver airport cost the city $1.1 million per day for months in 1994 and delayed the opening of the new airport for over a year.[1] Hershey Foods lost millions when a new financial system it installed did not produce as promised in 1999. In January 2005, FBI Director Robert S. Mueller III announced the scrapping of a $170 million system called Virtual Case File after an independent research report concluded that the system's design "is not now and unlikely to be an adequate tool."

The leaders who decided to invest in these projects were not stupid. They were probably intelligent, dedicated executives making what they thought at the time was the best decision. But an experienced technology decision maker like me could tell from the very beginning that they were doomed to fail. If it was so easy for me to spot, then why did these executives decide to do these projects? Even more important, given the track record of most decision makers, why do business leaders continue to make the same mistakes over and over? We will explore not just the answer to those questions, but what they could have done differently that would have saved them from the failed projects.

This book is especially important for entrepreneurs, CEOs, business owners, and executives—leaders all—whose organizations rely upon technology, but who have a difficult time understanding what makes a good decision and a bad decision. Sometimes I talk with entrepreneurs and business leaders who tell me that they don't make any technology decisions. But research shows that leaders make between one and five significant technology decisions each day, and the majority of leaders dedicate up to 12 hours per week gathering information to make decisions.[2] Just the fact that business leaders think that they are not making technology decisions shows how large the gap is. Here is the fact: There are no businesses that aren't impacted by information technology. All businesses are influenced by information technology either directly or indirectly, and all business decisions are technology decisions.

The Impact of Information Technology on Business

Jim Collins reported the following conversation in his best-selling book.[3]

Taking a short break from the rigors of writing this book, I traveled to Minnesota to teach sessions at the Masters Forum. The Masters Forum has held executive seminars for the past fifteen years, and I was curious to know which themes appeared repeatedly over those years. "One of the consistent themes," said Jim Ericson and Patty Griffin Jensen, the program directors, "is technology, change, and the connection between the two."

"Why do you suppose that is?" I asked.

"People don't know what they don't know," they said. "And they're always afraid that some new technology is going to sneak up on them from behind and knock them on the head. They don't understand technology, and many fear it. All they know for sure is that technology is an important force of change, and that they'd *better pay attention to it.* [Emphasis added]

The impact of information technology over the past few years cannot be overemphasized. The most recent publication of the World Economic Outlook in 2001 by the International Monetary Fund identified the change as a "revolution." The impact of information technology on economic growth went from 17 percent (from 1974 to 1990) to 25 percent (from 1991 to 1995) to 50 percent from 1996 to 2000.

The comparative investment businesses make in technology has skyrocketed in the past two decades. During the 1970s and early 1980s it was typical to see from 3 percent to 5 percent of business expenses spent on technology. Since the late 1980s, it is much more typical to see between 7 percent and 45 percent (depending upon the type of business). Figure I.1 shows the investment in information technology products. Furthermore, exports went from less than 1 percent of GDP (gross domestic product) to 11 percent of GDP. (In case you are wondering, that's roughly $1.3 trillion!)

WHAT AN ENTREPRENEUR CAN DO

How can we ensure that we are making the right technology decision at the right time? How can we be sure that we are getting the value we expected? How can we avoid the mistakes of the 91 percent of failed projects? What can we do to maximize our limited resources? That's what this book is all about.

The solution to technology problems is a combination of experience and research. Research shows that top-performing companies are very careful about the money they spend on information technology. They work hard at ensuring that they are making the right information technology decision at the right time. The harder task is to clarify exactly *how* those top-performing companies made the right information technology decision at the exact right

Figure I.1
Information Technology Investment in the Unites States*

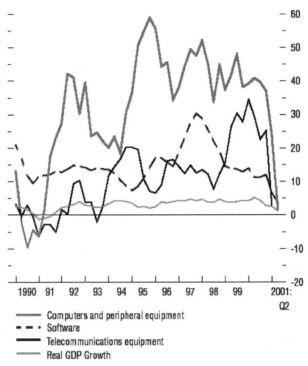

Computers and peripheral equipment
Software
Telecommunications equipment
Real GDP Growth

Source: U.S. Department of Commerce, Bureau of Economic Analysis.
*Real gross fixed investment.

time. That's where experience—one thing this book offers—can step in to get the job done.

The consequences of a failed information technology project can be dreadful and unexpected. A bad decision can cost money, careers, companies, and lives. With a little more knowledge, however, bad decisions can be avoided.

It Ain't Rocket Science

Just because making the right decision at the right time is rare doesn't mean that it is difficult. It may seem like enchanted magic to those who haven't done it yet, but it is easier than it looks—once you know how. This book will tell you what the vendors and technology people won't—the secret to making the right decision at the right time.

You might be asking: If it is so easy, why don't those who are knowledgeable share this information? The most accurate answer is that they might not know that others don't know what they know. Or they don't even know what they know because the knowledge has become intuitive and implicit. But there might be another reason. For most vendors and consultants, sharing the inside secrets would likely hit them in the pocketbook.

Nicholas Carr[4] and Paul Strassmann[5] are right on target when they claim that business leaders spend too much money on information technology and don't get enough value. There is a huge knowledge gap between those who know, and those who don't, and those who don't know are paying the price to those who do know.

These esteemed researchers aren't saying that information technology is not important (despite the provocative names of their books). What they are saying is that IT no longer guarantees a competitive advantage all by itself. The alignment between IT and the organization is the determining factor between winners and losers in business. Many businesses spend a lot of money, but don't know how to achieve that magical alignment, so their IT alignment is wasted.

You Can't Learn to Ride a Bike from a Book

Alas, you may read this entire book and still not benefit from the lessons right away. Books, seminars, workshops—they all can introduce the concepts and set the stage, but they are just a beginning. To learn something, really learn it, we need to actually experience success doing it multiple times. We need constant reinforcement, encouragement, and guidance. David Sandler understood that when he wrote the book *You Can't Teach a Kid to Ride a Bike at a Seminar.* He likens the process of learning to ride a bike with learning how to do other things (in his case, selling). We can't learn anything overnight, and we can't apply knowledge if we don't get the right kind of circumstances to practice with. Consider this book an ongoing reference as you work to manage technology better in the coming years. The technology terms may well become out of date, but the guidelines discussed here have stood the test of three decades of time. *They* will not go out of date. The more often you recognize the situations discussed here, and apply the lessons learned, the more you will get out of this book.

A SMORGASBORD OF COMMON SENSE

It may sound cliche, but I stand on the shoulders of giants. If you're an avid reader of Drucker,[6,7] Peters,[8] Deming,[9] Covey,[10] Collins,[3,11,12] Hammer,[13] Strassmann,[5] Carr,[4] and Weiss,[14] you will recognize the underlying current of their commonsense words flowing throughout this book: Pay attention to the customer. Focus on what you're good at. Begin with the end in mind. Lead, don't manage. Establish good, principled relationships. Distinguish between that which can be changed from that over which you have no control. The process, not the technology, is important. Be passionate in your search for excellence. Common sense sells.

Despite having eaten at the table of others' labors, the full responsibility for this particular meal is mine. Like a cook who can take the raw materials and knows just what to add to serve up a delicious meal, my unique experiences have led me to observe trends and connections that seem to be hidden to many others. I hope you find this book to be a smorgasbord of chewable advice and succulent knowledge to which you return for sustenance again and again. If this book is a spectacular success, it will be for two reasons: (1) the quality of the ingredients provided by the masters, as well as (2) the support, encouragement, and feedback of those listed in the acknowledgment pages. There are literally hundreds of people who, over the years, have sparked an inspiration, contributed ideas, or helped with logistics. They deserve all the credit.

Read on as we share the secret recipe for successfully planning our information technology strategy.

1

What Information Technology Is and Why We Need to Map It

Before we can manage information technology, we must learn enough about it so that we do not appear to be philistines in the digital age. This knowledge will make it easier to direct people adequately and make the right decisions. Do not fear; this book will not be a dull recitation of buzzwords. (However, for your reference an introduction to information technology concepts can be found on my Web site, http://ETMAssociates.com/ITConcepts/. Just enter the password INeedATechMap.)

This first chapter focuses on defining information technology, calculating the risk of not understanding it, and explaining the concept of the technology map and why you need it.

WHAT INFORMATION TECHNOLOGY IS

What comes to mind when someone says "information technology" or "IT"? Well, for many people, nothing comes to mind. They don't recognize the term. IT terminology keeps changing so it is difficult to keep up. Other terms that mean virtually the same thing are *computer*, *personal computer (PC)*, *microcomputer*, *data processing (DP)*, *electronic data processing (EDP)*, *information processing*, *data systems*, *information systems (IS)*, *computer systems*, *mainframe computer systems*, *document management*, *information management*, *systems management*, *communication networks*, *electronic communications*, and *cyberspace*.

For this book, information technology is a bit broader than any of these individual components. Let's define *information technology* as "the people, processes, software, and hardware that make up the information flow in the operations of an organization."

Notice that *people* is listed first, and *hardware* last—purposefully. A common point of confusion is thinking that information technology is just the hardware and software. People and processes are much more critical components. We can't discuss any one without discussing all the others.

Furthermore, the connections between these components are more important than any one of the individual components. A common root cause for failed technology systems is an incompatibility between the people, the processes, and the hardware/software chosen. It is often the case that, if evaluated individually, each component works just fine. People may be dedicated and hardworking. Processes may be well defined and top-notch. Hardware may be the best that money could buy. Software may be well designed and bug-free. But together, they just don't work. We can't talk about technology without talking about the relationships among all the components.

Having said that, this book is not really about information technology itself. This is an entrepreneur's guide on how to manage information technology, which means how to manage the people and processes, as well as the software and hardware. This is a book on making decisions about information technology.

Technology leadership is as important for the managing executives of a large Fortune 500 company as it is for the new entrepreneur. There is a difference, however. Executives and managers can rely upon the people in the technology division within their company to actually do the managing (although as you read on, you'll learn why they shouldn't abdicate to them). Entrepreneurs, on the other hand, often don't have the same level of resources, and their level of risk rises with their lack of knowledge about the technology. While everyone can use this book, for entrepreneurs the information is absolutely vital and found nowhere else.

The first step in understanding the importance of information technology is to calculate the risk of making the wrong decision regarding it.

Calculating the Risk

Very few people go to the trouble of calculating the cost of ignorance in any field, much less information technology. Often it seems that not knowing something is not our fault, or a petty issue, or simply not important. Because each problem by itself seems so small, we falsely believe we can ignore it. Many businesspeople think that learning the details of technology is beneath them—similar to the unwillingness of senior leaders of a bygone era to learn how to type (i.e., "That's what secretaries are for.").

I had one client, Jackie, who insisted that she had a few minor problems, but they were "nothing she couldn't handle" and it "wasn't causing that much of an issue." After doing an assessment (see Appendix B), we narrowed down her problems to two very common ones. Her company was: (1) spending money on software that didn't work as promised; and (2) unsure that the computer systems were going to be safe in the event of a disaster. After a little thinking, she realized that in addition to the $12,000 she had spent in one year on a particular software application that still wasn't working, there was the $4,000 she had spent for a week of a consultant's time and the $3,000 salary she had paid the other two people in her company who were working on the problem. Then she realized that she had to add the missing $80,000 in increased income that she had expected from the working software, and the $10,000 that she had expected to save by retiring the old computer system the software was supposed to replace.

Just one small failed project, caused by the fact that she didn't know something she should have known, cost the company over $105,000. That's a big chunk for a company with only $2 million in revenues and losses that year of $75,000. And Jackie told me she could think of three different technology projects that had similar outcomes. The key is that these problems would have disappeared had she just taken the time to understand the technical issues instead of ignoring them.

Like many business leaders, Jackie viewed the technical issues as "not under her purview." Information technology issues are the director of information system's problem, aren't they? Getting the *Enterprise* to hit warp speed was Scotty's problem, not Captain Kirk's, wasn't it?

Well, here's the question: Did Captain Kirk expect Scotty to hit warp 20? Of course not—everyone knows that the best the *Enterprise* could do was warp 10. Did Kirk expect Scotty to run the ship without dilithium crystals? Of course not. Everyone knows that a starship needs dilithium crystals. Business leaders need to have enough general knowledge and understanding of IT issues so that they don't have expectations beyond what's possible. If business leaders expect that a new system can be implemented without first spending six months cleaning up the data, they are demonstrating a lack of knowledge about IT. If business leaders expect people to be just as productive on a new system after only one week of training, they have unrealistic expectations. These kinds of information technology failures are costing businesses billions of dollars every year. So the answer is no: IT issues cannot be separated from business issues, and therefore must be the entrepreneur's problem, the business owner's problem, and not the IT director's problem.

It is difficult for us entrepreneurs to get our heads around the cost of ignorance. Consider the question of how much a business should spend to keep the systems up and running in the event of a disaster. When I ask the question "What is your information technology worth to you?" most entrepreneurs have a hard time answering. The whole thing is too big for most people to get their minds around. But if a business owner spends too much money on disaster recovery to keep the business "safe," he or she risks losing the business, because the costs can exceed the profits needed to keep the business going. The business's competitors might only spend 10 percent on disaster recovery. If there really were a disaster, the business that invested in disaster recovery technology might continue while the competitor would not. But if there isn't a disaster, the business owner would go out of business and the competitor would continue!

We can calculate properly the value of our IT by taking it just one system at a time. What if there were a fire in the room with the computer? Well, we'd lose the computer. Let's say that the cost to replace the hardware and software was $15,000. The data are even more important. If we have to hire people to re-enter just one month's worth of data, it might cost—say, three people at $15 per hour for two weeks—$3,600. Multiply that by 12 months, and the cost would be $43,200. Suddenly the cost of a special computer-safe fire extinguisher isn't that much (but the cost of a completely outfitted backup site might be too much).

Let's look at another example of risk calculation, this time dealing with the cost of technical support incompetence. I have a friend, Bob, who is a CEO of a relatively small company, and he complained to me about having to send his laptop back to the technical support people three times before they finally replaced the whole thing. He considered it an inconvenience, but not worth the effort to fix.

But then I walked Bob through the real cost of the incompetent technicians who took three tries to get it right. Bob's time is valuable. Imagine that, at his salary, packing up and shipping the laptop three times would cost about $450. Add to that $30 a piece for shipping, and $225 for the techs' time. And, of course, the final cost of replacing the laptop at $4,000. Now we're up to $4,765. If this is an average cost of a problem, and there are 50 problems like that a year—that's $238,250. Not chicken feed.

One of the most important parts of the equation, however, is the cost of lost opportunity. Bob was highly involved in the sales process. He was just about out of commission the entire time his laptop was gone. How much more could he have made for the company? Which opportunities were lost because he was trying to get his laptop working?

The high cost of lost opportunity was brought home to me when I was speaking at an event run by a chapter of the Association of Information Technology Professionals (AITP). One of the members, Chuck, a VP of sales, talked at length about his knowledge management system, an electronic library of information made available to those who need it. The knowledge system aggregated information about the products of his company as well as facts about their competitor's offering. The knowledge system cost about $300,000 to put together. Chuck's bosses were constantly howling about the high cost.

Then one day Chuck was on the phone with the company's top customer—a company worth well over $15 million in annual sales. The customer was unhappy and threatening to take his business to the company's competitor. Chuck was desperate. Thinking quickly, while he was on the phone with the customer he pulled up everything he could on the competitor from the knowledge base—and he came up with a fact about the competitor that, once revealed to the customer, made the customer stay with his company. He relayed this story to his boss, and complaints about the cost of the system were never heard again. Cost: $300,000. Savings: $15 million in five minutes. That's quite a return on investment (ROI).

Here's a short exercise. Calculate the value of increasing your knowledge about information technology. Choose a typical initiative or project in your company, then put a value on each of the items listed in Table 1.1.

Multiply your results by the number of typical projects in a year. This is just a rough estimate, but once all the amounts are added together, you might have a better idea of the value of learning more about information technology. This is a lot of risk.

Table 1.1
Calculating the Risk/Cost Benefit of IT Knowledge

Category	$ Cost
Replacement value of existing hardware/software	
Value of our time	
Value of others' time	
Cost of lost opportunity	
Increase in income	

WHY WE NEED A TECHNOLOGY MAP

Whether you are a technology person who has learned the business side, or a businessperson who has learned the technology side, you probably already have, inside your head, a technology map.

A *technology map* is a mental map of how technology works—how the different components of the systems in your company fit together. The map gives us a good understanding of how technology interacts and fits together. The map demonstrates the layering effect of IT.

What does that mean? Technology layers fit together like the layers of an onion, and each one can be peeled, one by one. Entrepreneurs make better technology decisions when they understand how to peel the onion, when they can envision the map and all the related layers. If we have a map of all the different layers and the way they are connected to each other, we can see where new concepts, buzzwords, and descriptions should be placed on the map. We can see where some items inherit certain characteristics because of their location or their relationship to the other items on the map. We can more easily see what portions (if any) can be replaced. We can also more easily tell when something is missing.

Think of it this way: A translator knows that there must be a verb somewhere in the sentence even if she doesn't know which word is the verb. If a translator is reading a sentence and can't find the verb, she knows that something is missing, and that the sentence is incomplete. Similarly, a technical person knows that there must be an operating system in the technology even if she doesn't know which operating system is there. If it's not obviously apparent, the technical person would ask the vendor about the operating system and would know by the answer which hardware the software runs on.

There are several reasons why we need a map. By envisioning the layers in a mental map, we can translate between the specific examples in our own systems and the general components that exist in the industry. We know which vendors we should be talking with. We will know what we can, and cannot, buy.

One of my clients was a large regional bank. At this bank, the department heads made many of the technology decisions. The loan department was headed up by Sam, an experienced executive in banking, but not so experienced in IT. Sam saw a demonstration of a loan-decision support application at a conference—and he was dazzled. Sam knew that his existing system (which was PC based) could not do all the marvelous things that this software could do. He figured that he could make more loans of higher quality and would need fewer loan officers with this new software. His ROI calculation showed that it would pay for itself within a few months. So he adjusted his department budget and wrote out a check for $100,000 to buy the software. When the installation tapes arrived, he sent them down to the system administrators in the information technology department to install.

There was only one problem: The software ran only on a mainframe computer. This particular department of the bank ran only small microcomputers. Sam had never even thought to ask on which kind of computer the software ran. He didn't realize that even if the systems people made arrangements to use the software, it would have taken four times the cost of the software to install a mainframe and hire the expertise necessary to run it. (So much for the ROI.)

You wouldn't buy new tires for your car without first checking to see if they fit the wheels, would you? And yet entrepreneurs and business leaders purchase technology all the time without first checking to see if it fits into the existing environment.

Because a technology map gives us a starting point for questions, we can use it to help us detect the difference between hype and reality. Furthermore, the technology map will help entrepreneurs understand how to tell when is the best time to make purchases.

Probably the most important reason we need the technology map is so that we can talk sensibly to those who are actually implementing the technology. Having a well-formed map will gain the respect of the information technology folk.

Sam wasted $100,000 simply because he didn't have a technology map. But that wasn't his biggest problem. Even more important, Sam lost the respect of the people under him and became a laughingstock. The technical folks still circulate the story, years later, with glee. They can't wait to tell new people joining the company about Sam's "great" software purchase. I was there less than a week before I heard the story (to many guffaws), but I wasn't surprised when I checked it out and found that it was true. To avoid the same fate, we can work to improve our own technology maps.

There are hundreds of stories similar to this one—you can probably think of a few yourself. But how do we avoid these mistakes?

Getting over the Hump

Due to the complexity and newness of much of technology, it is easy to understand why business leaders commonly respond, "I don't need to know that," when someone tries to explain it. In such cases, they let other people make the critical decisions for them. The problem is that the people making the decision often don't have the same vested interest in the business, or they have different criteria for success than the business leader. They won't necessarily make the right decision.

Is it any wonder the technology rarely accomplishes the desired return? In an even worse scenario (because the technology leaders don't understand the underlying technology but can't admit it), the decision makers can be "wowed" by polished salespeople striving to make a sale. Since the salespeople often don't understand the technology themselves, they make promises they just can't keep, and the buyer is always the loser.

Even if business leaders do try to attempt to understand their own information technology, they may become frustrated by the confusing technical jargon and contemptuous attitudes of some technical people.

In my role as a technology educator, I have heard thousands of complaints about how difficult technology concepts are to learn, and how impatient technology people are in explaining them. The funny part is, I have also listened to countless CIOs and technical people who complain about the overwhelming challenge and complexity of business and corporate culture.[15] I agree—corporate culture and business acumen are extremely hard to learn. I remember in 1986, as a school teacher starting my first business, I encountered the term "marketing" and had no idea what it meant. I tried to get my brother-in-law (who had a business degree) to explain it to me, but it seemed like it took me forever to understand the concept. My brother-in-law became impatient with my inability to understand what, to him, was a simple business concept. But I was a teacher. I had no context for the term.

Good business leaders learned all those business concepts over many, many years and within the context of running businesses. Business leaders immediately know the following terms: *finance, sales, marketing, operations, process flow, capitalization, expenses, receivables, payables,* etc. These terms are easy for businesspeople to understand but, believe it or not, hard to explain outside the context of a business. Similarly, technology people immediately understand terms like *operating systems, network interface cards, Internet protocols, printer drivers,* and *Web monitors* without even thinking about it. But they are difficult to explain outside of the context of information technology.

IT terms are not difficult; they just haven't had time to permeate our culture yet. The next time you feel frustrated because an IT person seems to be talking Greek, consider this analogy. Imagine that it is your job to help some people who were magically transported here from the 1840s. Now give them a road map and explain to them how to drive to New York.

Today, we can count on people having a certain amount of general knowledge about cars, roads, maps, and so on. For example, when we look at a map, we know immediately that the big thick lines are interstate highways, the smaller red lines are two-lane roads, the big blue splotches are bodies of water. We already know that we are going to get into a car and drive on those roads, and we intuitively understand the relationship between the car we drive and the representation of the roads on the paper. We also know different brands of cars (Porsche, Cadillac, Mercedes, Toyota, etc.), and we can picture them in our minds. We even know a bit about the social status of the people driving them based upon the brands. We know that if we go on a long trip, we will stop for gas on the way. We already know how to put gas in our car. We know that eventually we will need to change the oil and put in new brake pads. We grew up with the knowledge. We don't have to explain any of that to someone today, so giving them a map and telling them how to drive to New York would be simple.

But the people who grew up in the 1840s don't have the benefit of that background knowledge. They still live in a world filled with horses and buggies. They've never been in a car. They don't know what a paved road is. If we were tasked with explaining not only the map, but all the background information that goes into the context of what the road map is and how it works, we might show a bit of impatience and frustration, too.

But the difficulty just increases the importance. Don't you, as an entrepreneur and business leader, really appreciate when the technology folks learn a bit about the profit-and-loss nature of business, or work harder at getting along with others? Similarly, technology folks generally have much more respect for business leaders who learn a bit about the categories of information technology. To speak with them, we need a technology map.

Categories, Brands, and Providers

To make sense of the map, it must be put into the context of the categories, the brands, and the providers of the information technology within our businesses. We need to understand what we have, as well as the characteristics of each brand and provider within each category for each layer of the map.

To give a nontechnical example, if we purchase a Porsche, we know that we are going to get an expensive, fast car that others envy. That tells us something about where we should store it. We wouldn't put it unattended in a crime-infested center city lot. But if we buy a Hyundai, we know that we will get an inexpensive, affordable ride. We wouldn't build a beautiful garage for it, and we wouldn't expect to open it up by going 120 mph on the highway, either.

Now for a technical example. If the layer we are replacing is a database and we are considering DB2, Oracle, SQL, or Sybase, we would need to know that DB2 and Oracle are robust and expensive, SQL is cheaper and easier, and Sybase is entrenched as the database of choice for Wall Street systems. We also need to know that DB2 needs a mainframe computer from IBM, Oracle does not work well in any Windows environment, and SQL does not work well in a UNIX environment. Putting SQL on a mainframe would be like putting that Hyundai in a huge custom-built marble garage; it wouldn't make any sense. Putting Oracle on a Windows-based machine is like trying to drive the Porsche on a dirt road. Furthermore, if we only need to support 20 people accessing the database, we would know that Oracle is overkill (like buying a 747). Nor would we try to squeeze 200 people into a tiny plane, which is what putting 200 people on SQL would be like.

> If these terms are not recognized, you may want to first review the Information Technology Concepts book from the http://ETMAssociates.com/ ITConcepts Web site. Also keep in mind that these examples are oversimplifications for illustration purposes. The vendors would not necessarily place limitations on their software.

Understanding New Technology

Having a technology map enables us to quickly understand new technologies even if we've never heard of them before. Back in 1998, I was asked to take over a mainframe conversion project in my role as a vice president at a large credit card company. I had a deep understanding of some of the branches of the map (applications, databases, and networking), but I didn't know anything about mainframes or development tools. Because of the map, I was able to quickly relate new terms and concepts to what I already knew. The words were different, but all the layers were there in one way or another. Keep in mind that I had to make these translations. Even mainframe programmers and systems analysts often have not developed a technology map. Since they've only worked on one system that is not separated into components and is purchased all from a single vendor, they don't understand it the same way.

For example, in a PC, two of the layers in the main hardware are the central processing unit (CPU, the brains) and the hard drive (HD, the storage). On a mainframe, the equivalents are the processor (the brains) and the direct access storage disk (DASD, pronounced "dazzdy"). The first time someone used the term *DASD* and I asked what that was, the person gave me a long drawn-out explanation that I didn't quite understand. But I sensed a similarity, so we kept circling the concept until I figured out that DASD is like a hard drive.

I used the same trick when I first heard the term *IPL*. I quickly figured out that to IPL a mainframe is the same as booting up a PC. Same concept, different terminology. Piece by piece I found all the mainframe terms for the already familiar PC terms I knew.

The best place to use the technology map is when working with vendors. Imagine that a vendor is telling us about a new product called Malugas. We have never heard of it, so we ask what it is and the vendor tells us that Malugas is a Web server. If we understand the technology map, knowing that Malugas is a Web server tells us what it does (monitors the network card for requests to see Web pages across the Internet). We would also immediately be able to name four or five competitors (like Apache, IIS, or iPlanet). Furthermore, without even asking, we will understand what kind of hardware it sits on (multiuser server, either Windows NT, Windows 2003 Server, or a flavor of Unix, but not Windows XP or any other desktop system). We would also know what kind of software interacts with it (browser programs such as Internet Explorer, Firefox, or Safari).

But what if we were told that Malugas is an enterprise database? We would immediately know what it does (stores related tables of information), be able to name four or five competitors (like Oracle, SQL, DB2, or Sybase), know what kind of hardware it sits on (probably a multiuser server, definitely not a desktop), and what kind of software it interacts with (application programs coded in many different languages like Java and Visual Basic). This immediate recall of all the different characteristics of each layer or branch enables technology people to understand the strengths and weaknesses of each new product that is introduced by placing it on the map. The new product gains all of the characteristics of the current brand and provider already in the category on the map.

Difficulty of Sharing Maps

Over the years as I've taught people the importance of this concept, I have tried numerous times to illustrate a single all-encompassing technology map. Every time I tried to diagram the technology map, however, I realized that:

- It represented only the last environment I was in and was often inappropriate as an example for the person to whom I was showing it.
- It was too shallow in some areas and too deep in others for the purposes of the person to whom I was showing it.
- It was often already out of date and incorrect, and it often represented categories that no longer existed.

The upshot is that each technology map is unique, and one person's map may simply confuse other people (especially if it is the only example they see). I might show you an example of my company's systems (which are highly virtual and Web based), but if your company relies upon mainframes, it would just be confusing.

In Appendix A, you will find several example maps. Hopefully the variety of maps will help you understand the potential scope and size of your own information technology map. But remember—each company's map is unique. The important activity for you is to develop your own map. That said, Figure 1.1 is just one part of a sample map that reflects the unique system of a particular company's IT system.

Starting Point: Hardware and Software Inventory

We don't need a map of Utah if we are driving around in New York. But if we are driving in New York, we'd better have a map of New York. We don't need to understand every single type of information technology to make good decisions, we just need to understand our own.

Figure 1.1
Partial Technology Map

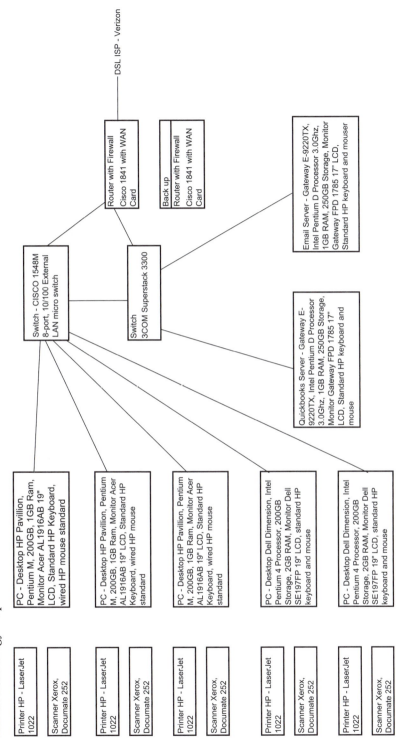

This is part of the technology map (Appendix A) done by Mariya Papazova. Used with permission.

We should start with our own inventory of hardware and software. For each layer we should know the name of the application, and the names of the vendors, and where they fit in the industry among their competitors. We need to know if we are using the Lexus of the industry, or if we are riding in a Chevy.

You may find that it is harder to get a simple inventory than you expect it to be. Leslie is one of my clients, the vice president of information systems (IS) at a $100 million manufacturer. At the time, in 1999, Leslie was new to her role in IS. When she asked her staff to provide an inventory of hardware and software, she was given a short list that included one minicomputer, 27 terminals, three routers, and five software programs. She immediately realized that this could not be the complete list (after all, there was a PC on her desk and it was not on the list). In this company, since the departments themselves purchased their own PCs and servers, the IS department did not keep an inventory. Her staff offered to walk through the data center and count what was there—but there was no way to tell what else was in use at other locations.

This is not a minor matter, and in this case not having an up-to-date inventory cost this company huge dollars. Remember the year this happened—1999, just before Y2K (the year 2000). Y2K is well known in IT circles because so many systems were built without the foresight to use four-digit years (due to the high cost of memory in the early years). During that transition year, when 99 was greater than 00, many systems would fail to function.

Leslie was told by the CEO when she first started that she had only two weeks to make a decision regarding the new purchasing system, which had to be installed by December 31, 1999. Two weeks was not enough time to get a complete inventory for 200 employees spread out over three locations. Leslie was forced to make a decision without knowing what hardware and software the company already owned.

Leslie chose a Unix-based purchasing system. She thought she had made a great choice, and that everyone would love the neat new features of the sophisticated system.

The problems started right away. First, the new system required a certain kind of software called a terminal client to be installed on the PCs. Unfortunately, the terminal client only worked with Windows 98, and many of the PCs in the departments were still using Windows 95 (some even Windows 3.1).

Additionally, the new Unix-based system was still a green screen (no colors, just text) and used function keys to access and manipulate the menus. The employees were used to the graphics color screens of the old system. Employees expected that a new system would include movable windows, menus across the top, and submenus available on objects—all of which could be clicked on with a mouse. The written requirements that had been given to Leslie did not describe any of this; it was just assumed that a new system would be graphical. A common problem in requirements documents is that they don't list features and functions already included in existing systems. Requirements documents often focus on new features the users want but don't have.

As you can imagine, the employees resented using this purchasing system, and many simply refused to learn it. After several years, the seriousness of the bad decision became clear. The new software never achieved the hoped-for gains because the people doing the purchasing either wouldn't use it because it was green screen or couldn't use it because the terminal client software wouldn't run on their machines. Even after the CEO issued an edict that all orders must go through the new system, most people continued to use the telephone and fax to order items.

The CFO had calculated the ROI at the beginning of the project. The CEO was expecting an annual savings of $4 million through volume discounts. But because few buyers used it, there was limited opportunity for grouping the orders of different departments for volume cost savings. The result of running the new system was that the company was spending an extra $2 million each year and saving nothing. Instead of the calculated 80 percent of the orders going through purchasing, or even 35 percent, which was the percentage that went through the pre-2000 purchasing system, only 10 percent of the orders went through the new purchasing system. If Leslie had held off on deciding about the purchasing system until she knew what already existed, there would not have been a problem.

In addition to having an up-to-date inventory, we also have to know the capabilities of our existing technology. Again, this is more difficult than it sounds.

I have a good friend, John. I admire John—he is a highly intelligent person and at the top of his field. However, John is not very knowledgeable about computers. He called me up one day to ask me where he could either buy software or hire someone to send out an e-mail to about 30 people. I tried to explain to John that he could use his contact management system to merge an e-mail to a distribution list, which was called an address book in his particular e-mail system. But, John was convinced that he needed specialized software and a technical expert to accomplish this task. He ended up spending $1,500 on specialized software before he discovered that, indeed, all he needed to do was learn how to merge to an address book on his own system.

For a small or new company, keeping a hardware inventory is as simple as having someone create a spreadsheet with basic information on each system. Table 1.2 shows a very simple department with a partial PC inventory. A software inventory might be similar but would also include a version number and source for the original media rather than hard drive space or memory. Once we get beyond a few hundred employees, we would want to keep the information in a database rather than a spreadsheet, but the columns would be the same.

A common problem is phantom inventory. If you ask most IT managers if there is an inventory, they will say yes. The problem occurs when you

Table 1.2
PC Hardware Inventory Sample

Current User	Brand	Type	Operating System	Hard Drive	Memory	WRITEABLE DVD?	Serial No.
Mainster, Jane	Systemax	Pentium IV	Win XP	80 Gig	255 Megs	YES	104723188
Schmoe, Joe	Ultra	AMD	Win 98 SE	10 Gig	224 Meg	NO	104660099
Harper, John	Dell	Pentium III	Win XP	60 Gig	255 Megs	YES	104723206
White, Sal	PowerSpec	Pentium VI	Win Vista	400 Gig	4 Gigs	NO	202110980400
Hooch, Ed	PowerSpec	Pentium II	Win XP	40 Gig	126 Megs	NO	20210983454
Network Server	Systemax	Pentium III	Windows NT	200 Gig	3 Gig	NO	4593823421

ask to see it. That's when we find out that the list either doesn't exist or is extremely out of date. It is not enough to simply ask if there is an inventory. The entrepreneur or business owner should actually ask to see it and check it for accuracy. Since keeping track of this information is tedious and boring, no one will do it unless a leader asks to see it.

One of my clients assured me that her hardware and software inventory was completely up to date. When we finally got the actual list, we learned that it had been—four years earlier. No one had updated it since Y2K, despite many upgrades and new employees since then.

In a large company, the manual labor of keeping these lists up to date is very time consuming, so many companies purchase specialized software that can go out on the network and collect inventory information on each PC as it logs in. Software that inventories software and hardware is often called *system management* or *asset management software*. I've found that trying to automate asset management is usually very expensive and problematic, sometimes causing more time to track down anomalies than it saves through automation. It is often more efficient to require each department to maintain a simple spreadsheet inventory and on a regular basis (such as quarterly) consolidate all the spreadsheets and check them for accuracy.

Often, entrepreneurs and business owners recognize the need to write out a technology map, but they get overwhelmed in the beginning. Don't let the sheer volume of knowledge dissuade you. Start with the inventory. Just look at it for a few days or a few weeks. Use the maps in Appendix A as a guide. Try to envision the categories that each piece of hardware and software fits into. Ask technology people questions about how different items in the inventory relate to each other. By doing so, you've already started creating your technology map.

Keep in mind that you don't need to get it right the first time. Accept also that there is no such thing as getting it exactly right because the technology itself changes, and the categories may change each time you buy something new. There is no single right or wrong answer. The important thing is to get something down on paper, and to have a mental understanding of the layers. After a while, you won't even be aware of how the map becomes the foundation that enables you to add new information, constantly updating and staying knowledgeable about information technology.

Next Steps: People and Processes

So far, we've only discussed the hardware and software aspects of the technology map. Remember, however, that information technology is not just hardware and software. The technology map involves people and processes as well. I will discuss these layers more in Chapters 3, 4, and 5. Furthermore, the hardware and software itself opens up a whole new world of vendor relationships that will be explained further in Chapters 6 and 7. We have only just introduced the concepts and the beginning of the framework in this chapter.

Before you go on to the next chapter, find out if there is a complete hardware and software inventory for your own organization. Take a look at it. Can you see the layers and how they fit together? Compare the sample technology maps in Appendix A to your lists. Do you see anything that doesn't make sense? Do you see anything that you only had the vaguest notion of before, but which becomes much clearer when you see the names of the categories and characteristics?

Add additional details for each item in each category of your own technology map as you encounter people, processes, vendor relationships, and networking as you read each chapter of this book. No matter how much you currently know, plan on spending some time in the coming months to improve your own technology map so all the holes are plugged in and you have a complete understanding of the technology map of your organization.

BEFORE WE BEGIN: THE PURPOSE

Stephen Covey says, "Begin with the end in mind," so it is with this sentiment that I've decided to put the resulting purpose of the technology map in the very next chapter instead of at the end of the book. In order to really become a competitive advantage, we must use the technology map to pounce like a panther.

SUMMARY

- ☑ Information technology is the people, processes, software, and hardware that make up the information flow in the operations of an organization.
- ☑ Calculating the risks of information technology helps to establish the value of information and provide guidelines for cost limits.
- ☑ A technology map is a mental map of how technology works—how the different components fit together. The components are layered and integrated.
- ☑ We each need to develop our own unique technology map in order to make good business decisions involving technology.
- ☑ A good starting point for developing our technology map is a complete hardware and software inventory.
- ☑ The next step is to evaluate the people and processes involved in the technology map.
- ☑ The ultimate purpose of the technology map is competitive advantage—the pounce like a panther concept.

2

Pounce Like a Panther

Throughout this book, we are going to discuss various rules and guidelines for entrepreneurs to follow in making decisions about business strategy that involves information technology. As you will see, in many ways this book advises a conservative approach; don't buy until you can be sure, don't believe it unless it's proven, and so on.

This chapter, however, is both a contradiction for everything else in the book and its most important guideline. This chapter outlines the specific situations where all of the advice in the rest of the book should be thrown out the window. To truly understand this chapter, you must go on and read the rest of the book. But this chapter will provide the culminating vision of the technology winner, so it will help put all the other chapters in perspective.

So here it is—the real secret to successfully using information technology for a competitive advantage: Pounce like a panther.

Panthers have a very specific method for hunting. Not being as big or as swift as some of their competitors like elephants or cheetahs, panthers like to climb trees overlooking a path where their prey tends to pass. Then, at just the right moment, they pounce down on the prey. Similarly, we can pounce on new technologies, like a panther, but only in that very specific situation where the right technology is there at the right time.

HOW TO POUNCE LIKE A PANTHER

When we look for certain instances for specific technologies that, when used at exactly the right time with full alignment of the business processes, we can transform a business and rocket it into stratospheric growth and profitability. This chapter is about how and when to recognize those truly strategic moments when inching out on a limb of a tree—even if it is a bleeding edge—is the right thing to do.

There are many steps to pouncing like a panther:

- Have a vision; a hedgehog concept.
- Ignore technologies that don't align.
- Keep track of standards bodies.

- Keep track of vendor success.
- Keep track of competitors' technology level.
- Know where all the holes are.
- Play with new technologies.
- Be patient for the right technology.
- When you see it, pounce.

Have a Vision, a Hedgehog Concept

A vision is essential. As Stephen Covey makes clear:

> More than any other factor, vision affects the choices we make and the way we spend our time. If our vision is limited—if it doesn't extend beyond the Friday night ball game or the next TV show—we tend to make choices based on what's right in front of us ... If our vision is based on illusion ... our choices [will] fail to create the ... quality results we expect. If our vision is partial ... we make choices that lead to imbalance ... [A vision] clarifies purpose, gives direction, and empowers us to perform beyond our resources.[16]

Fred Smith, founder and CEO, and Rob Carter, CIO, grew Federal Express from 186 packages a day (the average in 1973) to over 5 million packages a day. In the early 1990s, in both academic and industry writings, Federal Express was used so much as a technology success story that by 1999 I was sick of hearing about it. I figured that the magic of FedEx was probably more due to the needs of the market than to any particular technology strategy.

Then I met Fred and Rob at a conference, and I understood why they were continually used as *the* success story. Not only was their success clearly a case of correctly applied technology, but they are both very good at explaining exactly what they were thinking at the time and describing how things evolved. Their success was not an accident—and it behooves us to learn from them.

Their success started with a vision: to deliver packages overnight from anywhere to anywhere. Back in 1981, long before the Internet, and without any existing technology to rely upon, Rob Carter and Fred Smith laid out the technology needs for their vision of on-line everything. Not in general terms—in specific terms. The technology they needed to make the vision a reality wasn't feasible when they developed the vision, but over the next two decades it became feasible.

Fred Smith described his business idea in a paper as a student in an economics class in 1965:

> For instance, if you were a computer manufacturer like Burroughs or Sperry or IBM or Univac—all the people in those days who were competing for bank business—you'd go in and talk to, say, a banker in Amarillo and tell him he really ought to get rid of all his clerks and replace them

with computers, which would be able to do the work much more cheaply, quickly, accurately, and so forth. And the argument was totally compelling except for one fact: The minute that computer went dark, the bank couldn't function anymore. When you automate a human function, either that device has to work all the time or you have to be able to fix it rapidly. It was that simple an observation ... You'd need a faster, more dependable, and more far-reaching kind of delivery system.

If you've heard the story that Fred wrote this paper as a graduate student, or that it was a business plan for FedEx, or that he got a C in it, you've heard an urban legend. Fred doesn't remember what he got on the paper, and it wasn't a business plan, just the spark of an idea.

We can learn two lessons from this insightful paragraph. The first lesson is the direct lesson that unreliable information technology is worse than no information technology. Once computers enter the picture, they can't go down without disrupting the entire business. Smooth computing means profitable computing.

The second lesson is more indirect, but the point of this section. To adopt the innovations that would help their business, FedEx needed to wait for the technology to become available, and feasible. In 1965 logistical information technology did not exist. But Fred Smith and Rob Carter kept the vision in mind throughout the years. They watched and they waited. When the time was right, they pounced on the technology—after it had been proven by others, after it became financially feasible, but before their competitors had adopted it.

Fred and Rob utilized technology to plan and maintain a series of systems that could fulfill their agreed-upon vision. In 1994, they introduced on-line tracking of packages (long before the Internet was the ubiquitous network it is today). By 1996 they were providing shipping information on-line, and by 1997 they were also providing return information. In 2000 they enabled customers to actually see the proof of delivery signature— immediately—on-line.

Note that Federal Express didn't always get it exactly right, either. In 1980 they launched Zapmail, a product that electronically transmitted documents from computer to computer. It was ahead of its time, and before the fax machine matured and then e-mail took over those functions. Zapmail flopped—big time. But Federal Express just picked itself up, brushed itself off, and tried again with a more successful service.

Not everyone can be a Federal Express. And not every business is served by the same technologies from which Federal Express benefited. But every business can improve by pouncing on the right technology at the right time.

In the late 1990s, Larry Bergman (COO) and his team at Boscov's, a large regional department store on the East Coast, had a vision that can be summed up in the headline of an article about it: Out the Door in 7 Minutes.[17] Fast growth at Boscov's left it with a challenge: bottlenecks and slow throughput in the distribution warehouse. Sometimes it would take months for items to get to the selling store. For some items a delay wasn't a big deal, but for some items, especially items in the fashion world, Larry figured they were losing millions in sales.

At the time of the vision, there were no automated sorting conveyer systems that could handle the varied items sold by Boscov's. There were no standards for electronic invoicing. But Larry watched, and waited. As various and sundry technologies became available that would enable the vision, they were implemented so that over the course of three years, Boscov's succeeded in getting items to the stores an average of 170 days faster than before.

First they found ways to encourage more of their suppliers to use advance shipping notices (ASN). ASN is an e-mail that says "we just sent you a delivery of these items and we estimate it will arrive in four hours." The advanced notice enabled Boscov's to double-check the order and prepare to receive it. Next they increased the use of bar code scanning, chose a better monitoring system, and began to deal with errors differently. Finally, they installed a new sorting conveyor belt—a superhighway compared to their old one-lane road. The vision "out the door in 7 minutes" had not changed, even while newer technologies were being employed to support the vision. Everyone—from Max Devlin, warehouse worker, to Olen Shaffer, shipping manager, to Bob Goonan, director of logistics—knew the vision was getting the items through the system quickly and accurately with minimum wait time.

The vision comes first and has to do with our own business goals or desire to fill a market need. The vision is essential to guiding adoption of future technology, not the other way around. In other words, if we see a new technology and think "here's a good use for that technology," we are working backwards. I believe that was one of the problems I had when I invested my heart and soul (along with significant funds) into a business that provided live videoconferencing systems for customer service. We saw the technology, and we were trying to find a good use for it. Not a good idea.

Furthermore, the vision must be known to everyone in the company. We discuss ways to communicate the vision in more detail in Chapter 5, so for now I just want to note that the vision can't be hidden away in the corner like a business plan that an entrepreneur is afraid to show people because they might "steal" the idea.

Jim Collins described the importance of developing and communicating the vision by using another wild animal, the hedgehog. Collins researched companies that were *Built to Last* and companies that went from *Good to Great* in an attempt to differentiate the key elements that made those companies successful. He determined that each successful business has a core strength, a core principle, a value proposition, a vision. Collins called this central vision the *hedgehog concept*, based on the idea that a hedgehog can do one thing (roll itself into a ball) very, very well, and is highly successful using that one well-known technique of defense. Collins notes that companies that have gone from good to great know what they do well and focus only on that capability, selling off divisions (even profitable ones) that don't directly support their hedgehog concept. Great companies pay attention to that one strength. Great companies don't waste time or energy trying to pay attention to everything.

Collins gives numerous examples of companies that are highly profitable while they stay focused on their hedgehog concept, but begin to decline the moment they start to focus on something else. He also describes the difficulty people have in recognizing hedgehog concepts, but provides some guidelines for identifying and communicating it so that everyone in the company buys in to the same vision. For a hedgehog concept to work, everyone in an organization must be rowing in the same direction.

Having a hedgehog concept doesn't necessarily mean that companies can't diversify. Diversifying a product line does not mean that a company dilutes its hedgehog concept. The hedgehog concept has more to do with meeting a need in the marketplace (which can be met in a variety of ways) than it does with a specific product or service. But in all cases, the hedgehog concept was the guiding principle used by the leaders of these successful organizations in designing their strategy.

Technologies, especially potentially strategic technologies related to the hedgehog concept, can help forward the core strengths of a business. Any technology that can do that is worth some investigation, some research, some added attention and capital dollars. Later in the book we will advise entrepreneurs and business owners to stay off of the leading edge and stick with tried-and-true stable technologies. However, the only time it makes sense for a company to be on the bleeding edge is when the company is investigating possible technologies that would launch new capabilities in the company's hedgehog concept.

Ignore Technologies That Don't Align

Have you ever gone fishing? Did you memorize all the names of all the fish in the ocean first? Of course not! We don't need to memorize the names of all the fish in the ocean before choosing the bait in order to start fishing. Similarly, we don't need to learn about all the technologies—only the relevant ones.

The biggest problem most leaders have is not that they are not aware of, or watching, the technologies that would align with their business. The biggest problem is that they are also watching all the technologies that don't. That is a mistake because it will distract them.

A company priding itself on its wonderful customer service should know all about the customer relationship management (CRM) programs on the market, although that doesn't mean, necessarily, that they've already implemented a CRM. But a business focused on the customer needn't spend the same amount of time and effort investigating back-end general ledger or financial systems.

If a company has a hedgehog concept of being the "most accurate and fastest shipper," investigating wireless radio-frequency identification (RFID) tags might be a good investment of time. But the company shouldn't spend the same amount of time investigating which is the best word processor to purchase, or which PC manufacturer has the fastest processor—because neither of these technologies are related to that particular company's hedgehog concept.

The same would not be true for a company that provided medical transcription services, however. For that company, spending time looking at RFID tags would be a complete waste of time. A state-of-the-art word processor and document management system investment, on the other hand, would be a strategic technology aligning with the hedgehog concept.

As Chad Dickerson, a noted columnist and CIO, said: "Just as one man's trash is another's treasure, one man's commodity is another's competitive edge."[18]

As will be explained in later chapters, except for the hedgehog concept technologies, the best strategy is to stick with what you already have, or follow the crowd for anything new you might need. No one ever got fired for buying Dell and Microsoft. We are best served by choosing whatever our competitors are using. Don't sweat it, or waste time. Our best strategy is to completely ignore product brochures and articles touting new information technology that doesn't directly relate to our hedgehog concept.

At the same time, we need to follow the progress on technologies related to our hedgehog concept with a keen eye and our ear to the ground.

That's not to say it is easy. To me, focusing on aligned technologies is such a commonsense bit of advice, I had trouble understanding why so few businesses do it. Why don't decision makers follow this strategy? The research I've done points to various reasons this issue is such a problem.

First, those who know and understand the strategic vision of the company (typically the business owners and/or entrepreneurs) are often not technically literate enough to understand the underlying infrastructure, which is necessary to know which technologies to watch. Their technology maps are incomplete, and they haven't spent enough time trying to complete them. Typically the technology leaders of the company understand the underlying infrastructure enough to know which technologies to watch in support of the vision because they have a complete technology map. But they either don't know, or don't care, what that strategic vision is.

As explained more in the chapter on managing people, technology people get into this field because they love technology, not because they care about making money or supporting someone else's vision. Successful companies can only pounce like a panther when the technology people are fully aware of, have bought into, and are willing to support the central vision or hedgehog concept of the company.

Another related problem, also uncovered in my research, is that often the chief financial officer (CFO) is involved in the decision to the detriment of the decision-making process. Indeed, one of the most common mistakes in technology strategy in businesses over the past 10 years has been investing in back-end enterprise resource planning (ERP) systems without paying attention to the impact on the customer. CFOs, being adept with spreadsheets and return on investment (ROI) calculations, can often make the case sound good. And, as the people holding the purse strings, they can often smooth the approval process. But the fact is, without a complete alignment with sales and operations, a back-end financial system will do more harm than good.[19–21] Many companies discovered this as ERP system after ERP system failed to deliver on what was promised. The problem wasn't the ERP system, the problem was that the ERP system was selected and implemented by the financial division of the company, with little thought toward sales, marketing, or operations, the true blood of the profit-making corporation. In the cases where the ERP system was chosen, customized, and implemented by the entire company rather than a single division, there was much more success. Studies also show that the amount spent on training had a significant impact on success, but more of that will be discussed in Chapter 3.

Furthermore, focusing too narrowly on the ROI calculation can lead to the exact wrong decision (discussed more fully in Chapter 5). Pouncing like a panther on the right technology at the right time has to do with strategy, not financial calculations. It must be customer driven, not financially driven.

Keep Track of Standards Bodies

There is an old joke in the technology industry: The wonderful thing about standards is that there are so many to choose from.

A *standard*, literally, is an approved way of accomplishing a technical goal that is published by a standards body such as the Institute of Electrical and Electronics Engineers (IEEE); International Organization for Standardization (ISO); the World Wide Web Consortium (W3C); and several others (e.g., IEC, CEN, CENELEC, ETSI, ITU-T, and OASIS).[25] Some of those standards bodies are as old as the hills (such as IEEE which was established on May 13, 1884), and others are just babes in the woods (such as W3C which formed in October 1994). (As an aside, IEEE was originally called American Institute of Electrical Engineers. In 1963 it merged with the Institute of Radio Engineers [originally founded in 1912] to form the new organization Institute of Electrical and Electronics Engineers [IEEE].)

Old or young, a standards organization is usually needed to broker negotiations for shared standards so that businesses can capitalize on interrelationships. Standards bodies are involved in the politics of a standard as well as the technical aspects of it.

The workings of standards bodies may be better seen with a nontechnical example. The size and shape of a freight container (one that can be moved from train to truck to ship to plane without emptying the contents) was one of the standards published by the ISO. Vince Grey, former secretary and chairman of ISO, talks about getting around the politics of establishing a freight container size.[22]

> One of the first problems we ran into was various countries trying to have the international standard reflect their own national practices. We really didn't want to do that. The trouble was, that when we decided to get into the middle type of container size, the ones that are like a truck body, the metric countries wanted to confirm the container sizes that had been in use in the UIC (International Union of Railroads). I'm bringing it up because I think how we approached that subject may have value. Instead of locking horns, and saying "no way!", we accepted these container sizes and called them Series 2 containers.... But when it came to the market place, no one bought [them].... It's better to get on with the work as long as you can achieve the basic goal and let the merits of each series be judged by the users.
> Anyhow, once that last peg was put in place at that Moscow meeting, so that people could go out and procure standard containers, the industry just took off! Everybody started placing orders for containers. Until that time, the fear was that you would spend a lot of money buying the wrong containers.

So why must we know about standards? Because in order to know when to pounce like a panther, we must know when standards are "real." It's not just a matter of seeing which standards are published, but in following the politics behind them and recognizing which standards are likely to be used by an industry, and which ones are likely to be phased out.

Once we've identified our hedgehog concept and have envisioned the technology that will improve and strengthen our ability to provide the product or service to our clients, we need to identify those bodies that manage the underlying standards supporting the technological devices involved in that technology.

Imagine that you are a movie distributor back in the 1980s. You would have been acutely aware of the impact of the competing VHS versus Beta tape format standard on the industry. If you had chosen to distribute all your movies on Beta only, you would today be out of business. If you had invested in both VHS and Beta, you would have lost your Beta investment, and perhaps because of overreaching, your business too.

The optimum path, back then, would have been to continue to focus on whatever you were doing before video players were widely and cheaply available. Then, the moment it was clear that VHS would win the tape format war, pounce on the VHS format. This strategy would have helped you avoid your competitors' mistakes of wasting time and money on the wrong format. Following the standards bodies would have let you clearly see that moment much earlier than waiting for the market to reveal the trend.

Let's work through an example involving a well-known technology standard—the network that connects your computers. You may have heard that your wiring and network card are Ethernet, but what you may not know is that Ethernet is another name for the IEEE standard number 802.3. Back in the 1980s, Ethernet was just one of two popular competing standards (Token Ring, 802.5, was the other). Back in the early 1980s, if we didn't know that there were standards bodies defining wiring standards, we might not have known there were two potential solutions.

Let's imagine that we own a company that provides marketing research services to the transportation industry in 1985. A local area network is essential to our hedgehog concept because our employees need to communicate and collaborate using a network. Further imagine that we have just leased a building and must decide what kind of wiring to install. Our director of IT had previously worked for IBM, so she recommends Token Ring. If we didn't know any better, we might take her advice.

If we choose Token Ring for the wiring, however, we would be wasting a great deal of time and money. We would end up replacing the entire thing within a few years. The standards committee that defined Token Ring stopped actively working on it in the early 1990s, and it has since disbanded. Ethernet was cheaper, and it seemed to work just as well for most companies, so the better choice was Ethernet, despite the fact that technically Token Ring was superior to Ethernet (just as Beta was superior to VHS).

At the risk of pre-empting some of the issues we will discuss in Chapter 4, a situation in which the technically inferior but cheaper technology wins is a common scenario. Technologists, however, often want to use the superior technology rather than the optimum technology. To give one example, my brother can be described as nearly legendary in some circles for his technical prowess. He held onto his Beta video system for years after everyone else had given up on Beta tapes. He still occasionally rants about how much better Beta was, and he would detail to anyone who would listen why VHS was a poor substitute. I still know people who swear by Token Ring, and resent being forced to use the unstructured shout-on-a-wire Ethernet networking.

It makes sense to pay attention to the more enduring technology rather than the technically superior one. Pouncing on the wrong technology (even if it is the technically superior one) can be detrimental to our ability to pounce on the right technology. The cost to replace the entire Token Ring network would make the switch unfeasible for many years, but as time went on Ethernet became more and more essential to smoothly running networks. New devices such as switches and routers were released only for the more common network type, Ethernet, but not for the less common Token Ring.

Knowing the standards bodies, which standards they are working on, and which standards are competing with each other is an essential step to understanding the underlying technology. Generally, when there are competing standards we want to wait until there is a clear front-runner before pouncing. In the case of our network, by 1989 it was pretty obvious to anyone watching that Ethernet would beat out Token Ring as a standard even though it would be years before it stopped being supported by the industry.

Why are there competing standards? Once the standard is, well, standard, the technology equipment manufacturers have to do one better than the standard in order to have a competitive advantage. As a matter of fact, the standards of today are usually the innovations beyond the standard of yesterday. But innovation means that the equipment is no longer following just the standard. The Ethernet (802.3) standard, for example, is not what most people have today. The most common configuration is a combination of 10BASE-T Ethernet (10 megabit per second, 802.3) and Fast Ethernet (10 times the speed, called 802.3u). Of course, the next wiring standard will be one of two competing Gigabit Ethernet protocols. Both are 100 times faster than the original Ethernet. One is called 1000BASE-X, IEEE standard number 802.3z, and the other is called 1000BASE-T, IEEE standard number 802.3ab. There is also a completely new one called 10 Gigabit Ethernet (802.3ae). While knowing exactly what these standards are is not important, understanding that they exist and who publishes them is important. Since there is no clear winner among the competing Fast Ethernet standards, for example, we would know that now is not the time to replace our "slow" 802.3 10 megabit per second network devices with, say, 802.3ab. We might guess wrong and waste our investment. If we keep up with the activities of the committees, however, at some point a clear winner will emerge. That would be the right time to pounce.

Why is waiting for a winner important? Competing standards are often not interoperable. You can't have a network card "talking" at Gigabit Ethernet speeds (1000) while the hub port is "talking" at Fast Ethernet speeds (100). They must match, or the network doesn't work. Since you can't replace just one piece, switching to a different standard is a big deal and will cost a great deal of money.

Are you wondering which comes first, the product or the standard? Products using the standards are usually developed before the standard is published. Indeed, it is often the research and development arm of the vendors who submit the standard for publication. Token Ring, for example, was researched, developed, and submitted by IBM. Ethernet was researched, developed, and submitted by 3COM. So if a standard is published, there is already at least one vendor using it.

"Wait a minute," you might say. "Why would an organization pay for the research to develop a new way of doing things, only to turn around and submit that way for a standards body to publish? Wouldn't they want it to be proprietary, so only they have it and can charge more for it?" In a different industry, like drugs or chemicals, yes. However, information technology products are useless unless they interface with other information technology products. So a vendor can't keep its way of doing things proprietary and still interface with other pieces of the puzzle. If a vendor develops a way of doing things, but it is not adopted by the rest of the industry, that vendor goes out of business.

That's not to say some vendors haven't tried. Apple, for example, has a history of not submitting its standards for publishing by standards bodies. Instead it tries to maintain complete control over the entire system—hardware, operating system, software. They've even sued, and won, to prevent other vendors from using their methods and protocols. Some say that this is the reason Macintosh is an expensive niche machine that never grew to the level of PC-based industries. Other examples are the proprietary network protocols of the 1980s like Novell NetWare, IBM's SNA, and Microsoft's NetBIOS. Unlike the general TCP/IP protocols of the Internet, these networks could only interface with their own systems. All of them eventually disappeared, as proprietary technologies tend to do.

In summary, it is important to understand and follow the standards (or have a trusted adviser who is doing so on our behalf) that relate to the type of technologies that relate to our hedgehog concept, as well as the relationship between those standards and the products on the market, so that we can know when to pounce.

Keep Track of Vendor Success

As noted previously, the products and services sold by IT vendors have a relationship with the standards published by standards bodies. But the success of the vendors themselves also has a profound effect on knowing when to pounce. As I will explain in the chapter about vendors, it is important to seek out vendors who have financial stability. We want to stay away from vendors who grow too quickly, whose growth is spurred more by venture capital than actually selling a product or service that meets a need. The smaller the company, the harder it is to have the necessary staying power to contribute significantly to the industry, a subset related only to the newest product or service.

Therefore, when the industry is full of new vendors in a particular product or service, it is probably too new for us to pounce on. To give some current examples (as I write this book), the vendors selling voice over Internet protocols (VOIP) have not yet had a shakeout. There are still 15 major VOIP vendors, and 34 minor players. The government regulation of the industry has not quite stabilized, definitions aren't yet solid, and the business models of the vendors are still in flux. (Should they charge by the minute? A monthly fee? Charge for the device? How is the income shared with wiring providers?) At the present moment, unless directly related to a hedgehog concept, VOIP is not a technology anyone should be considering for replacing existing systems (although there may be a case made for new installations). But by the time you read this book, that may have changed.

At the point that consolidation has begun, we want to start watching to see whether the industry will disappear or mature. The signs that maturity is coming are subtle. The industry will have consolidated to three or four major players who are no longer dependent on venture capital but who are making a profit by selling their product or service. The regulatory environment has stabilized and there are no pending lawsuits that might change the business model. Definitions are solid, and business models have been tested.

The signs that the industry is not quite ready for prime time and has not yet matured (and may never mature) are similar but telling. The consolidation has resulted in a few puny or dying companies. The underlying technology upon which the entire industry is based has hit some problems that have not been overcome. For example, the videoconferencing industry has been limping along for decades because inexpensive connections do not yet have the required quality. The highly hyped network computer of the late 1990s never grew into any kind of industry and is pretty much as dead as a doornail now.

The moment to pounce, then, is just after consolidation, when there is a strong financially stable winner or two in the field.

Keep Track of Competitors' Technology Level

In addition to watching the standards and watching the success and consolidation records of the vendors in the field, we also want to keep track of what our competitors are doing. One way to get this information is to use a competitive-intelligence consultant or send employees over to speak with their employees or observe their operation. We can purchase their products and look for clues in the invoice or paperwork. Often, though, all we need to do is ask our IT vendors; their salespeople will often know exactly what type of system all the major players in any industry are using.

Once we have the information, we use it to adjust our own strategy. This is a strange case of not being too early and not being too late. If the other companies in our industry are still on green-screen mainframe terminals, have no Web base, nor any integration with their suppliers, we don't want to be in a hurry to implement any of those technologies. Remember that as long as our competitors are using and maintaining the same technologies they've been using for dozens of years, their cost basis for technology is near zero. If they can lower the cost of their products and services below ours, and not give up too much on features and benefits, it is not to our advantage to invest in new technologies that will raise our cost basis for slightly incremental improvements to the products or services. In other words, it is too early to pounce.

At the same time, if we find out our competitors are investing in all new technology that will (supposedly) increase their market share or lower their costs or increase their quality, we don't necessarily want to jump on the bandwagon and invest in the same new technology. It might be that our competitors will implement it, and it will fail because it was too expensive, hyped, or not reliable enough. All we need to do to succeed is to sit back and wait for our competitors to do all the hard work to find the faults of the new technology.

If the technology our competitors invest in does not turn out to be a complete failure, that's when we should pounce! While our competitors are still struggling with getting their systems to work reliably, we can learn from their mistakes and implement the next generation of the information technology. Remember that vendors learn from clients' mistakes as well, so the vendor will come to you with a much deeper well of knowledge in how to implement the new systems. Even if our competitors are relatively successful in their new technology implementation, the second time a new technology gets implemented always is faster and cheaper than the first time, the third time cheaper yet, the fourth time even faster, etc. My experience says that by the time a technology has been implemented over a dozen times, the projects will start becoming smooth as silk—but not before then.

Some people might say, "But what about first-mover advantage? Once our competitors get their new technology implemented, they will have the advantage, and we won't be able to catch up." Well, the truth is; first-mover advantage is a myth.

"But what about the great examples, Amazon or eBay?" you say. Again, the truth is that there were many on-line booksellers and quite a few auction sites already on the Internet before Amazon.com or eBay.com. Their founders benefited by looking at why the others had failed. Cook and Proulx, the founders of Intuit and the highly successful Quicken and Quick-Books software (often used as a first-mover example), joke that they had a forty-seventh–mover advantage.[23]

There are very few cases where the first company to implement a new technology actually succeeded. We think that the successful companies we hear about were the first ones because we didn't hear about the failures that came before them. As Mickey Rooney says, "You always pass failure on the way to success." The key to being the success and not the failure is to avoid being a front-runner until the perfect moment in the race (usually just before the end) when we can pull ahead.

Know Where All the Holes Are

Innovation and technological advantage almost always come from plugging up a hole in the existing information technology. A *hole* is a function or feature that would be really great to have—but which doesn't exist in any of the current technologies. The technology map we've talked about can help us establish where the holes might be, but more often than not the hole must be defined by the need, not by the technology.

An example revolving around a personal need that is still a hole might make this concept clearer. A few years ago, I realized that I really needed a storage place for my ever-growing data files. Between client files, photographs, videos, databases, my research, and my writing, I've aggregated quite a load of essential electronic files—about 25 gigabytes. (About two years ago the size was only 10 gigabytes, and that was after I spent three days cleaning out and archiving files I no longer needed. I recently considered another cleanup, but I realized that at this point in time, three days of effort is more valuable than the space, so I didn't bother.)

I'm constantly sending subsets of this data to my employees for various tasks they need to accomplish—which is a pain. It would be so much nicer if there were a password-protected virtual storage facility where I could store all my files. That way, I could just set up access authorization for my employees and I wouldn't have to waste my time finding and sending through e-mail or creating a CD for my employees when they need the files. Furthermore, someone else would be backing them up and maintaining them.

I investigated for months. I tried no less than five different companies that promised to provide exactly what I needed: a virtual storage area on the Internet where I could place my files and give access to the files to my employees.

So where is the hole? None of these services, not one, could give me instant access to my files across the Internet. Some promised to do so, but in every single case the time necessary to access the file exceeded the time-outs on the connection, and I rarely was able to work on the files virtually. In the end I gave up, purchased a portable hard drive and carried it with me when I saw my employees so that I could quickly download whatever files they needed into their systems.

It is hard to get vendors to talk about holes until they have a solution. They deal with the lack in one of two ways. They ignore the problem, considering it unsolvable or outside of their purview. Alternatively, they act as if they already have a solution, even when they don't, and will fail to understand your explanation of why their solution is not good enough. Once a vendor has a solution, however, they will tout it to the heavens for a while. Once every vendor has the solution and it is no longer a differentiator, they will go back to ignoring it.

For example, back in the 1980s, there was a major hole regarding managing the memory on personal computers due to a problem known as the 640K barrier. To solve this problem, virtual memory was developed, and dozens of memory management companies popped up so that people could use graphical programs, like Windows, which needed more than 640K of memory to run. But once memory management was built into the operating system of the personal computer itself, the hole disappeared, and so did all those memory management companies.

Another example: As recently as 2005 most anti-virus packages did not do anything to prevent spyware. Anti-virus programs were designed to eliminate computer viruses—little unwanted programs that actually damaged files or systems. Spyware is a little unwanted program that doesn't cause any direct damage, but watches what we do as we use our computer or surf the Internet and reports back to the vendor our behavior, ostensibly so that they can figure out what our needs are so that they can sell to us. It causes no direct damage, although it slows down our systems. A hole appeared—soon plugged by anti-spyware programs, which had to be purchased separately. It only made sense, however, that anti-virus and anti-spyware programs would merge so that most systems are protected from both viruses and spyware by the same program. The hole disappeared.

To provide a business-oriented process example, there was, at one time, a hole when it came to calculating shipping costs. In order to calculate how much profit businesses receive on every sale, they have to know the shipping costs of the sale. But shipping costs are variable based upon the size, weight, source, and destination of the package as well as which shipping vendor was used. The costs were therefore unknown until the box had actually been weighed and stamped by FedEx or UPS or DHL or the post office. Because the actual costs could not be known at the time of the sale, most companies simply set shipping and handling charges to some number that they hoped was more than the cost, and went on their merry way.

But this could cause problems. In the early 1990s, I was responsible for the warehouse at a systems integrator firm. Every month, the warehouse manager was responsible for reconciling the estimated and actual shipping costs, and he came to me with a problem pattern he happened to notice. After investigation, we discovered that the salespeople were entering a low-ball figure for the shipping costs. The price to their customers was lowered without impacting the salespeople's net profit, on which their own commissions were based. But at the end of the month the company was losing thousands of dollars in shipping. Since this was before the Internet, we had no choice but to start charging the salespeople's commission the following month for overages from the previous month because there was a hole—no way to accurately calculate the shipping costs.

Nowadays the hole has been filled. Most financial packages can link automatically with the chosen shipping vendor who takes the size, weight, source, and destination of the package and accurately calculates the shipping cost. Once we know where the holes are, we can keep checking new technologies to see if the holes have been filled or not. To pounce optimally, we need to be aware of the hole, and the fact that it has been filled.

How do we find the holes if they are not readily apparent? We keep asking questions until we find something that a system can't do. It may help to know that a hole is usually related to one of six different requirements:

- Ease of use.
- Integration and connection with other needed function.
- High quality.
- Size.
- Security and privacy.
- Reasonable cost.

It may be that we can get the feature that we want, but it is very difficult to use and requires the skill of a technologist. One example of this is the Web browser. Before Web browsers such as Internet Explorer, Netscape, Safari, or Foxfire were available, Internet surfers from 1973 to 1995 memorized and used esoteric commands to get around the Internet. Web browsers filled the hole.

Alternatively, the system might be easy to use, but it is not integrated with some other related device or software with which it needs to be integrated, such as navigation systems that aren't hooked up to Global Positioning System (GPS). Or, the feature or function is integrated, but we can't get the quality high enough. For example, we can get a grainy videoconference connection but not a television-quality videoconference connection.

On the other hand, we might be able to get the quality that we want, but not enough memory or space. We can feasibly get 25 megabytes of on-line storage, but not 25 gigabytes. If you have too many contacts in your electronic Rolodex, you might bump into the number of contacts issue when trying to store them on a personal digital assistant (PDA) device. I tried five different PDAs before finding the HP Handspring which, with the extra memory module, can handle most, but still not all, of my contacts.

We also might be able to get the quality, but not in the size we need. For example, we can get a 3-inch videoconference window, but not a 17-inch monitor-sized conference window.

Security and privacy are often a lagging hole because vendors don't work on these until there is a well-publicized problem. E-mail is not secure and cannot be used to send confidential information such as credit card data, health records, or personnel records. Quite a few Web sites still don't accept credit cards because security is such an issue and a secure Web site is expensive.

Finally, we may be able to get all of the requirements we want, but it costs an arm and a leg, outside of the reach of all but the most affluent. Large companies can afford all the most up-to-date secure Web site technology so that they can accept credit cards, but the small mom-and-pop shop still feels the hole.

Of course, we also have to be careful that we don't lose existing capabilities when we plug up the holes. One of my clients purchased a new financial system to replace the green-screen mainframe system they had been using. The hole they were plugging up was the "easy to use" requirement because new employees found it very difficult to learn the old system. Until they implemented the system, however, they didn't realize that the accounts receivable on the new system was not directly integrated with the general ledger where deposited checks were recorded. They ended up entering each check twice: once for the deposit and once to record the payment against the invoice—something they didn't have to do on the old system. As mentioned earlier, it hadn't even occurred to the employees writing up the requirements for the system to include the question "When you enter a check for deposit, can you mark which invoice was being paid?" because their old system had that feature and they assumed any new system would also have that feature.

Another of my clients, Jim, decided to switch to a new Web site hosting service because it promised to provide a secure Web site with a shopping cart that would accept credit cards. Unfortunately, Jim hadn't consulted me before making the switch. He discovered the Web site had no way of syncing automatically with his inventory system as his previous hosting service could do. Jim had gained security but lost accuracy.

Every system has holes; the key to success is in knowing where the holes are and finding a way to work around them or live with them while keeping our eyes open for the solutions that give us everything we currently have, plus plugs up the hole.

Play with New Technologies

How do we check to see if the holes have been filled? We play. We establish a test lab and install new systems to see if they fill the holes without losing existing capabilities. In the chapter on dealing with IT people, we discuss an excellent way to keep information technology gurus focused on improving our internal systems without tempting them to break the systems in order to play with new technology. We give them a budget to purchase, install, and play with any new technologies that support our hedgehog concept. But we can do the playing ourselves as well as long as we know what the existing capabilities are and where the holes are.

For example, for over 20 years I have been dreaming of a specific system that does not yet exist. I envision an Internet-based contact management/calendar/e-mail program, similar to the original Lotus Organizer, ACT!, GoldMine, or Outlook, that works seamlessly for a small group. This program would sync automatically with a wireless calendar/videoconference/camera/phone/Web browser/music device, but will be able to access many of the functions even when in an area that doesn't have connectivity to the Internet. Other people, like my employees, would have password-protected access to my calendar and direct access to the files on the corporate Web site (all 25 gigabytes). The calendar portion of this system will provide me with a report each month that graphs different categories of activities. The contact manager will hold all 4,000 of my contacts, which are also available to my employees. Each contact's address will be automatically connected to a mapping program and will give me verbal directions from my GPS location at the touch of a button. All for less than $500 a year. And all very easy to use.

I already have all of these capabilities, but there is no single solution that provides all of them, and the combination is way beyond the $500 a year cost basis (and there are quite a few manual processes that I programmed or designed for myself that are not generally available). Every time any software or hardware related to any of these capabilities comes out, I investigate it. Devices like the Blackberry are getting closer to accomplishing the vision (much closer than when I first had the vision back in 1987), but none have yet succeeded.

For example, the iPhone came out with much fanfare on the weekend I was writing this section. I had a simple question: Can the iPhone maintain and sync with my calendar? If the answer was yes, I would buy one to play with to see if it could meet my other needs. I went to the Web site to get an answer to the initial question. Of course, the first problem was that my Windows-based system did not have a QuickTime component it needed to even watch the commercial about the iPhone, and they had no text-equivalent (a harbinger of things to come and typical of a media-driven vendor, I believe). I didn't want to download the commercial and watch it with Windows Media Player because the file was 318 megabytes—a huge program not worth the download time. Lucky for me, I have both PCs and Macintoshes at home, so I just went into the next room, launched Safari instead of Internet Explorer, and watched the entire 30-minute guided tour (i.e., commercial). Unfortunately, it did not answer my question. Nothing on the Web site, either. Eventually I went onto a series of on-line forums where people were discussing the iPhone and discovered that the IPhone doesn't even have a calendar program. Furthermore, there seemed no way to convert contact information from my existing contact manager. No calendar? Re-enter all my contacts? I don't think so. I didn't even have to buy one to play with to find out it was worthless to me.

In summary, if we know the capabilities of our own system, and we know where all the holes are, we can quickly look at each new technology to investigate if it fills the holes without losing existing capability.

Be Patient for the Right Technology

It is hard to simply sit back and wait for the right combination of events to align so that we can pounce. More than 15 years ago, a friend of mine, Jan, called me up to find out what combination of software and hardware would allow her to start a transcription business. She'd seen a demonstration of a system that could automatically type up the spoken word. She envisioned a business where doctors and lawyers would speak into a phone and have their words automatically converted to text and e-mailed to them. I told her that what she was envisioning wouldn't work, because that the hardware and software that she wanted didn't exist yet. She was sure that the technology was just around the corner, and would be available within the next year or so.

Fifteen years and we are still waiting. Last month I was speaking with some other people, Bob and Mary, telling them about my friend Jan, only to have them inform me that they are actually in the medical transcription business. Furthermore, they had just purchased the hardware and software to do what I described. Their clients (mostly doctors) speak into a phone and their words get recorded. Until recently, a human being listened to the recordings and typed up the information. However, Bob was sure that the system they had just purchased and implemented would eliminate the need for typists. It would automatically generate the text.

Of course, after some in-depth questioning on my part, I clarified that currently the system only helped; it was 80 percent effective. Currently the new system was costing more to have the typists correct the mistakes than it used to cost to have them do the typing from the beginning. But Bob was sure that within a short time the system would get more accurate and it would stop costing more to correct than to type. If he'd been my client,

I would have told him point-blank that he had wasted his money. These systems were 80 percent effective back in 1987, the height of the natural language processing research. In 20 years they have not improved their track record much. The necessary technology was beyond the capabilities of any but the most powerful supercomputer system today. The typists have been, are, and will be cheaper for years to come.

No one is immune from impatience. Seven years ago, I allowed someone to convince me that videoconferencing over the Internet was not only possible, but currently being done. My impatience for that technology colored my views. If I had been more patient, I would have saved the hundreds of thousands of dollars that I lost when I invested in a company trying to sell videoconferencing technology before its time.

Trying to push the envelope are companies selling video e-mail services, videoconferencing services, voice over Internet protocols, video on demand, end-to-end enterprise network management, natural-language processing, voice-recognition services, customer relationship management, radio-frequency identification, and many, many more "new" services. We all want these capabilities, and they seem so near to the capabilities we do have that it is hard to understand why we are still waiting. Remember that the panther may end up waiting for weeks on the limb of that tree until the prey comes walking down the path. Hunger pangs do not make the prey appear. Wishing does not make it so. There is no way to force the prey to appear.

Some entrepreneurs try to force the needed information technology by investing in research and development. They hire programmers or engineers to plug the holes or develop the needed information technology. The difficulty with that path is the high cost. If one company pays millions to develop an easy-to-use shopping cart so that they can sell their items online, and another company just waits two years for easy-to-use shopping cart software to become available commercially, which one will win out in the end? The company who waited, because its cost basis will be many times lower than the first company. Once again, until the right time, we must be patient.

When You See It, Pounce

After having watched for years and years, following the guidelines in this book, when the exact right technology comes along, we will recognize that critical moment in time. Our vision aligns with the people, the process, the hardware, and the software. We have only one thing left to do. Pounce.

When the just-right technology finally matures, we need to jump into it with every muscle, every brain cell. Great companies allow themselves to be completely transformed by new technology—every division, every department, every decision maker, every employee. Pouncing is not incremental. It is not inching out on the tree limb. Every person, every process, every system usually has to change to incorporate truly new technology. Only by being willing to transform the entire business to take advantage of the new technology—only then will we accomplish far more than any stuck-in-the-old-way competitor can keep up with.

The jump cannot be accomplished without the watchful waiting first—because hype and lack of knowledge will keep us from being sure when the transforming technology is ready. If we jump as soon as we wade in we will get fooled. We need the research lab, the careful testing, knowledge of the holes. We need to be absolutely sure.

Jim Collins noted that technology is an accelerator. If we choose the right technology, one that fits into our hedgehog concept, then it can accelerate the entire business to great new heights. But if we choose the wrong technology or the wrong time to implement the technology, then that very same technology will accelerate our demise.

I have personal experience with the accelerating power of technology—both positive and negative. I started my very first company in 1986, Computer Educational Services (CES), a computer training and consulting firm. I had already had the vision of contact manager/calendar/file management during the infancy of CES. I wanted to be able to access my files from any of my three offices (home office, training room, and administrative office) and from either the PC or the Macintosh. The files were only a few dozen megs' worth back then, but no less important to me and, a decade before the Internet, much harder to access. In my quest for the technology to fulfill my vision I got to know certain people who ended up being critical to my success. One was Warren "Pete" Musser, the CEO of Safeguard Scientifics, a venture capitalist who invested in Novell NetWare in 1987. We appeared together in an entrepreneur's panel for alumni at Lehigh University. When I met him, being focused on making my vision a reality, I asked him what he knew about accessing files from either a PC or a Macintosh on a single server. Pete told me that I could do what I wanted with Novell NetWare, and he made arrangements for Novell to give me a copy of NetWare 286 (along with the shelf full of manuals) so that I could share files from the server from either the Macintoshes or the PCs in my training room. Of course, in the end the file sharing didn't work as seamlessly as I would have liked. And I'm still waiting for a contact manager/ calendar/file management system. But my knowledge of this difficult-to-use network operating system led me to great success in the infant field of networking so the vision still helped me.

It was because of my knowledge of networking that I was able to impress Ray Melcher and Ed Barrett, the owners of Hi-TECH Connections, a systems integrator firm, by solving a problem on a multiuser version of WordPerfect that their network engineers were unable to solve. Eventually I transformed my company from an applications training and consulting organization to an enterprise network management training and consulting company, which turned out to be much more lucrative, and sold it to Hi-TECH Connections.

My knowledge of networking had accelerated my business to unbelievable heights. But I've also seen the downside. The third company in which I invested jumped on videoconferencing technology, as mentioned, before its time. Our focus on the technology accelerated us straight to bankruptcy within a few short years. So timing, as they say, is everything.

IMPLEMENTATION: POUNCING LIKE A PANTHER

Entrepreneurs who have followed all these steps in their own industry are more likely than anyone else to see the magic moment when the technology that fills the hole is feasible. Let's summarize.

We start with a vision, a hedgehog concept. All of our employees know our hedgehog concept, what we are good at and how our clients benefit from working with our company. We know which technologies relate to our capabilities to meet the client needs.

We carefully watch and keep track of technologies that align with our vision. We avoid wasting our time on technologies that don't. We keep track of standards bodies, and know exactly which standards are current, which ones are likely to become real, and which ones will probably fall by the wayside.

We keep track of vendor success. We know which subindustries within the information technology world are blossoming and which ones are floundering.

We keep track of our competitors. We know what level of technology they are using. We know what the customer's expectations are, and whether we (or our competitors) are fulfilling those expectations with existing technology.

We talk with the people on the front lines, so we know where all the holes are. We know what kind of work-arounds we are currently using. We spend quite a bit of time playing with new technologies to see if they fill the holes. We extensively test to ensure that we won't lose existing capabilities when we implement the new technology. We remain patient for the right technology, and we avoid succumbing to the power of wishful thinking. The right technology comes along, and we recognize it. We are ready. Okay ... Pounce.

SUMMARY

- ☑ Start with a well-known and agreed-upon vision.
- ☑ Know which technologies relate to the vision, and keep track of their progress.
- ☑ Avoid wasting time on technologies that don't relate to the vision.
- ☑ Keep track of standards bodies, know which standards are current, and which ones will probably fall by the wayside.
- ☑ Keep track of vendor success. Know which industries are blossoming and which ones are floundering.

☑ Keep track of the competition, and stay just behind them.
☑ Know where all the holes are, and be patient for new technology to fill the holes.
☑ Spend time playing with new technologies to see if they fill the holes without losing existing functionality.
☑ When the right time comes, pounce like a panther.

3

Why Non-IT People Find IT So Difficult

THE ROUGH START

I know how difficult it is to understand information technology because I had that same difficulty myself—in the beginning. When I worked on my bachelor's degree to become a teacher, not one word about computers was mentioned. Nonetheless, in my very first job, in 1982, I was given a computer (an Apple IIe). Being the dutiful teacher I was, I took a class in how to use computers. But when I tried to apply the knowledge to the computer in my classroom, it didn't work. I took another class. I still couldn't use the computer. A third class—and I was still completely lost at sea when I tried to use the computer in my classroom. My father was a computer programmer, but the mainframes he worked on were completely different from the beige box on my desk. I was highly frustrated.

I was so dumb that when I borrowed PFS Filer (a database) from the technology resource room, I couldn't understand why I couldn't edit all the student names and addresses I had entered after I had returned the program. The concepts of application and data and storage were foreign to me. It wasn't until the fourth computer class that I figured out what I was missing. Finally I had met a teacher who taught me about word processing, spreadsheets, and databases, and understood how they worked instead of trying to teach me how to program using a computer language. This experience, and my subsequent career in becoming an entrepreneur and starting a business to teach people how to use computers, made me think quite a bit about information technology and how we attain knowledge about them.

Assessing Technological Skill

There are two main characteristics (shown in Figure 3.1) that identify any particular person's ability to work with computer systems: experience and ability.

How long does it take a person to learn to play a musical instrument? A day? A week? A month? A year? More?

Chances are you said "more."

Figure 3.1
Experience/Ability Chart

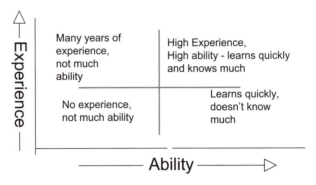

I took piano lessons for 10 years. I practiced enthusiastically every day. The result? Well, let's just say that even my friends grimace when they hear my plodding attempts to play a piano piece for the first time.

It doesn't matter how much I practice or how many years I study, it takes me about six months to learn to play a new piece so that it doesn't elicit the nails-on-chalkboard response from other people. I simply have no talent at playing the piano. If I work on the same piece for a year I might even sound good enough that the uninitiated would think that I was pretty good. But in truth, when it comes to musical instruments, I have high experience but low ability.

My husband is just the opposite. He can pick up any musical instrument in the world—with no prior practice or instruction—and figure out how to play it very quickly. He's never had a piano lesson in his life, but unlike my pedantic pounding, his songs are beautiful music. His ability with music is extremely high.

Technology is a little different for me now. I can sit down to any computer application program, and within days or weeks be using it like I was the original developer. In the 1980s, when I taught individual CEOs how to use the computer programs on their computers, I often would walk in to the lesson having never seen the programs before. But I could always figure it out as we went along. By the end of the lesson, my CEO client would think I'd been using the program for years. I have high ability with technology.

But I recognize that others are not so lucky. My husband calls me every time there is the least little change in the computer screen he is used to. His ability with technology is low, although his experience is high because he's been using technology longer than I have been.

For people who have low ability with technology, their experience on one system might make it appear that they are very good in technology, but their experience is not able to be generalized. I can play the piano, but I can't play a guitar or a flute.

If we don't have some way of assessing people's ability with technology, the hardware and software chosen will be more appropriate to the IT people who make the decision. Because IT people tend to be able to quickly and easily come up to speed on a new technology, they often make the assumption that most people are the same way. Nothing could be further from the truth. For 90 percent of the population, productivity on a new system occurs after years of using the system. Training can shorten this time period, but no matter what it takes most people time to become productive on a new system.

So here's the problem: What happens when the system changes every two years? For most people, they just start feeling comfortable on a system—just start to become productive—and the system changes and they are back to square one. The speed of change in technology is the biggest reason why people with low ability find IT so difficult.

Why does it take so long? Studies of knowledge have led many experts in the field to believe that the issue is one of indexing—making connections to other knowledge, even if this other knowledge seems unrelated to the current information being learned. People who pick up knowledge quickly either have already built indexes to hold that knowledge, or they know how to create their indexes in order to connect that knowledge. The daunting task of building the indexes is time consuming and more difficult the longer you have lived without them. The next generation of workers, of course, developed the indexes as children growing up. They are way ahead of today's generation of business leaders.

Furthermore, using a computer is a combination of both intellectual and kinesthetic skills (eye-hand coordination). Like learning to drive a car, most people learn to use a computer by using a computer. You can't learn it from a book. The more people use technology, the more quickly they pick up new technologies. The more similarities between new technologies and the technology they have already experienced, the more quickly the new methods will be learned.

People with high experience and high ability tend to gravitate toward highly technical jobs. We will probably find more of them among the information technology divisions of the company. They tend to be the most flexible regarding information technology. They will learn new technologies quickly, and they will be able to rely upon past experience to help them make the most of any information technology they use.

High-experience, high-ability people, however, are not appropriate for all jobs. They tend to get bored easily, and do not do well in jobs that require attention to detail or unchanging tasks. They also don't tend to do as well managing people, or where a high degree of collaboration is necessary.

Specific jobs using a single system are sometimes better suited to people with lower ability. For example, an accounts payable position entails using the same system over and over again in the same way. Another example would be someone who enters shipments into a warehouse receipts program every day. In these cases high experience in the system used would be a bigger plus than general high ability. As a matter of fact, this combination can be spectacular. If a person with low-technology ability gets into a groove with a system, his personal productivity goes into a super-summit mode. It would be very hard for a competitor to match that level of productivity.

Understanding the Nature of the Gap

To be personally more productive, we have to do more than learn just the basics. We need to learn all the little tricks and techniques for using a system more effectively. Furthermore, we cannot assume that our employees are taking it upon themselves to become more knowledgeable and experienced in any particular technology. When queried, people will usually say that they already know how to use a particular technology. Even if they realize they have much to learn, they find it difficult to admit when they don't know something, and often don't want to spend the time to learn more. This is human nature.

Let's take a nontechnical example. Imagine that we are running a large business in widget distribution. We hire people. Some do sales; some do billing. Some do business development. Some do purchasing. Now imagine that occasionally we hire someone who knows how to use the telephone, but for the most part, the people we hire have never had to use a telephone before. They pretend, of course. They pick up the handle, hold it to their ear and talk, imitating the people who actually know how to use the telephone. But they don't actually know how to dial the phone and ask for someone. Should we just ignore the fact that they don't know how to use the telephone? Of course not. We would insist that they learn how to use the device properly so that they can do their jobs more effectively. We would bring in special trainers, if need be, because learning to use the telephone is such a basic requirement of the job.

Of course, in today's environment everyone already knows how to use the telephone. But what if they didn't? Imagine you are one of the people who doesn't know how to use a telephone. You go into the office, and everyone else acts like using the phone is so easy a toddler could do it. They all seem to have no trouble using it. Would you go to any of those coworkers and say, "How do you know what number to dial? What should you do when it rings?" Of course not. You might be embarrassed to admit that you don't know, and you won't want to face sneers or jeers from people who do know (although they are no better than you; they just had someone show them already).

But we can't allow the gap to continue to widen. As time goes on and the majority of people learn how to use this technology, the problem will get worse for the few who haven't yet learned it. The fear of appearing dumb prevents people from learning more about how to utilize hardware and software more effectively. Unfortunately, ignoring the problem tends to backfire. An obvious example is the CEO who insists on the fancy laptop—but who has never opened it up. This is apocryphal. There is even a Dilbert cartoon about a laptop that Dilbert gave his pointy-haired boss. Dilbert carefully explained that it had to be shaken upside-down in order to reboot. Amazingly enough, it looked just like an Etch A Sketch.

The less obvious but more common example is the person who enters the column of numbers into a spreadsheet, and then uses a calculator to add up the column of numbers and enters in the total. (You would be surprised by the number of people who do this!) Or the people who press the [Enter] key at the end of each line when they type into a word processor—especially when they want the second line indented (and they don't know how to use the indent function).

As entrepreneurs and technology leaders, it's important that we recognize the huge gap between those who have been using information technology regularly and those who are relatively new to the process or use it infrequently. Information technology is easy—when you already know how it works. Information technology can be devilishly difficult—when you don't already know how it works.

In most cases, there is no pressure to be an effective information technology user. Few managers insist that their employees become personally productive using technology—often because they themselves have not done so. They don't understand its importance.

It often takes quite a bit of creative encouragement to get people to learn it. As noted, due to embarrassment or learned helplessness, few people will ask for help in learning to use a personal computer more effectively. An entrepreneur or business owner can cultivate a business culture that encourages learning.

First, it is up to entrepreneurs and business owners to get over their own humps. Believe me, I know how difficult this is. In the 1980s, a great deal of my computer training business was individualized confidential and private instruction for the CEOs of many of the larger businesses in the area. These senior leaders could not ask their employees to teach them without losing status. They could not take a class (many of which are not paced properly for highly intelligent leaders who didn't have any context for information technology and therefore needed a completely different approach to learning it). What they desperately needed, and what I gave them back then, was a customized program of instruction, spread out over the course of six months to a year, in blocks of 90 minutes, two or three times a week. I called it "The Executive Program," and it was many times more expensive than any other instruction. But the executives who went through it back in the 1980s are undoubtedly much more well-informed today about information technology topics because they got over the hump early. Those who didn't are now 20 years older, and still on the wrong side of the information technology hump. And now they face competition from youngsters who grew up with computers.

Once they've gotten over their own hump (and even if they haven't), it is up to the leader of an organization to establish a culture where people are not made to feel inferior because they don't yet know how to do some function on the computer, while at the same time demonstrating the importance of the knowledge. It is up to the leader of the organization to encourage people to ask questions and figure out a more effective and efficient way to do everything they currently do.

It makes the most sense for us, as business leaders, to take responsibility, find out where our employees are in their level of knowledge, and train them on the gap between what they know and what they don't know.

It is also important to understand the extensive time involved in the process. Information technology is not something that can be learned in a day-long workshop. Not even a week-long training class. Not even a month-long course. Learning to use information technology effectively, when starting from square one, takes years and years.

Most important, it is up to the leader of an organization to recognize that while people are learning new technology, they must be given leeway regarding their productivity. We can only expect drastically increased productivity once they have fully learned the new technology.

Making the Assessment

I wish I could say that there is a specific test that we could give prospective employees to determine their technology ability and experience. There is not. I've given you a sample general personal computer assessment in Appendix C, but the truth is that an assessment has to be based upon the particular needs of a particular job. I've found that, in most cases, an informal assessment by the supervisor works better than a formal paper-and-pencil assessment. High-ability employees are more likely to already shop on-line and to belong to on-line communities such as LinkedIn or YouTube or MySpace. These are Web sites where you can join a community, set up a profile, post your comments or videos, and interact with others in the community at no cost. High-ability people have frequent conversations with friends and family in e-mail or using instant chat programs. You might also want to ask employees if they would like the opportunity to learn a new software. Those who are willing to volunteer are more likely to be high ability.

Experience is a bit more difficult. Experience can be both wide and deep. If an employee knows how to use 10 different computer programs, her experience is wider than if she only knows two different programs. But if an employee has used only one or two programs for the past 15 years, his experience is deep, not wide.

Level of experience can be estimated by simply observing the employee using the program. An employee with strong knowledge of a program will work very quickly and take many shortcuts; she will seem to fly through tasks. An employee with a low level of knowledge will use the menu (often the slowest method), read everything on the screen, and take much longer to accomplish the tasks. With a high-experience person, an observer will have trouble keeping up with how he got from screen A to screen B. With a low-experience person, an observer might feel slightly impatient because she seems to take forever to get anywhere.

One way to create an assessment for new people is to first work with someone who has high ability and high experience in one of the programs utilized by your business. Watch what they do and how long it takes them to do things. Then assess others' capabilities against those measurements.

Here's an exercise that would assess, for example, the technology skills for the word processor: Go into a document that someone within your company has sent you recently and change whatever option you must to reveal the invisible codes. (In Microsoft Word, it's usually a button with a ¶ on it.) Look at a paragraph that's been indented. If the person has a ¶ at the end of each line and has manually lined up the indent with either spaces (.) or tabs (⇒) then she has never learned to properly use the word processor, and is wasting time each day lining things up manually. Another test: Did she use a template, or did she manually make all the changes needed to the normal template? (You can tell by going into the File—Properties choice and seeing if the template says "normal.dot" or something else.) Does she use Styles, or does she manually change the format for every word and paragraph? Watch your employees copy and paste. Do they painstakingly go back to the main menu for everything, or do they use the toolbar buttons or shortcut keys (Ctrl+C to copy and Ctrl+V to paste)?

Of course, you may want to do this test on your own documents, and get someone to show you any of the markers you are missing. Styles and templates, for example, are much more efficient than manual formatting. But their use demonstrates an advanced knowledge or ability because they are known and used by very few people. You may think that these are small things, but all the hundreds of small things add up to significant difference in productivity over time—hundreds of hours a year. If your people are not as educated in using the software as they could be, they are wasting valuable time every day.

Accepting the Learning Curve ROI

I once worked with a client whose secretary, Rosemary, typed everything on a word processor, but she never saved anything—ever. She typed it, and then exited out of the word processing program because she didn't see the need to save. In other words, she was using the word processor as if it were a typewriter. For her it was quicker and easier to retype the document than to learn how to retrieve a saved document because Rosemary could type up a one-page letter in five minutes. It would probably take an hour for someone to show her how to save and name a document the very first time. This short-term hit to productivity was why the fairly intelligent manager, Pam, continued to allow her secretary to retype the documents instead of saving and retrieving them (not necessarily a bad thing). Pam wasn't willing to wait an hour for a document, and though she knew that Rosemary wasn't using the system properly, she wasn't willing to demonstrate the proper way, or encourage Rosemary to take a class so that she could learn the proper way. Pam did not even complain about the fact that it took much longer to get a change made to a document because Rosemary had to retype it from scratch each and every time. In Pam's mind, the difference was minimal and few enough documents needed to be changed.

The problem is that the company is losing out. By enabling Rosemary to use the word processor like a typewriter, the company is losing the electronic history of documents that would be helpful to the person who takes over for Rosemary after she retires. True, the ROI on a single letter is negative because Rosemary could type, print, and exit in less time than it would take to learn to save. However, the cost of copying, organizing, and storing copies of all those letters would be a drain on the entire company. Furthermore, the difficulty in making a single change may mean that the company was avoiding needed changes unnecessarily. When looking at the whole picture instead of just one document, the ROI on learning to save documents makes a lot of sense.

Of course, there are times when we have to drop our quest to do it a better way and simply get it done any way we know how. It is not easy to know where to draw the line. In a few cases, the front-end learning curve is not worth it for a single event. It makes little sense, for example, to learn how to mail merge (automatically create a letter for each name and address in a separate list) if we only send out one mail merge every five years to 20 people. In that case, we should simply save a template and enter the name and address manually. But most times, learning to mail merge is well worth the learning curve because once we've learned how to do something, we will find 10 others ways to utilize that knowledge to make things more efficient. It may be, for example, that we only send out one mailing every five years because it's so hard to do. Once we've mastered mail merge and it's a five-minute task instead of a 10-hour task, we may well use it several times throughout the year—increasing sales and profits and making 200 or 300 times return on our investment.

There are also times when we have to give up trying to change the people in our employ and just let them do things either manually or using whatever system they prefer. It is a smart strategy to wait until the extremely reliable and fast employee retires to try and implement a new system because chances are, we will completely lose the productivity of that employee if we switch systems and force him to use it.

Unfortunately, because it's difficult to quantify the return on the outset, often managers are unable to take that initial hit to productivity during the learning curve. In many cases, managers aren't really sure what's worth it and what's not. The difficulty is that the larger the gap between the employees who can easily use information technology and the employees who find it harder to use, the worse it gets. Not only will the people themselves be less productive than the technically knowledgeable ones, but there will also be more resistance to changes and new technologies.

Overcoming Initial Resistance

There is always initial resistance to any new system. However, once the benefits of technology become obvious, no one ever goes back. When was the last time you saw an office filled with typewriters, index cards filing systems, telex systems, or round finger dialing telephones? Once people use word processors, contact management, e-mail, or spreadsheets, they rarely go back to doing it the old way. Once people discover how easy it is to find information on the World Wide Web, they never go back to wasting time trudging through library stacks. But first someone must show them how to use the word processor, contact manager, e-mail, spreadsheet, or Web browser. And someone must encourage them to use these tools appropriately.

Overcoming resistance to new technologies can sometimes require creativity and effort. Overcoming resistance is always possible when the benefits of the technology are real and experienced firsthand by the users. But the perception of benefit cannot be forced.

Jane, a CIO for a network of hospitals in California, tried five different ways to implement a computerized physician order entry (CPOE) system. They tried four different vendors. They tried PCs, tablets, and PDAs. No matter what they tried, the physicians demanded that the system be removed.

Why? It takes a physician five seconds to fill out a prescription on paper. The fastest physicians took two to three minutes for a computerized version. According to Jane, the doctors were frustrated, and felt that the system was stealing money out of their pockets because of the crippling impact on their productivity. Even when the system was finally implemented, it took about a year for physicians to recover to 90 percent of their original productivity.

One of the most difficult areas to deal with regarding resistance is sales-support software. Sales administrators would love for their salespeople to utilize information technology to the max because it would give them more control over the process (they believe) and enable salespeople to make more sales in less time. Certainly, there are some information technologies that are very helpful to salespeople. Wireless communication, cell phones, dynamic inventory information, and remote sales order capability can increase sales. But customer relationship management (CRM) programs often meet with strong resistance from salespeople. Like the physician who loses time on every prescription, CRM programs often interfere with the sales process and steal important relationship-building time away from salespeople. I've seen cases where the best salespeople in a company refused to use administratively mandated programs, while the worst salespeople in a company used them eagerly. If the benefits were real, the opposite would be true.

The best way to overcome resistance is to have a large number of users, not just a token few, involved in the decision making regarding any new system. George, CEO of a large regional teaching hospital, learned this lesson the hard way.

Ten years ago the administration tried to make the emergency room (ER) entirely paper free. The project planning lasted about six months and was done mostly by administrators, and the system was installed within another six months. George mandated its use by all doctors and nurses in the ER, but most of the doctors and nurses refused to use it. The hospital eventually scrapped the project.

For a more recent medical administration automation (MAA) project, George used a different tactic. There was still a high level of resistance initially. But this time the administrators involved many doctors and nurses in the project planning. They then spent two years in planning and then another year in piloting the system on various floors. Unlike the paperless emergency room system, this time they also included a great deal of ongoing training and support in the plan.

The results of the pilot clearly told the tale. Staff who had worked on the floors *with* the new technology were refusing to go back to work on the floors *without* the new technology. Once the doctors and nurses experienced the benefits, they became fans of the new system. Word spread to others, and for the most part resistance disappeared.

In summary, there are five keys to overcoming resistance to new technology:

- Make sure the users of the system are the ones who get to make the plan and choose the system (not administrators or information technology folk).
- Spend more time planning than implementing.
- Allow for a generous start-up time while the new technology is being learned without the pressure of quotas or other measurements based upon pre-technology processes.
- Make sure that there is ongoing support and training—not just at the beginning of the implementation, but for years afterwards, too.

WHAT WE NEED TO KNOW ABOUT TRAINING

Research is pretty clear that trying to save money by limiting training is not very smart. Organizations that have invested in new financial systems, but did not invest in training, did not do as well as organizations that invested in financial systems and the training for them.[24] The key was the percentage of the staff involved in the training. In one study, companies that involved higher percentages of their staff in training had higher returns from their information technology investment. Another study found that organizations that spend roughly 20 percent of project funds on training succeeded, while organizations that allocate a mere 4 percent to 6 percent to training (a much more common amount) tended to fail more often.[25]

You may think that this is common sense—I certainly do—but I've been surprised, again and again, by decisions of senior leaders to cut the training budget, or to plan only for initial and not ongoing training, or choose to train only a few people.

Why do entrepreneurs make the decision to cut the training budget so often? Why is the training budget one of the first things to go when money gets tight?

For one thing, training quality can vary widely. If one company purchases a training tutorial for 5,000 employees at a cost of $100,000, and another company custom-designs and implements live training for five different levels of employees with an experienced trainer at a cost of $100,000, are they both equivalently trained? My experience says "no," but there are lots of vendors of on-line tutorials who will disagree with me.

For another thing, it is rather hard to trace specific financial returns to training. The cost of training can get very high. As noted earlier, 20 percent is not too much to spend, yet very few companies invest that much.

Consider this fact the next time you are about to commit $5 million to implement a new system and the project manager, who is about to launch the project including a 20 percent budget for training, budgets $1 million for training. Instead of retorting: "What do you mean we need to budget $1 million for training—are you crazy?" it might make sense to remember the value of a failed project. Would you rather invest $5 million in a successful project or $4 million in an unsuccessful project? Implementing a new system without paying a significant amount for training is like buying a car and then refusing to purchase any gasoline for it.

The third reason is how training appears in an ROI calculation. According to generally accepted accounting principles (GAAP), training should be listed as a one-time expense. This might put the ROI on the negative side, and doesn't accurately reflect the valuable ongoing benefits of training. One way to adjust for this problem is to include the training dollars in maintenance kits, documentation costs, and upgrade costs, all of which are capitalized and depreciated over time. The ability to capitalize the training costs is why so many vendors are willing and able to bundle training dollars with the software and hardware—they know that they wouldn't get those training dollars any other way. While not illegal to bundle training costs, it is better, in my opinion, to have the training dollars spelled out. But if the financial arm of a company places limitations on the amount of training because of its impact to the return on investment calculation, then I see nothing wrong with encouraging a vendor to bundle the costs. Good training is, after all, one of the most valuable components in the purchase of a new system.

Of course, getting training from the vendor of the hardware and software may work fine—but it also may have problems. For one thing, because of the difficulty of getting recognition of the importance of training, hardware and software vendors know that they have a captured training market. That means the training from the vendor of the hardware or software often simply isn't very good. Vendors don't have to pay top dollar for really great trainers or put as much effort into the quality of their training. They don't have to try so hard because they can fill up their classes with trainees who are getting the training, in their minds, "for free." Unfortunately, when the quality of the training goes down, the value of the training goes down as well. It's like trying to run a car on a mixture of gas and water. The magical effect that training has on making systems pay off disappears when the training is not of a high enough quality.

I'm not saying all vendors have poor training. Some do a very high-quality job. But you can't always count on that—so it makes sense to check it out before you accept the training as part of the package.

Just-In-Time Training

Another key to employee productivity is just-in-time training. Rather than sending people off to day-long or week-long workshops, it makes much more sense to ensure that anytime an employee needs a particular set of training, he can get it. Need to use the invoicing module for the first time next Friday? Schedule a few hours of training on Wednesday or Thursday. Need to send out 150 letters to people using a mail merge next Tuesday? Schedule a few hours of training on Monday.

People tend to learn more (1) when the training is immediately relevant and (2) when the training is hands-on. Just-in-time training can ensure both of these things in a cost-effective manner.

How to Tell the Quality of the Training

So how can we tell if the training we are considering is high quality? First, it relies upon live trainers—and trainers who do both training and consulting for a living. Trainers who do nothing but training rarely have the real-life experience that is the essential secret ingredient to high-quality live training.

Second, the training is flexible enough to accommodate the needs of the people taking the training. When a training group is relatively large, it's impossible to meet all the needs of everyone. But sometimes, even if the training group is small, the curriculum requirements restrict the ability of the trainer to answer questions and get into the kind of details that will really help the trainees. So courses with a too-strict curriculum are actually detrimental to high-quality training.

You might think that I would add high-quality materials to this list, but in practice I've found that although materials can add to the quality of training, they are not essential for high-quality training. Furthermore, the high cost of material development often outstrips its benefit, especially in the constantly changing world of IT. The experience and talents of the trainer are really the deciding factor between an okay training and great training. A great trainer can add great value just by sharing experiences. A poor trainer can have the best materials in the world and it won't help the quality.

Additionally, in my experience, there is no substitute for live training with an experienced and talented teacher. I have found many tutorials to be a complete waste of money.

Matching Hardware and Software to Ability and Experience Levels

Characteristics should also figure prominently when we make a decision on hardware and software. To mitigate the effect of the difficulty in learning new technologies, we can assess people's skill in technology and match the hardware and software types to their ability levels.

When dealing with employees with high ability, we can choose software with more power. Software has more power when it is possible to program within the program with templates, macros, ad-hoc reporting, and so on. Word, Excel, and Access are all much more powerful programs, for example, than PowerPoint, Works, or Encarta. When dealing with employees with low ability, ease of use should be the guiding factor when choosing a program. Easy-to-use programs are sometimes not as powerful, but they are much more effective among people who have less need of power. Most people will never use the advanced features of software anyway, so why confuse them with the option? Often, a good pairing comes from someone with high ability customizing the programs for people with lower ability.

Problems can occur if there is a mismatch. If we give simple technology with few options to people with a great deal of ability and experience, we limit their productivity. They will be frustrated at what they know they could do if they were only given the proper tools. At the same time, we can't give sophisticated and complex systems to people with low ability or experience, or the capabilities will be wasted and the people will still not be able to get the information they require. In the end, balance is the key.

SUMMARY

We can mitigate the difficulties that non-IT people experience with IT by:

- ☑ Assessing people's ability and experience in technology.
- ☑ Encouraging personal productivity with technology.
- ☑ Not allowing the gap to get too wide.
- ☑ Understanding the learning curve ROI.
- ☑ Overcoming initial resistance.
- ☑ Focusing on quality training.

4

Why IT People Are So Difficult

Let us now turn our attention to that 10 percent of the people who actually develop, install, and maintain all this information technology. If it hasn't become apparent to you yet, let me point out that technology people are not the same as non-technology people. The stereotype of the geek, pockets filled with gadgets, hunched head-down at the computer, effortlessly gliding around the virtual world (while a face-to-face meeting would tie the tongue and put knots in the stomach)—is not always far from the truth. Chapter 3 was about general staff—administrative, sales, marketing, and operations employees. This chapter focuses specifically on managing information technology staff, as well as IT vendor personnel.

First, they seem to have completely different motivations from most businesspeople. Second, they often don't have the same people skills as non-technology people. Third, they sometimes pursue technical excellence and logic to the exclusion of common sense. Fourth, they may have developed a sense of entitlement, especially if they have achieved guru status in the IT world. In order to use their skills effectively, we will need to adjust for these differences.

WHY ENTREPRENEURS NEED TO KNOW THEIR IT STAFF

Some small business owners can avoid the pitfalls of managing IT people directly, because their businesses are small enough that they don't actually have any hard-core IT people on staff. They either rely upon vendors, or struggle along without any real IT guidance. However, IT vendors are filled with IT people, so it would behoove all entrepreneurs and business owners to read and understand this section.

Many of today's entrepreneurs will find this section extremely useful because they may be trying to build a business around the skills and talents of a particular IT guru or team. Ethernet, Linux, enterprise network management, the public Internet—all of these innovations and hundreds more came out of virtual teams of technologists in a relatively short amount of time. They were built within a special IT culture of knowledge. But it was rarely the technology gurus themselves who did the business building. For most, there needed to be a partnership between IT people and non-IT people.

In my own background, two of the start-up companies in which I was involved were based upon the technical expertise of gurus (other than me). One company was based upon the brilliance of enterprise network management engineers, and the other was based upon the superstar capabilities of Web site developers. In both cases, the success of the business was directly related to how well the leaders of the organization managed the gurus of the organization.

Once I was hired by the CIO and CEO of a midsized manufacturer because their director of IT was difficult. They wanted to fire him. They were unsure what would happen to the network, however, since neither the CEO nor the CIO knew anything about how the network was set up. All they knew was that this director of IT was spending too much money and giving them a hard time. He was disrespectful to them. He was ignoring their directives and going off and doing things on his own. So I came into the organization as a consultant ostensibly to write up a report on network security, but really I was there to learn as much as I could about the network so I could quickly secure the network when they fired the director of IT, and to help them find a replacement.

What I found was surprising. In every nook and cranny I checked, this director of IT had made the right decision. As I looked at the history of the network, I could see how he had taken a very backward system and, bit by bit, and for very low cost, transformed it into a high-performing, secure tool for the administrators of the corporation. He had also taken a look at the old-legacy manufacturing system and started down the road on an excellent replacement plan.

To top it off, he was not paid very well for his efforts. As I started the search for his replacement, I could see that it would cost three times his salary to find someone with the breadth and width of his domain knowledge.

I delved a bit more deeply into the conflict he was having with the business leaders. Apparently, they had given him some directions he felt would compromise the network. They told him to ignore security protocols and switch over to an obsolete operating system. Initially he argued with them. He was not very tactful in his responses to their "boneheaded" commands. Finally he simply ignored them and didn't return their calls. But he was still working 60 hours a week ensuring that they had the best infrastructure they could possibly have at the lowest possible cost. I was able to convince the CIO and CEO to keep him, and he is still working there as I write this.

This story demonstrates the pervasiveness of the difficulty when non-technologists try to lead technologists using standard hierarchical "I know better than you" command structures. It also demonstrates that good technologists often have poor people skills.

There are many experienced technologists in the field, but few who can both do the work and work with people. Often, executives have to make a choice. Is it more important to have superior technology at a low price? Or is it more important to have people who get along together and have substandard technology?

CHARACTERISTICS OF IT FOLKS AND GURU

As noted, many entrepreneurial businesses are dependent upon the skills of an IT guru. Unless they are managed right, gurus themselves can be the obstacle to their own success. They have a tendency toward arrogance and often get involved in petty technological religious wars (like Microsoft versus open source) rather than focusing on accomplishing the task at hand. Even if the entrepreneur is not counting upon the specific talents of a guru for the growth of the business, all businesses need brilliant technological people to quickly fix issues.

Despite all the drawbacks brilliant IT people are often essential for success. Technological people of lesser skill may end up being nicer, but they also tend to spin the wheels of never-ending problems and may do more harm than good when it comes to fixing issues that impact productivity of the whole company. Gurus keep the computers running smoothly and solve every problem that comes up. We can't live profitably without them.

If your company has been lucky enough to find brilliant technology people, then you know what a big difference it makes in how productive your company can be when using technology. But if these same people have become a thorn in your side, don't despair. Don't make the mistake of letting them go. Smoothly running computer systems are often worth the risk of fracturing a few feathers. We just have to learn how to manage them.

Techno-Jargon

Very few people understand the language of information technology. Techno-jargon is the terminology that IT folks use to converse. Believe it or not, techno-jargon is not purposefully used to exclude non-IT people. Techno-jargon is used because IT folks must discuss issues at a level of detail that is beyond what most people know about IT, and the jargon provides the shades of meaning necessary to have accurate and meaningful conversations. A doctor can't just say the leg is broken; there are several bones in the leg that might be affected. A doctor, when talking to another doctor, would need to specify an intertrochanteric fracture of the femur bone.

Furthermore, the jargon gap is due, in part, to a time lag before the concepts permeate the culture. The vocabulary is not well known among the general business population yet. Businesspeople, after all, have just recently even begun to think of technology as part of the operation, so there is a gap between their knowledge and the vocabulary. The gap will eventually disappear and what was once considered lingo will be part of the general knowledge.

Don't believe it?

Well, imagine that you have just been magically transported back 95 years. Walk around a typical small town and talk to the people who live and work there. Ask someone to tell you what a parking brake is. Try to explain to someone how a carburetor works. Look around for a gas station or a car mechanic. When you don't find them, ask a few people where they are, and note the look of puzzlement on their faces. How many people would you meet who would know that you have to change the oil in your car every few thousand miles? How many would know that it makes no sense to put your foot on the gas and the brake at the same time?

Back in the early 1910s, information about automobiles was not generally known. The terminology was specialized, and only known to the few who had built their own cars. Those who actually owned these cars were different from everyone else—so they likely hung out together and developed their own specialized culture. When problems arose they would check with their buddies instead of a commercial establishment. Garage mechanic was not yet a job classification.

Think about it. Today, most people know what a car is, what it looks like, how to drive it, perhaps even how it works. They know that a car has a body, an engine, and that it runs on gasoline. They know how to turn a steering wheel, they know that cars can't be driven under water, and they know that a Porsche is faster than a Hyundai. They know the oil has to get changed regularly, and they know that if they don't fill up the tank before they run out of gas they will get stuck somewhere. Think about the amount of general knowledge there is about automobiles among everyone—from children to senior citizens. Words that were techno-jargon in the 1920s are now commonly understood terms.

Now try to imagine what it would be like to purchase a car without understanding any of those terms. Can you imagine looking at a brochure and not understanding what is meant by a V-6 engine or power steering or anti-lock brakes?

IT folks understand buzzwords and jargon, and have a hard time explaining them to people who don't understand them. IT folks see many business leaders making decisions about technology products and services without understanding what they are buying, what components are included, or how it all works.

How many business leaders have you encountered who would know that trying to put Windows XP on an AS400 machine is akin to putting the engine of a Volkswagen Bug inside the body of an Oldsmobile Regency? Did you even know that? How many people know that occasionally you have to optimize the hard drive space, and re-index the databases? Or that you can't run an enterprise network management software on the same machine as a relational database? Any IT person would recognize all of these terms and would know, without having to think about it, all of these general IT facts. Most businesspeople would not, but they make business decisions that are influenced by all these facts.

That isn't to say we haven't made progress—we have come a long way. Today, terms such as *Web site, Internet, e-mail, personal computer, printer,* and *flash drive* are pretty commonly understood. Most people can name Microsoft, Hewlett-Packard, and Google as large technology companies. More than 10 years ago that might not have been true.

But we still have far to go. How many CFOs can explain the difference between an operating system and an application? How many CEOs can differentiate between a BPM system, a CRM system, or an ERP system? How many know that virtual private networks are neither virtual, nor private, nor networks? How many know that Quality of Service has nothing to do with quality or service?

An *operating system* is the low-level instructions that interface between the programs and the hardware. The *applications* are the programs like Office, SAP, Oracle, Outlook, etc.

BPM is business process management software. *CRM* is customer relationship management software. *ERP* is enterprise resource planning software. In my opinion, all of these terms are used inconsistently by everyone, but generally they all relate to enterprise-wide applications used in business.

A *VPN* is called a virtual private network, but it is really just a way of encrypting information for privacy because the Internet has no built-in security. Using a VPN is akin to putting all of your messages in a locked Kevlar bank envelope before sending them through the U.S. postal mail.

Quality of Service (QoS) refers to being able to distinguish between different types of messages on a private Internet. QoS does not exist on the public Internet. On an Internet, if a videoconference system and an e-mail system share the same network, installing QoS on the routers will allow the routers to be programmed to hold the e-mail message traffic while letting the videoconferencing traffic go through uninterrupted.

Suffice it to say that IT folks sometimes feel like they are speaking English while everyone else is limited to Latin.

Logic and People Skills

If you have ever tried to manage someone who has superb technology skills and knows it, you may recognize that technological brilliance often precludes the ability to work well with others in a team. They get testy when forced to deal with real problems that interfere with the elegance of their systems. According to them, if everyone would just conform to the logical world of computers, everything would be peachy keen—no one would be frustrated. They often feel that they are being forced to work in a world filled with bumbling dunderheads who don't know a kernel command from a universal resource locator call. They are frustrated at dealing with people who can't memorize command-line syntax or even troubleshoot a corrupted driver. Most people use Windows and mice to click on menus, but real IT folks like to enter the commands directly because if they know the syntax they can accomplish many things more quickly and more powerfully than if they are limited to a menu.

In Unix computer systems, the central core is called a *kernel*. A command directed to the hardware directly through the core programming language is called a *kernel command*.

A *universal resource locator* (URL) is the address of a Web page. To make a URL call is to write a command to read the contents of a Web page, as in http://google.com, which is the URL call to the home page of the Google Web site.

Command line syntax is following the rules for writing commands. For example, *dir/w* is a command to provide a short wide list of all the files in a folder. *Dir\w*, for example, would be the wrong syntax.

A *driver* is a file with instructions for using a peripheral like a printer or a flash card. Because a driver is written by a manufacturer to work with the operating system and hardware of other manufacturers, they often don't work correctly or get corrupted.

You will recognize the true gurus because they will want to automate everything. They are exasperated by a world that doesn't see the value of technology the way they do. They will spend six hours writing a program to automate a two-minute manual task done four times a year. You may think I'm exaggerating, but I've seen it myself. Actually even though I'm not really an IT guru, in my early programming days I was guilty of doing the same thing!

People who get along superbly well with computers often do not get along as well with other people. The rules of the computer world are complex, but stable, logical, and predictable—easily understood once you've cracked the code. The real world of relationships, on the other hand, is fraught with illogical and unpredictable behavior. In a computer system, variables are easily controlled. People are not so easily controlled. Face-to-face encounters with people demand flexibility. Rejection is a potential risk to one's self-esteem. Some technology people take a preemptive strike against rejection by acting rude and insolent from the get-go. They seem to have no respect for authority or hierarchy.

To deal with the lack of people skills, the most important prerequisite is to be understanding of the behavior. Think about it this way: Non-IT people think IT is complex and difficult, and people are easy to get along with if you are just friendly and helpful. IT people think that IT is easy to get along with if you just understand the logic, and people are complex and difficult to deal with. Just as non-IT people would appreciate a little more patience when they have trouble with IT, IT people would appreciate a little more patience and understanding when they have trouble with people.

Although rude behavior should never be tolerated, a certain amount of gruffness should be expected.

Sometimes it helps to minimize contact between IT people and non-IT people. I know one company that set up a system of e-mail requests rather than phone requests. The less time the IT person needs to spend dealing with non-IT people, the fewer problems the business will have.

Non-Business Motivations

Typical business leaders, with their core talents at managing people and making strategic business decisions that produce profits, are often totally flummoxed by the dedicated IT people who aren't governed by the same internal motivations as most people. Just what makes them tick?

The best technologists are typically highly intelligent independent thinkers, dedicated to doing a good job. As noted, they also tend to be poor communicators who don't play well with others. But there is an exception: IT people congregate with other IT people, who then provide their true motivation for work—recognition. The best IT people wish to impress their virtual peers.

The rules governing the dynamics of technology teams are simple—the most elegant algorithm or the most in-depth insight wins. Hierarchy is established immediately after public demonstrations of domain knowledge, which determines which role will be played by which guru (as tacitly agreed upon by all members of the team). Only performance matters. No one cares about looks or congeniality. Each takes turns showing off to each other.

The motivations of suits (a derogatory name IT people often use to connote businesspeople) are often unappealing to IT people. One time I carefully set up policies to govern how my IT staff would earn raises, or corner offices, or offices with windows. I shouldn't have wasted my time. It turned out my IT staff couldn't care less about money. Or a corner office. Or any of the normal trappings of success. What they care about is knowledge and getting information technology to do things. All 10 IT folks chose to stay in their windowless cubicles in a shared space rather than be separated off in their own windowed offices! (They did take the raises, of course, but personally I don't think they were very motivated by them.)

Obviously the answer to this issue is to recognize that the trappings of success that motivate businesspeople may not work for IT people. We may need to spend more time and effort discerning their true motivations.

Aversion to Multidisciplinary Teams

Between the lack of interpersonal skills and a different base of motivation, we can see why teams that mix businesspeople and technology people often don't work. For one thing, businesspeople can't immediately ascertain who has the most talent, so they have a hard time understanding the IT hierarchy. A brilliant algorithm won't necessarily increase sales or lower costs, so it is not important to businesspeople. As a result, they often don't pay the proper respect to the achievements of the IT folk. A non-IT person might give more respect to the nicer IT person (who doesn't know as much) than to the truly brilliant IT person who has the best chance of solving their IT problems. That's akin to treating the janitor like royalty and ignoring or insulting the VP in the office.

We often have to find alternatives for IT folk that don't require them to interact and play nice with others on a non-IT team.

One common strategy that doesn't work well is the matrixing solution. A *matrix organization* is one in which project teams band and disband and in which a traditional hierarchy is hard to discern. In a matrix organization, IT personnel report to several different people and are responsible for prioritizing among the requests of them all. My experience is that matrixed IT people end up pleasing no one. They are put in a position where they can surreptitiously spend all their time working on esoteric technical issues without any real-life application, telling each person demanding their time that they are working on a problem for someone else. Instead of solving problems, they create new ones.

One strategy I've found that does work well is to appoint a liaison to work directly with IT people so they don't have to attend team meetings. Also pairing a non-IT person with an IT guru tends to work well. The non-IT person must have enough IT knowledge to gain the respect of the IT person, but they don't have to be super technical (just tolerant). The non-IT person can do the documentation and training for the systems while the IT person can develop, configure, and install the systems.

The Hero and the Challenge

I don't know many IT people who have *not* experienced the thrill of being the hero. Because there aren't that many people who understand IT, often IT people can quickly and easily fix problems that completely mystify everyone else. I can tell you that there is no better feeling in the world than to be the knight in shining armor to an office full of non-IT people.

However, I've noticed a very bad trend. IT people, in seeking opportunities to repeat this feeling, may subconsciously manufacture crises that they are then called in to fix. Even if not precisely manufactured, IT people may not do all they can to ensure smooth-running systems. They scorn documentation and often will not share their secrets of configuration or programming. They do not have any motivation to ensure that systems can run perfectly without them. Just as businesspeople can become addicted to the urgent rather than the important, IT people often become addicted to the crisis solution rather than the stable system.

Face it; the stable smooth-running system is no fun. Once a system is working perfectly, most IT people will feel compelled to tinker with it, ostensibly to incrementally improve it, but resulting in constant changes that require further tinkering to fix. Vendors encourage this behavior by continually providing patches and upgrades they must install.

The truth is, a smooth-running system needs no maintenance, no upgrades, no work. With the exception of bona fide security patches, there should be no need to install or update anything. However, there is no glory in keeping a smoothly running system going. IT people can't be the hero that rushes in to save the day if everything runs smoothly. They might be ignored. Or worse—the leaders might get the mistaken impression that IT folk are not needed and fire them! I've seen this happen. If systems run too smoothly, you might forget that the IT folks who got the systems running smoothly are the *only* people who can keep them running smoothly. IT is still too complex for a second IT person to come in and take over. In other words, the configuration of a smoothly running system is unique and would take months (if not years) to fully understand. Organizations cannot afford to eliminate their IT people (or their IT vendors).

But how do you get IT people currently addicted to being the hero to change their focus and instead ensure smoothly running systems? The answer is to build smoothly running systems into both their formal performance review and an informal pat-on-the-back habit. Keep measurements of how long the system has been running without a problem and how many backups have been done without incident. Don't count help desk calls (because that will discourage people from calling), but conduct surveys and count satisfied users.

To keep IT people busy while the systems are running smoothly, direct them toward the future of the organization. Provide them with a budget and a test lab. Have them keep on top of the standards bodies and install and test each new product or service that comes out in the domain of the hedgehog concept of the company. Feature their results in a quarterly or annual presentation to the senior leaders. Get them involved in planning the next generation (5 to 10 years out) of IT systems. Most of all, treat them with a lot of respect for their knowledge and skills.

Not-Invented-Here Syndrome

The not-invented-here (NIH) syndrome is not unique to information technology, but it is much more of a force, I believe, in causing troubles for good relationships with IT folks.

People with the NIH syndrome believe that they are the *only ones* who can develop the solution to the problem or figure out the best way to handle a process. Gurus are especially prone to this disease—often developing entire libraries of code rather than reusing code that another developer publishes.

Doesn't that mean the company owns more of the technology then? One would think that if a really talented technologist works for a business and develops a library of procedures and code while in the employ of that business, the business would be able to continue to utilize the code after the technologist leaves. Certainly they have the legal right to do so. But procedures and codes are often completely unintelligible to anyone except the original developer who wrote them. They are rarely transferable to another system. Furthermore, system configurations include thousands of variables that are only known to those who set them up. Losing a top technologist is often a major blow for a small entrepreneurial company.

The NIH impulse also leads organizations to hire their own programmers or develop their own customized software rather than take advantage of third-party or commercially developed packages. Too often, in the buy or build question, the IT people will always recommend the build road despite the fact that the buy road is more cost effective and leads to smoother computing.

Protector of the Gap

Like most people, IT folks like to be needed. But the language and general knowledge gap between IT and most people enables them to take advantage of the situation to their own benefit; sometimes subconsciously, sometimes not.

Early on in my career, I was talking with a programmer who was charging the owner of a corporation quite a bit of money to code a program to calculate a sales index every day. The formula was very complex, and took the owner about 15 minutes to calculate every day. Because the owner put a high value on his time, the ROI on the programming project was positive even though coding the program cost thousands of dollars. In my initial meeting with the owner, he beamed with pride at his use of information technology to save time, and he boasted about getting it so cheaply since the programmer was charging less than the going rate for programming.

When the programmer showed me what he was doing, I realized that the entire program was unnecessary. I asked him why he didn't simply teach the owner how to enter the formula into a spreadsheet. It would take only five minutes to enter the formula, and the answer would appear instantaneously each morning when the owner entered the daily numbers since the formula would automatically recalculate. The programmer's initial reaction was knee-jerk. "You can't tell them how easy it is to use a spreadsheet! Then they wouldn't need to pay me to program for them!" Since the owner was my client, I went ahead and explained how to use Lotus 123 (the most common spreadsheet at the time) to do the calculation. The programmer was not happy with me because he lost the contract, but once he thought about it, he realized it was the right thing to do. (Because I praised his skills in front of the owner, the programmer was hired for the next—legitimate—programming job, so in the end he didn't lose anything.)

We can't expect people to work against their own best interests. I don't blame this programmer for his reaction; his livelihood was at stake. It is this same impulse that made many a mainframe programmer deny that microcomputers and spreadsheets would ever amount to anything. It's the same impulse today that causes Web developers to emphasize the complexity in developing a Web page. I'm not surprised by how difficult it is to get IT people to explain technology to a businessperson; Their salary depends upon the businessperson not understanding IT.

Mutual Mystification

The gap of knowledge makes "mutual mystification" occur often. Mutual mystification is when a businessperson and an IT person are talking to each other but are completely unaware they are talking at cross-purposes or talking about two completely different things. Years ago I witnessed this exchange between a vice president of information technology at a bank and the lead sales engineer for an enterprise-network-management software product.

> *VP of IT*: Can this software check the entry of the clerk so that the transfer always goes through?
> *Sales engineer*: Absolutely—yes. Every time a packet gets sent, an acknowledgement is returned so that the sending computer knows if it was successful. The transfer always goes through.

The VP ended up thinking the sales engineer answered the question in the affirmative. In reality, nothing could have been further from the truth. After they spoke in that manner for about 30 more minutes, I finally jumped in to clarify and translate for the sales engineer what the VP meant. Once the sales engineer understood what the VP was asking, he admitted that the program he was selling was not designed to do that. But I can imagine this type of conversation happens all the time—without someone there to translate.

Imagine asking a road builder working on a new road, "When the road is finished, can the cars on it be painted blue? Will they ride smoothly?" The road builder would answer, "Yes, of course," even though the road builder has no idea what color the cars will be or if they will ride smoothly. The road builder knows that the work being done will enable a smooth ride for cars (with good shock absorbers, of course) of any color. Just because the road builder said that blue cars would ride smoothly did not mean that the road builder would provide the cars, nor that they would all be blue.

Such cross-communication is why entrepreneurs and business owners, upon finding out that the software they just implemented won't do a required task, will often say, "But I asked my IT people if this software did this task and they said it did!" The businessperson and the IT person are mutually mystified when they are disappointed in the results.

Technology Wars

The topics constantly change, but there is always a technology war going on between vendors or between standards or between ways of doing things. I refer to technology wars as religious wars because of the passion and fervor of the technologists who wage them. IT people are almost always on one side of the war or another, and it impacts their ability to do their jobs.

In the past, technology people have lined up on various sides regarding mainframe versus microcomputer (microcomputers proliferated unchecked); Ethernet versus Token Ring (Ethernet won); NetWare versus NT (NT was the clear winner); Sybase versus Oracle (Oracle came out on top); NetBIOS versus TCP/IP (TCP/IP won). The winner takes the market share lead, and the loser resolves to a niche market or disappears altogether.

I can think of one clear example back in the early 1990s. The IT director of a small manufacturer had heard about Microsoft NT (in 1994), so he hired an NT guru into what had been a NetWare-only shop. The anguished CEO called me a few months later when problems arose—all the NetWare staff had quit, and the new guy didn't know Novell. The senior managers had not even been aware that bringing in an NT expert would signal the end of Novell to the existing staff. The senior leaders had naively assumed that the IT staff would welcome a different operating system and be happy to learn it from the new guru.

The biggest current battle is Windows Server versus open source. Open source is not a vendor, but rather a movement of IT people who believe that the software code should be free. In loosely organized technical teams, they work together to create software that is sometimes technically superior to what we can buy. It is always, however, more difficult to use because it is written by and for IT people, not non-IT people. Additionally, it is often incompatible with Microsoft products because many open source developers are rebelling against the high cost and lack of power in easy-to-use Microsoft products. Microsoft competitors such as SUN and IBM have embraced the open source movement hoping that it will break Microsoft's monopoly.

Mark, a client and friend, is the CIO of a large nonprofit organization. Because Microsoft gives huge discounts to nonprofit organizations, Mark has a Microsoft shop with Exchange, Outlook, Office, SharePoint, and so on. But his technical employees are all staunch open source advocates. Instead of spending their time figuring out how to use all the Microsoft products, they spend their time developing alternatives to those products using open source tools on Linux systems. As a result, there are constant problems on the network and nothing seems to work smoothly. I suggested to Mark that he should choose one or the other (Microsoft or open source), but he does not see the current battle as the cause of his problems.

Though we don't want our businesses to get involved in the wars, it is important to know what battles are being waged and where your IT people stand in it. Otherwise, the skirmishes can hurt business.

MANAGING IT PEOPLE EFFECTIVELY

Remember that it doesn't do any good to rail against the perceived faults of IT people. Those faults may be the reason IT people are so good at what they do. People who are personable, friendly, profit-oriented, and good team members rarely develop the logical, dedicated focus necessary for high levels of IT knowledge.

Once we recognize the characteristics, we can manage technology people effectively. To summarize from this section, follow these guidelines:

- Give the IT people recognition for their role.
- Focus them on what they do best, and supplement them on what they don't do well.
- Give IT people leading-edge technology in isolated labs.
- Provide IT people with liaisons to teams instead of forcing them to be part of the team.
- Prevent crises by rewarding a smoothly operating system.
- Understand the technology wars in which gurus are involved, and be willing to live with the consequences of taking sides.

As noted earlier, IT people thrive on recognition. They usually don't care much about money or status—they care about recognition among their peers for their knowledge. They want to give their opinions, and they want to be taken seriously. We don't necessarily have to follow every suggestion they make, but they will fume if they are not asked. So smart business entrepreneurs discuss all potential strategies with their IT people before decisions are made.

Second, IT people will work hard, harder than most other people, but they will not do what you want them to do (like plan and organize their work, write up documentation, or communicate with others). Instead, they work harder to further their own knowledge and push the limit of the technological capabilities of the systems. Don't expect them to understand the business needs or appreciate profitability as a reward. Establish guidelines so that they focus on what is helpful to the business, and minimize administrative functions for them as much as possible.

Third, gurus will not be happy spending day after day on maintaining older technologies. The importance of maintaining stable, smoothly running systems that require no active work is at conflict with finding exceptional IT people who hate monotony. We can attract and keep gurus while preventing them from doing research using the operational network as their personal lab by providing them with a separate budget and letting them spend a portion of their time investigating various options for the future. There is nothing a guru loves more than playing with the latest and greatest technology. If you can get the guru to focus on your hedgehog concept and think about innovation, you may receive a return that is many times the value of the time and money they spend on it. This will also help with the hero-seeking issue. An IT person may become a hero by finding that perfect information technology that aligns with the hedgehog concept of the business. That works much better for an entrepreneur than having systems break all the time as IT people tinker with them.

Fourth, don't expect good team member skills. Find other people to manage projects and write up documentation. IT people, gurus especially, will be happier if they can focus their intellect on furthering the technological limits of your company in the core business areas and keeping the systems running smoothly. If you aim them right, their happiness means more profits for you.

Fifth, build in measures that reward no-problem systems. Do not overly reward the knight in shining armor who comes into work in the middle of the night to solve a computer problem. Show more appreciation to the technologists who prevent such crises. Otherwise, quest for recognition will lead to constant crises that IT people are only too happy to solve.

Sixth, understand the current technological wars going on and understand which side of the battle your IT people are on. It would be best to find IT people who don't strongly take sides in the current technology war, but that's rare. The next best thing is to know the technical direction of your business, and choose IT people whose opinions are compatible with it. If they are on the wrong side from the technology direction of the company, find others. Don't expect IT people on different sides of a war to get along.

Talented IT staff can easily fulfill a very valuable role that brings significant strategic value to your business—but only if you manage them well. By following these few simple guidelines, you can maximize the skills and talents of your IT employees. They will be happier and do more for your business in return.

SUMMARY

We can manage IT people more effectively if we:

- ☑ Understand the nature of technology professionals.
- ☑ Give the IT people recognition for their role.
- ☑ Focus them on what they do best—supplement them on what they don't do well.
- ☑ Don't force IT people to work in multidisciplinary teams.
- ☑ Prevent crises by rewarding smoothly operating systems.
- ☑ Understand the technology wars in which gurus are involved.
- ☑ Give IT people leading edge technology in isolated labs.

5

The Essential Balance: Matching the Process

It's been a few chapters, so let me take a moment to reiterate the definition of *information technology*. Information technology is the people, processes, software, and hardware that make up the information flow in the operations of an organization.

We've discussed, in detail, the people aspect. Before we delve into the hardware and software, we need to look at the glue that holds all the other components together: the process.

BALANCE IS KEY

Let's look at an example of how a mismatch between the experience and ability levels of the people, in combination with a poor process, can ensure failure even with the best hardware and software.

At one company where I worked, the senior executives invested in an extremely powerful OLAP system to analyze the budgeted and actual expenses. OLAP stands for On-Line Analytical Processing, in this case a particular program called Hyperion. The software gives a company the ability to slice the numbers in a myriad of ways, providing a cube of data based on three (or four, or five) different factors at the same time. It is a highly sophisticated system. All the experts in the field of budgeting waxed poetic about the great ability of this software to quickly analyze and chart dozens of dimensions in a multidimensional cube.

As an analytical person who loves to play with financial numbers, I enthusiastically delved into this software and quickly learned how to get the most out of it. My superiors noticed how good I was with the new software and put me on the team responsible for implementing it.

The power of the system was its capability to dynamically review live financial numbers and drill down into the data as needed. I got extremely good at analyzing the numbers and finding patterns and anomalies to investigate. But my expertise and facility with the software did not help my employer. Analyzing the numbers was not my job.

The people who should have been doing the analysis, finding the patterns and identifying anomalies to investigate, were the senior leaders. The software was designed for them to play with the numbers and conduct the analysis themselves. The problem was that the ability and experience levels of the senior leaders were extremely low. (Many had not yet mastered e-mail; they had their secretaries print out each e-mail message, to which they dictated a reply that their secretaries then typed into the system.) They did not have the time to learn how to use this powerful tool, and they did not have the experience to pick it up as quickly as I had.

The beauty of OLAP is its ability to keep drilling down into live data, seeing chart after chart in order to visualize the numbers and identify the issues. Unfortunately, the benefit of OLAP is lost if the senior leaders have to describe to someone else what they want to see. Printing out a picture of the cube of data is worthless, and could more easily have been done with Excel or some other graphing program. The company would have been better off hiring a few more analysts dedicated to creating charts of the numbers and giving them to the senior leaders upon request. You can pay a harem of analysts for the cost of a single multimillion-dollar OLAP system.

So the first problem was a clear mismatch between the ability and experience levels of the users, and the power of the software. But the next problem was even more influential in the difficulties in using the system.

Despite pointed requirements and strong pressure from me, managers across different departments failed to standardize terminology and agree on definitions prior to implementing the software. The result was the clichéd situation of GIGO (Garbage In, Garbage Out). To make the information available to the senior leaders, the underlying source data had to be hand massaged to clean it up sufficiently so that it reflected accurate data. That meant that the data couldn't be analyzed in real time, and instead had to be done in monthly batches. Since the beauty of an OLAP system is its ability to drill down into live data, the one thing it was designed to do could not be done.

The organization had spent millions implementing this new system, and still had inaccurate, old, and unintegrated data. This is a very common problem. Businesses often try to bolt a technology onto a poor process—when what they need to do is fix the process itself. In this case, fixing the definition problems at the source would have solved the problem of inaccurate and unintegrated data at a fraction of the cost of the new system. Always fix the process before choosing a system!

ASSESSING PROCESS

Processes are those procedures that people use to accomplish tasks. They include both manual and automatic parts of the task. Each process must have an input and output—perhaps several inputs and outputs. An input can be a telephone call, a note, a report, an e-mail, or a time/date. An output can be a telephone call, a note, a report, an e-mail, and so on.

The easiest way to identify a process is to start from the end and work backwards. Many processes are easily described. For example, the process to schedule a meeting is this: I receive a phone call or e-mail identifying when and where the meeting will be held; I check my schedule in my PDA or on the computer to see if I'm free; if I'm free and have the interest, I enter the meeting location and purpose in my calendar at the meeting time. Some processes are more complicated, however. If I were a business process engineer trying to identify a process in an office that processes medical claims for an insurance company, the dialogue might sound something like this:

Business process engineer: What does your office do?

Worker: We process medical claims for Euwish Insurance Company.

Business process engineer: And how does that work?

Worker: Well, the insured call us up to submit a claim. We process it.

Business process engineer: What do you mean by "process it"?

Worker: We investigate whether it's a valid claim and if so, we send a check to the vendor who provided the service for the insured.

Business process engineer: So the end result is a check to the insured?

Worker: Yes—but there's a lot more to it.

Business process engineer: Okay, but let's work backwards. How are the checks printed?

Worker: Suzy prints them every Friday on that printer over there. Then she puts them in the envelopes and drops them in the outgoing mail bin.

Business process engineer: How does Suzy know which checks to print?

Worker: After a claim is identified as valid, the adjuster enters the check information on this screen into this program on this computer.

Business process engineer: How does an adjuster know what to enter?

Worker: The name and address of the vendor are on the invoice, along with the amount charged.

Business process engineer: How does the adjuster get the invoice?

Worker: They come in the mail.

Business process engineer: Who sends them?

Worker: The vendor sends them.

Business process engineer: How does the vendor know to whom to send them?

Worker: The insured gives them the address to send them.

Business process engineer: How does the insured know the address to give to the vendor?

Worker: The insured calls us to find out the address and the claim number.

Business process engineer: Claim number?

Worker: Yes. The claim number needs to be on the envelope so we know which adjuster to give the mail to.

Business process engineer: So the insured calls you to submit a claim, and you give them a claim number?

Worker: Not right away. The insured has to be verified first.

Business process engineer: So the insured calls and gives you the information about the claim. Who takes that call?

Worker: One of the workers in the call center takes the call.

Business process engineer: And what do they do with the information they get on the call?

Worker: They fill out one of these forms with the name, address, and policy number of the insured.

Business process engineer: And what do they do with it?

Worker: They give it to Sally, who looks up the policy number in the computer and verifies that the person is actually insured with us. You'd be surprised at how many people call the wrong insurance company, or who don't know the policy number, or think they are insured for something they are not. It's a real problem. Sometimes Sally is backed up for days at a time verifying insurance policies.

Business process engineer: Okay, the insured calls and gives a name and address and policy number to the worker. The worker writes the information on this form and gives it to Sally, who looks it up to make sure the person is actually insured. Then what happens?

Worker: Sally gives the form to one of the adjusters.

Business process engineer: How does Sally know to which adjuster to give the form?

This exchange, naturally, went on for another 10 minutes. But you get the picture—charting a process takes a fair amount of time and investigative work. It may be tedious, but for an information technology process to work effectively, every single tiny detail of the process must be known and documented. Note the frequency of the questions "How do they know which ..." and "What do they do with...." Once the entire process is known, it can be documented using flowchart boxes and arrows so that other people can see the process as well. It is important at each step in the process that these aspects of the step are written down: who, what, when, why, and how. It does not work, for example, to say "the mail is sorted." We must say, "The mailroom clerk sorts the mail and puts envelopes with people's names on them in their slot. Envelopes without names go to the receptionist."

Matching People's Skills and Process to Systems

Why do we have to go through the process of identifying the process? To ensure that the skills of the people (as defined in our assessment) and the technology properly match the needs of the resulting process. As noted earlier, problems are often identified when there is a mismatch between the skills of the people, the capabilities of the systems, or the flow of the process.

In the OLAP project, for example, if we had done a detailed process flow prior to choosing and installing the system, it would have been obvious that the system could not replace the manually massaged numbers. Can you tell where some of the difficulties are in the insurance process described in the previous section? Go back and reread the process to see if you can identify the problems before going on to the next section which will point a few of them out.

Identifying the Issues

Let's dig into this case a little more. After investigating the features of the system, the business process engineer discovers that the system itself has a capability to print the letter with the claim number and the address. Additionally, the business process engineer finds out that the system contains a module that would allow quick lookups of people by name and policy number that can, within seconds, provide the information necessary to identify whether or not the person calling with a claim is actually the insured.

The business process engineer returns to the office to find out why the adjusters aren't using the system capabilities.

> *Business process engineer:* In further investigation, I found some capabilities of the system. I was wondering if you were aware of them.
>
> *Worker:* What are they? You know they didn't give us very much training on the system, so there may be things that it can do that we weren't aware of.
>
> *Business process engineer:* For one thing, there seems to be a module that provides the information about whether or not a person is insured pretty quickly—it's designed to be used by someone accepting the claim on the phone and immediately giving the claim number.
>
> *Worker:* Oh yes—we knew about that. But we can't use it.
>
> *Business process engineer:* Really?
>
> *Worker:* The call center takes the call. They don't have this program.
>
> *Business process engineer:* And they can't get it?
>
> *Worker:* The call center people wanted to do it—they said that they are equipped to verify the claim and send out the letters, but our VP didn't feel comfortable that they would do it right. Besides—it would be too expensive. This program is $250 a seat. There are over 100 computers in the call center—it would cost us over $25,000 to purchase the program for the call center.
>
> *Business process engineer:* I understand—that is a lot of money. I'm wondering, do you know how much time does it take for Sally to receive all the slips of paper, verify the accounts, assign the claim, and have the adjuster get the claim letter to the person?
>
> *Worker:* Well it only takes a few seconds for Sally to verify the person once she gets the slip of paper. It takes a few more minutes for her to assign the account. If the adjuster is there, it can be done right away, but if not, however long it takes the adjuster to return to her desk. It could be a few days, even a few weeks, if the adjuster is really busy.
>
> *Business process engineer:* What does the person do in the meantime?
>
> *Worker:* What do you mean?

Business process engineer: Well I'm guessing that a person doesn't wait a few weeks to go to the hospital or see a doctor after an accident. If they don't have the claim number, what do they do in the meantime?

Worker: Oh I don't know. They have to wait for the claim number.

Business process engineer: But what if they can't?

Worker: They should wait for the claim number, otherwise the vendor will use the wrong address and they won't get paid.

Business process engineer: That must be a real problem.

Worker: You're telling me! It's insane—late bills, phone calls back and forth, angry vendors, angry customers. People are constantly giving the wrong address to the vendor, and then they get mad when the bill doesn't get paid!

Business process engineer: I can see that. Well—the other capability we discovered was the ability to send out a letter with the claim number and address—that can be done within the system, automatically.

Worker: Really? We didn't know that.

Worker2: I'm sorry to interrupt, but I knew that. I discovered it by accident one day. It saves me hours of time a week—that's why I'm able to process my quota every week—I don't have to spend so much time writing letters.

Business process engineer: That's great. How many people know about this?

Worker2: Oh—I think Janice knows, and Bill. I told Janice, and Bill found out on his own.

Business process engineer: Why doesn't everyone use it?

Worker2: Well, I told Mary, too, but she doesn't like to use it. So I stopped telling people about it. I told Sally about it, but she didn't want to force everyone to use it. For one thing, she was afraid our quotas would go up, and some people just aren't fast enough to keep up—even with the automatic letter printing.

Business process engineer: That's understandable. Thank you both for your help.

What are the capabilities of the system in this scenario? What are the capabilities of the people? How is the process helping or hindering the people and the capabilities?

It's easy to see that there are a number of problems here. The big lag time in getting the claim number and the address causes the insured to give the wrong address for billing to the vendors, who then get angry because they don't get paid. Then they bill the client, who gets angry after receiving a bill for something that was supposed to be paid for by the insurance company. The obstacle to fixing that problem is not technology—the system already has the capability to provide the claim number and address right away—on the phone in the initial call. It also has the ability to send out that letter—automatically, right away. You could say that the problem is people—the VP of the area won't let the call center do that part of the function. But the VP believes that he is saving the company money ($25,000) and ensuring that the job is done right (which he believes only his department can do). So he has the best intentions and is dedicated to doing the right thing. You could say that the problem is the process—except that from the perspective of the workers, the process is working just fine.

Another problem is the fact that not all the adjusters are quick enough with the computer to understand and use the automatic letter feature. The adjusters are working hard, and are probably dedicated—but remember that ability curve. Not everyone has the ability to utilize technology without a lot of experience. And Sally knows that management will not permit the quotas to change—even temporarily—while people get used to the new technology. She is doing the best that she can for her people when she refuses to enforce use of the technology to accomplish the task.

Presenting the Solutions

The difficulty is a mismatch between the process and the people and the technology. What is the answer? In this particular case, the business process engineer does find a way to improve the situation. Let's see how the rest of the dialogue goes.

> *Business process engineer:* I'd like to share some information with you, if you have the time right now.
>
> *VP:* Sure. What have you got?
>
> *Business process engineer:* Well, as you can see from this flowchart, the current process is working pretty well. Most people are able to achieve their quotas. Your overall customer satisfaction scores are pretty good.
>
> *VP:* Well, of course!
>
> *Business process engineer:* There are a few areas, however, that could use a little improvement.
>
> *VP:* By all means, tell me what they are. We always want to improve if we can.
>
> *Business process engineer:* Well, as you can tell from this flowchart, there can be a very long lag time between when people verbally submit their claims and the time they get the claim number and the address to which the vendors should submit bills.
>
> *VP:* Yes, my people are complaining about that all the time.
>
> *Business process engineer:* I've been told that you have investigated allowing the call center to provide the claim number to the people.
>
> *VP:* I'm not convinced that the call center people can handle that. They simply don't have the right skills. What if they give the wrong claim number? Then when the adjusters send the letter, it will be a mismatch. Besides—it would cost $25,000 to give them the software—I don't have the budget for that.
>
> *Business process engineer:* Yes, I believe you are right. However, I wonder if … well, how well do you know the head of the complaints department?
>
> *VP:* Jennifer? I know her very well. We have lunch together often. She's a really great person, but I wouldn't want her job. It's thankless! All those complaints.

Business process engineer: Do you think she would be willing to pay $25,000 out of her budget in order to decrease the number of complaints she gets?

VP: She sure would. If she could cut down on the complaints, she could cut down on overtime, which is extremely costly. She told me that last month she spent $45,000 on overtime alone!

Business process engineer: So perhaps she would be willing to use her budget to pay for the software?

VP: I'll bet she would. But I still don't trust the call center people to give the right claim number.

Business process engineer: What if the call center printed the letter, so the claim number they give over the phone and the claim number they send are always the same?

VP: I did discuss that with the call center manager. He said they don't know how to use a word processor and can't use the template we developed.

Business process engineer: But what if I told you that the system itself can automatically send the letter?

VP: I didn't know the system could do that!

Business process engineer: Yes—few people do. The first version of the software couldn't, but the one you are using does have that feature. I verified it—the automation would work—and the printers in the call center are already set up for using features like that—they have to send letters out for the life insurance department.

VP: Well, that does change things! I'll talk to Jennifer right away and then set up a meeting with the call center manager. This should be very helpful! Thanks.

Business process engineer: I didn't do anything. It was your people who pointed out the best way to do this. This has been a wonderful project to work on. I enjoyed it quite a bit. Thank you!

As you can see, when everyone has the proper information, they generally make the right decisions, though not always. The key to ensuring that the process, people, and system match is to have full knowledge about all three of them.

- Understand the capabilities of the people (both ability and experience).
- Understand the capabilities of the system (all features and functions).
- Match the process to the people and the system.

It often helps to diagram the process visually, as in the example shown in Figure 5.1.

Sometimes senior leaders purchase and implement new system after new system because they think the system is at fault. Or, they fire good people because they believe the people are at fault. In my years as a consultant, I have rarely found that either the people or the systems are at fault. In almost 99.9 percent of the cases, the problem is a mismatch between the system and the people.

Figure 5.1
Euwish Insurance Company Internal Claim Process

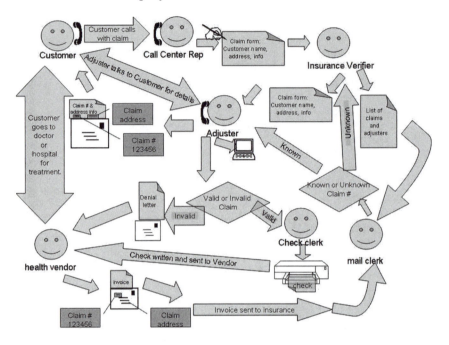

That's not to say that systems don't have faults. Every system has faults. A company may invest in a new system that gets rid of a fault of the present system, only to discover that there are new faults that they must get around. Nor is it to say that people don't have faults. All people have faults. Again—you may fire someone to get rid of one of their particular faults only to hire someone who has a different fault.

The key to success is not to find a perfect system or perfect employees. The key to success is to find a process that maximizes the strengths of the systems and people, and works around the weaknesses. Since process is the most flexible of the people-systems-process threesome, it makes sense to work hard at finding a process that matches the people and the systems before adjusting either the people or the system. To review a process, these guidelines are helpful:

- Review the process from end to end (i.e., not just one department, but from initial vendor to final customer).
- Accurately define the problem you are trying to solve.
- Brainstorm possible solutions.
- Envision the solutions to find alternative problems that might arise.
- Practice trial and error—try different solutions until one fits.

Often, finding the problem and solution is not the biggest stumbling block. The method that is used to identify the problem and communicate the solution is more important than the steps themselves. When investigating potential process-people-hardware-software mismatches, it is important to keep the following guidelines in mind:

- Find out why things are done as they are. "We've always done it that way" is not an answer. Find the real answer and assess whether the reason is still valid.
- Always maintain everyone's ego.
- Never look for, or lay, blame. Focus only on actions and the reasons behind them.

Go back to the business process engineer dialogue. What if the business process engineer had confronted the VP with what was found in a different way?

Business process engineer: I've found a problem in the process.

VP: Problem? What problem?

Business process engineer: If the call center is given the software, they can validate that the person submitting the claim is insured and send out the letters.

VP: We've already investigated that, and it won't work. It costs too much, and the call center people don't have the capability.

Business process engineer: But I've checked with the manager and they have the capability. And the head of the complaints department is willing to pay for the software.

VP: I said no. Now stop meddling. Pay attention to just my department— not what other people can do.

If the business process engineer says there is a problem, the manager will get defensive. Despite the fact that the problem is identified and the solution known, a defensive manager will not allow a problem to exist and will not allow a solution to be implemented because it would impinge on his or her own ego—a common human trait. We want to avoid making people defensive or indicating in any way that they've done something wrong when trying to solve a sticky problem.

Making the Decision Involving Technology

Just about now you may be feeling a bit overwhelmed by all the advice you are reading regarding managing information technology. Furthermore, the process has to match the system as well as the people. Every technology, when implemented, will change processes. Some change them only a little; some change them a lot. But attempts to force the hardware and software to fit an existing manual process are like trying to build a house on quicksand. It may stay up long enough for pictures to be taken (and senior leaders to pat themselves on the back for a job well done), but probably sooner rather than later it will fall apart and sink.

There are several keys to maintaining the delicate balance that must exist between people, process, and systems. The first has to do with decision making, the second with communicating the vision, and the third with redirecting when we get off course.

Making good decisions is a talent that most successful leaders develop over time and is an essential part of the people-process-system balance. We can easily see why by looking at the steps of decision making.[26]

- Classifying the problem.
- Defining the problem.
- Specifying the answer to the problem.
- Deciding what is right rather than what is acceptable, in order to meet the boundary conditions.
- Building into the decision the action to carry it out.
- Testing the validity and effectiveness of the decision against the actual course of events.

It's that last one that usually is difficult and time consuming. All people make poor decisions initially, but they then, generally, make better and better ones as they go along. Executive leaders often don't become successful until they are 40 or 50 years old. When they were in their twenties and thirties they made all the mistakes and have since learned from the poor decisions of the past.

Additionally, if we think about the actual stages of defining the problem—which usually include gathering information, delineating various options, identifying the advantages and disadvantages of each option—we can see that one of the most important factors regarding understanding the advantages and disadvantages is having all the knowledge necessary to define the options.

As described in an earlier section, both of these critical steps of normal decision making demonstrate problems when the decision is about technology. Technology hasn't been around long enough for most people to test the validity and effectiveness of their decisions against the actual course of events. Also, the people making the decisions haven't had time yet to gain the critical knowledge they need to properly define and assess the options. Many of the top decision makers in business today were educated long before technology became an influential factor. They may be knowledgeable in every business domain except technology.

Due to these problems, technology decisions (25 percent of the time according to my research) have been left up to the data-processing managers or the information systems experts. IT people, however, do not have the decision-making experience of today's leaders and due to their very nature often make very poor managers.

Understanding the roles involved in decision making is essential. That's more easily done if you keep these rules in mind.

- Don't abdicate.
- Remember that the vendor is not a decision maker.
- Ensure that both business and technology leaders agree on the goals.

Don't Abdicate

As noted in the first chapter, information technology is involved in every major business decision these days. That scares some decision makers. I've known several CEOs who left IT decisions entirely up to CIOs and IT managers because they didn't feel qualified to decide. They hand wave the details. It's easier for the emperor to allow the wizard to decide, of course, as long as the wizard is a trustworthy person.

Any abdication, however, is a problem. If the wizard were good at emperor-type decisions, he or she would be emperor, not wizard. The key is this: Information about the technology should not drive the decision—information about the business should drive the decision.

The bottom line? Only the person who thoroughly understands the business has the depth of knowledge necessary to align the proper technology with the business. The business leader must be involved in the decision making for technology, but he must be knowledgeable enough to make the right decision.

Remember That the Vendor Is Not a Decision Maker

Lack of confidence in their own technology knowledge, and the difficulties involved in obtaining the necessary information, often lead senior executives to relinquish the decision to the technology vendor. Abdicators often expect the vendor to tell them what can be accomplished with the new technology, how much it will cost, and how much money it will save the organization.

Entrepreneurs and business owners need to know the answers to these questions before talking to the vendors of any new technology. As noted in Chapter 2, a vendor will always be biased toward implementing technology, and it will always find financial and operational returns that seem to support its view. Despite what he or she may say, the vendor's job is to sell us technology, not to ensure that our business is healthy and growing for years to come.

As a buyer, we need to establish the parameters for the relationship, and we should clearly communicate that to the vendor.

Ensure Both Business and Technology Leaders Agree on Goals

A couple is driving down the road. The husband is behind the wheel; the wife has a map open on her lap. It's obvious they've been driving for quite a while.

"Where's the next turn?" he inquires.

"Two miles ahead, on the right," she answers.

As they approach a quaint cabin, they both seem to perk up a little when she announces, "Finally! Stop here."

They get out of the car, stretch a bit, and look around. He looks puzzled and says, "Where is this? I thought we were going to the beach."

"Oh," she answers. "This is our cabin from last year. I thought we were going to the mountains."

Technology decisions depend upon the strategic direction of a business. As with our couple, sometimes the business leader has a completely different idea of where the business is going than the technology leader. The majority of the time, a decision is made either by the business leader (the CEO or the COO) or the technology leader (the CIO or IT manager), but rarely both. Out of the 584 organizations that participated in the surveys I conducted, 26 companies, less than 4 percent, said that both the CEO and the CIO had been among the technology decision makers (though less than 1 percent had the CEO and CIO as the only decision makers).

As can be seen in Figure 5.2, about half of the companies declared that technology decisions were made by the CEO-president-owner (50 percent). In 48 percent of the cases, 278 companies, the CEO was the sole technology decision maker. Only 18 percent (122 of the companies) included CIO/IT director/IT manager as part of the technology decision-making team. Ninety-one companies (16 percent) allowed the CIO to make technology decisions with no other input.

Figure 5.2
Roles of the Information Technology Decision Maker

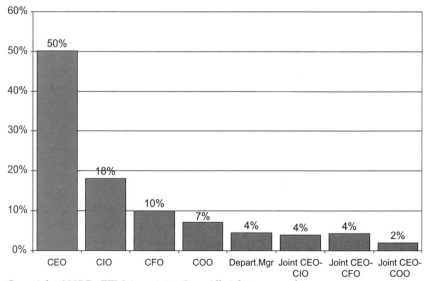

Are you wondering which fared better in terms of new technology use—companies in which the CEO or the COO or the CFO made the technology decisions, or companies in which the CIO made the decisions? Neither. Companies where the CEO made the decisions did about the same as the CIO alone, which was about the same as any combination of decision makers.

However, when the CIO and the CEO got together to make the decision, the effective use of new technology such as the public Internet increased. It is easy to see in Figure 5.3. Only one combination led to a majority of companies rated "Blossoming Internet Use" or "Internet Savvy" rather than "Bare Minimum Internet" or "Unversed in Internet" on overall Internet technology utilization.

It appears, then, that when both CIOs and CEOs are included on the decision-making team, they improve the overall use of Internet technology. (You might also notice that the organizations that used Internet technologies least effectively were those who let the CEO and the CFO make the technology decisions.)

Too often, I find business leader–technology leader decision-making partnerships in organizations today navigating toward different destinations. There are discussions about cost reduction and planning and whether they should take the highway or the back roads. There are not many discussions about which direction they are traveling, and where they are going.

As already noted in the discussion of abdication, the answer is clear. CIOs should not be making technology decisions alone. Neither should the CEO, CFO, COO, or any other business leader (especially the CFO, as it can be clearly seen in the graph that including the CFO in the decision-making

Figure 5.3
Internet Utilization by Decision Maker

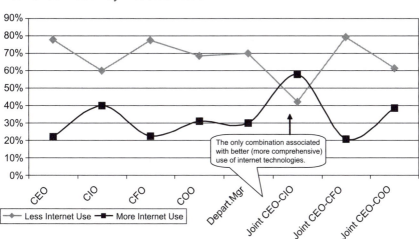

team always led to less Internet utilization). The best outcome appeared when both the business leader and the technology leader were involved in the decision-making process for technology projects, and when both agree on the final destination.

Process Development over Time

The longer a process has been implemented, the more productivity people will achieve with it. Many times, businesses don't get the expected value from their technology simply because the process changes too often for people to accommodate the changes. It takes people time to adjust to a new process. If the changes happen more quickly than people have time to adjust, they are constantly in that state of learning but not knowing. That state decreases productivity.

Systems become more valuable when people who use them have the ability and experience to get the most out of them, which only occurs over time using the same process and the same system. The more time people have to adjust the process to fit the people and the system, the more productive the technology can be. Finally, the more highly integrated and seamless the functionality of the system, the higher the productivity. These combined ideas can be expressed as a non-numeric formula as shown in Figure 5.4.

It does not matter how much we spend on technology, but it does matter how long the people, and the process, and the hardware-software connectivity get to work with each other as they move toward alignment with the hedgehog concept that provides the highest productivity possible.

COMMUNICATING THE VISION

In Chapter 2 we noted how important having a vision was. Now we will discuss the process of how to communicate that vision. In a recent research study, I asked successful executives if they ever had to go back and do a project all over again. If they had, then I asked what they would have done differently. The number one most common answer was "spend more time communicating the vision."

Figure 5.4
Formula for Productivity

Productivity = (People * Ability * Experience in technology) +
(the Process * Length of Time process in practice) +
(the Hardware/Software/Connectivity * Integration index)

or

P = (PE * A * E) + (PR * T) + (HSC * I)

There are several keys to communicating the vision:

- Start before the decision has been made.
- Keep the message simple and consistent.
- Design communication using multiple methods (visually, auditorily, kinesthetically, behaviorally).
- Reinforce the message frequently over a long period of time.
- Provide breadcrumbs in your message.

Start before the Decision Has Been Made

The worst time to start communicating a vision is after the decision has been made. No matter how participative we have tried to make the decision-making process, this will appear to everyone that the decision was made without their input. Human nature is such that everyone resents decisions that are made without their input. People are much more forgiving of a leader who goes against their advice than of a leader who has not even listened to their advice.

The easiest way to avoid this problem is to start the communication process before the decision has actually been made. We can plan personal contact with as many people as possible, asking them their opinion on the issue or problem we are trying to solve. This gives them a heads up that a decision is being made, and enables them to feel part of the decision-making process. It also begins the process of communicating a vision, because we can provide our vision as an option that we are considering. This process has the added advantage of actually getting input on the vision—which may turn out to be valuable. We may even modify our vision based upon the input. Often we think we know the perfect answer at first, but repeated presentations to interested parties are bound to improve the vision (or at the very least, how we describe the vision).

Keep the Message Simple and Consistent

Back in the days when I was an employee, I would always get a schizophrenic response to the assessment of my communication skills in my evaluations. On one hand I was told that I was a good communicator because I could write and speak well. My grammar is generally better than average (the product of tyrannical parents who constantly corrected me), and I'm highly animated and dynamic in front of an audience. On the other hand, I was told that I was a terrible communicator because my message was constantly being misunderstood by people. I was told that I was not clear in my communication, and that I didn't listen well.

It took me quite a while to figure out what my problem was (well, actually it took several expensive executive coaches hitting me over the head again and again with the lesson, but that's a story for another day). The problem was that I was too focused on my understanding of the issue or problem. Instead, I should have focused on the understanding of the issue or problem from the point of view of the person with whom I was communicating.

Furthermore, I was also a bit tyrannical when it came to accurately describing the circumstances, the problem, and the solution; I doggedly insisted on total accuracy in discussing technical issues. What I discovered was that complex and accurate descriptions often interfere with under-standing, like the husband who keeps interrupting his wife when she is tell-ing a good story. Although the techno-geek side of me always wants to give the whole story and teach everyone all the ins and outs of the problem and the solution, I learned through experience that I needed to give that up. I needed to listen to the people with whom I was communicating so that I knew what their current level of understanding was. Then I needed to figure out a way to communicate my message so that it matched their level of understanding. In order to see the vision, people have to under-stand it.

Design Communication

Rather than just hoping the vision gets communicated, it is important that we design the communication surrounding the vision using multiple methods: visual, auditory, kinesthetic, and behavioral.

The simple message can often be communicated with a short catch-phrase, but the longer explanation behind the catchphrase needs to also be carefully crafted. A logo or picture can also help communicate the phrase. Concrete examples and physical equipment or office reorganization or furniture placement may be able to help with the communication. We don't need to hire a branding expert or spend a lot of money on graphic design-ers. We just need to choose the central theme to go with our vision. At every opportunity, we use the same theme to reinforce the vision.

Most important, behaviors need to change to accommodate the vision. Starting from the top and working its way down as well as starting from the bottom and working its way up—all people involved must catch them-selves behaving the old way in order to purposefully change their own behavior to the new way to accommodate the new vision.

Measure through Performance Scorecard

The easiest way to change behavior is to measure the behavior we wish to see. The concept of the performance scorecard provides a method to accomplish behavior change through measurement.[27]

All of the measurements must align. I worked for two different compa-nies that claimed customer service was their differentiating factor. One, however, measured its customer service representatives on the quality of their interactions. The other evaluated its customer service representatives on how short they could make their phone calls. Which do you think pro-vided better customer service?

Reinforce the Message Frequently over a Long Period of Time

Two of the most important keys to the vision are frequency and duration. Jim Collins talks about the flywheel and the doom loop. The doom loop is when an organization keeps announcing all of these wonderful new programs with great fanfare, only to have enthusiasm and energy for the vision drop over time, whereby a new program or vision is announced. Within a few years, no one will pay any attention to new visions because they know that, within a year or two, everyone will forget about it.

Quality Management, Six Sigma, Process Reengineering—all are wonderful programs that can drastically improve performance of an organization. In a way, they all build upon each other. But if each one is tried, assessed, and then forgotten, no one benefits. Motivation can be sapped by too many improvement programs.

But if the same message is given, over and over and over again, year in, year out—people begin to get the message that the vision is real. It will not go away. Yes, it may get boring for the leaders to constantly quote the same statements and refer to the same pictures, but it is important to everyone in the organization.

At one of the companies I worked for, the phrase "Think Like a Customer" was printed over every single doorway, on every single computer screen. The dedication to the customer never flagged, never wavered. It was stated again and again. All of the performance scorecard measurements supported it. Stories of how we creatively helped our customers constantly circulated. Each time, people (we weren't allowed to call them employees) got a little jolt of pride. We worked for a company that cared about the customer. The message was consistent and stable. Frequency and consistency worked.

Provide Breadcrumbs in Your Message

In addition to the overarching vision, information should be communicated regarding where the organization came from, how it tried to accomplish the vision in the past, how it is accomplishing the vision now, and how it will accomplish the vision in the future. Like the breadcrumbs that Hansel and Gretel left to find their way back to where they had been, we must name the periods in the organization's past so that people know what the path has been. People within the organization should be able to track the different generations of technology and how they align with the vision. Constantly referring to both the past and the future enables everyone in the organization to maintain the balance even during periods of transition.

SUMMARY

- ☑ Assess the ability and experience of the people.
- ☑ Identify the features and functions of the system.
- ☑ Review the existing process.

☑ Look for problems: mismatches between the people, the system, and the process.
☑ Keep everyone's ego intact.
☑ Work with the people to modify the process in order to better match the people to the system.
☑ Follow good decision-making processes.
☑ Include technology experts, IT staff, and vendors in the process but don't abdicate the decision.
☑ Communicate the vision and how each decision fits into the vision.
☑ Start communicating even before the decision has been made.
☑ Keep the message simple and consistent.
☑ Design communication.
☑ Measure through a performance scorecard.
☑ Reinforce the message frequently over a long period of time.
☑ Provide breadcrumbs in your message.

6

Why IT Vendors Are So Difficult

Why is purchasing technology so difficult? Good question. It is very difficult to establish good relationships with information technology vendors for several reasons:

- Immaturity.
- Obfuscation.
- Speed of change.

Let's look at each of these in turn.

IMMATURITY

The patent for ENIAC, the first real computer, was filed on June 26, 1947. Since then, we have seen technology swell into a world-changing revolution over the past 50 years. With the exception of science fiction readers and writers, the world of today would be unrecognizable to the typical adult of that period. Fifty years, however, is not a very long time. As a result, many of the difficulties we have with purchasing new technology arise out of the immaturity of the entire field.

There are several issues that are influenced by the immaturity of the field. IT is a relatively new domain of knowledge without the background of other business domains. Being fairly new to the world makes IT difficult to understand. The typical leaders in today's corporations were more likely to grow up racing in soap box derbies than IMing (instant messaging) with their friends. And if you ask a typical teen what a soap box derby is, he will look at you as if you were losing your marbles.

Most people who rise to the position of decision maker in a company have learned from school or from experience quite a bit about several different business domains: sales, financials, customer service, logistics, and operations. There are thousands of years of history upon which to rely for most business decisions, and hundreds of business schools willing to teach them. The fields are well documented, and the terms are well-defined.

Business leaders either learned the optimum way of doing things within various areas themselves, or they found people who could be trusted to provide them with the right information to make the right decisions within those fields, or they educated themselves from the easily accessible sources of knowledge on those domains.

Information technology, however, is something new. There is not much of a track record, and no history to speak of. Documentation leaves much to be desired. The egos of supposedly self-assured decision makers prevent them from asking too many questions or revealing their own ignorance—especially when talking with vendors or consultants, or even their own technology employees.

Business leaders probably perceive that vendors and consultants treat them to arrogant chatter in an impenetrable language. Alternatively, vendors might stick to vague business concepts that don't convey the critical information necessary for optimum decision making and end up making the decision themselves. Either way, the business leaders lose.

Another problem is that the infrastructure is not yet in place for smooth technology communications. This is not without precedence. In the early days of the automobile, people had to pave their own roads to connect with the public streets. Even the public streets weren't all that great. Stops for animal crossings were frequent, as were bumpy dirt-covered roads. There were no end-to-end highways ensuring a smooth fast ride from one state to the next.

Contrary to popular belief, the public Internet is still in its infancy. It's closer to the covered-wagon-trail stage than to the superhighway that it will become within the next decade. There are many toll roads, and no agreement on how big the roads should be or how much to charge for them. Incompatible routes, frequent outages, and no guarantees are the rules of the day.

Today's Internet consists of more private networks than public interstate highways. Currently, we provide our own road (a private Internet) up to a certain point, and then we get on the open street (the public Internet). A typical problem is a big truck hogging up both sides of a little side road, preventing anyone else from passing (someone in your neighborhood hogging the bandwidth to download a movie or video). Another problem is when larger organizations try to speed up their own traffic by mixing private Internets with the public Internet. Private Internets are like railroads in the middle of a city. While they speed up the traffic for those in the train; they slow down all the traffic on the public roads around them. Like the railroad, the crossings between the public and private will eventually disappear until there are only a few left in small towns. At that point we will be able to count on a paved, highly stable infrastructure. Until then, using the public Internet will be a bit perilous.

Another major problem is that IT components aren't purchased already assembled or standardized. In the early days of automobile purchasing, buyers put up with an extremely difficult purchasing process. Many of them built their own cars and had their own mechanics on staff. Just because you could drive one car didn't mean you could drive another since, at the time, there were no industry standards in place.

How easy would it be today to purchase a car if you had to go to one place for the chassis, another for the tires, another for the engine, and another for the steering wheel? Imagine learning to drive if one car had a round steering wheel, while another vendor used a stick to steer.

The automobile industry matured, however, so that now you go to one vendor for all the parts of the car—already assembled and tested together. You can find mechanics in many places and you only need them a few times a year, so you needn't hire one full time. You know that the steering wheel will be round and that the brake is a pedal you push on the left, while the gas is a pedal you push on the right. You can count on the fact that the car will work as it was designed to work on the interstate highways that stretch out waiting to take us where you want to go.

When it comes to technology, we've actually devolved. Strangely enough, in the early days of computing, purchasing a system from a single vendor was the norm. But the breakup of monopolies like IBM and the popularity of Microsoft operating systems and personal computing software put an end to that approach. Think about how we purchase IT these days: We buy the hardware from one vendor, the operating system from another, and the application software from yet another vendor. Then we work with different vendors to configure the network: one for Internet service, one for the routers, one for the switches, one for the wiring in our building, and a different one for the cards that connect functions within our computers. We fully expect that certain parts will not work as designed, and will need to be replaced several times before they are correct. We hire programmers and developers to create or customize the software so that they work with our processes, which were designed by a totally different vendor or consultant. And there are only tiny, crowded public connections between our system and the outside world, so we still end up building our own highways in some cases. And that requires a whole host of other vendors.

The immaturity of the entire industry means constant shakeouts. Companies that once dominated the industry, like DEC or Commodore are dead (or at least gasping for breath) and companies that were started out of the college dorm just ten years ago (like Dell) have inhaled market share with each breath. Thousands of IT companies have started and ended in a very short period of time. Even a lowly school teacher without any formal training who had just a smidgen of talent with computers and no sales or business experience at all was able to build a sizeable technology consulting firm because businesses were willing to pay big bucks to gain the productivity technology promised. Even more amazing, within a short time that same lowly teacher (me) sold the whole business to another technology company for big bucks.

When acquisitions and mergers happen in more mature industries, the customer isn't impacted much. You can go to any grocery store today and buy the same Cashmere Boutique soap and the same Palmolive dish detergent that you could in 1928 before the merger of Colgate and Palmolive. But when mergers happen in a technology industry, the impact on customers is substantial.

A Fortune 500 construction conglomerate, one of my clients, purchased a highly touted computer system produced by a company called Data General in 1999. All the industry magazines at the time spouted glowing reports on how wonderful this new technology was. And, indeed, it had far surpassed any other system I'd seen in terms of reliability, speed, and flexibility.

But a few months after the company bought the system, EMC, a fast-growing vendor of storage devices, purchased Data General because of a new storage device it had developed. Within a very short time, all other vendors stopped supporting Data General hardware. It was very difficult to find technicians who understood it. New programs wouldn't run on it. Parts could not be found for it. My client was forced to purchase an entirely new system within three years.

The problem is not limited to hardware. A few years later, this company undertook a multiyear study to figure out the exact right financial system to purchase. After identifying all the requirements and evaluating all the systems, it finally chose one that met all its needs: the JD Edwards Real One system. Negotiations ensued, prices were established, and pilots were successfully run. Within a few weeks after the company signed on the dotted line, however, PeopleSoft purchased JD Edwards. Within a year, Oracle successfully took over PeopleSoft. JD Edwards Financial software is at risk of being orphaned, which means no one would be updating the code after a certain date. If the system is orphaned, the company would probably be forced to change again in a few years. Because technology requires a continual level of support from the vendor, mergers and acquisitions almost always bode harshly for the customer.

Even in stable technology corporations that hire hardworking, honest people, there is a risk. No IT vendor can be trusted to be around for the long term. We discussed in the last chapter how difficult it is to hold onto really good IT gurus. This problem plagues IT vendors. Customers just start getting comfortable with their vendors and, poof, the core guru of the service decides to find a better pond.

Also, because good technologists are hard to find, they tend to leave employment when they don't feel fully appreciated, which their lack of people skills causes to happen a lot. Just because a vendor project starts with superior technologists doesn't mean they will be there at the end.

The stock bubble didn't help. The irrationally exuberant dot-com feast had technology-related companies shooting for the stars, and sometimes getting there. Kids straight out of high school were able to get $90,000 a year programming for the Web. Think I'm exaggerating? When I was the CIO for a short time at Millstar, an e-commerce software development company, $90,000 was the standard starting salary for Web developers who knew how to program using a middleware program called Cold Fusion. Few had graduated from college, and all just happened to hit the job market with the right skills at the right time to be vaulted to guru status immediately. Venture capital was plentiful and everyone got jolly playing with the Web toys. New companies were popping up left and right. No one worried about profits or business process.

And then reality set in.

Information technology vendors did not do well after the dot-com crash. The sticky air of desperation still hovered over technology salespeople—those that survived—for years and years after the bubble burst. They jumped at every opportunity, and drooled over every marketing lead. The legions of unemployed programmers, project managers, and systems analysts finally thinned as people left the field and joined so-called normal industries. Salaries came back down to earth. But there are still plenty who are pining for the glory days, picking up short-term consulting jobs wherever they can and hanging in there until the fat paychecks for technology people return, which is just beginning to happen again as new audio and video technologies begin to pick up speed.

OBFUSCATION

Obfuscation, or the art of appearing to state something clearly while actually hiding the meaning, leads to several issues. For one, IT is fraught with hype. This is caused by the fact that IT seems to have amazing capabilities, but it also has limitations that make no sense to most people. Hype is fueled by these unrealistic expectations, and obfuscation can be used to write service level agreements that seem to meet expectations but actually don't.

How does hype hurt? I once worked for a CEO who loved to read industry magazines. However, he had no technology background. Every Monday morning he would come into my office and share some gem he found over the weekend—a carefully highlighted article or advertisement on some hardware or software. The truth is, he rarely even understood what the software or hardware product or service was, much less whether it could help us. The CEO was a trusting soul. He would read all those wonderful, glowing phrases and thought they really meant something. I finally stopped trying to educate him on the issue and just said "thanks" and filed the ad in the round filing system.

I wasn't alone. At a Society for Information Management meeting I attended, a CIO humorously proposed a motion that we lobby Congress to ban technology ad–filled magazines on airplanes for just this reason.

To demonstrate how easy it is to make a product sound like a winner, here are some actual ads from magazines (with the product names disguised). In the following examples of advertisements that use hype, see if you can tell what the products and services really do.

- What if you had someone to watch your back? Someone to integrate your back-end logistics with deadly efficiency. Someone to manage your warehousing, delivery and financial settlements. Someone to protect your entire e-commerce operation. What if one company could handle your entire back-end operation? That's the idea behind Product A. Built around an open and extensible transaction network, our integrated approach enables you to outsource any or all of the logistics behind your buy button. A partner to plan it, implement it, and stand by it. In short, someone to make sure it pays off.

- Customer Care is a Five Way Street ... A bundled "point solution" that handles one or two communication channels is no longer the answer. Product B, a complete and integrated Internet Relationship Management system, can arm your business with self-service and full-service customer care solutions over any communication channel.

- Introducing Product C. You enjoy suspense in a good mystery novel, not in a working relationship! To successfully manage all the complexities and risks involved in any business you need collaboration. With someone who brings all the experience, tools, and understanding to bear, in order to help you anticipate and deal with any unforeseen problem. Someone who will share with you knowledge, practices, risks. And results. Discover the Collaborative Business Experience, discover Product C, a partner you can count on day after day. A partner who is committed to helping you achieve faster, better, and more sustainable results. And puts it on paper.

If you have a good technology map, you can identify these products and services from the nuggets of fact among the mountains of hype in these ads. But to most people, these ads might sound like they solve all your problems. They make it seem as if technology is easy, and that if you just make the right choice, your problems will go away.

Vendors do not hype because they are bad people. Vendors hype because the market forces them to do so. If Vendor A tells a buyer something can't be done, and the buyer goes to Vendor B who tells the buyer that it can be done even though in the end it can't, the buyer is the loser, not Vendor B. If a buyer is looking for a particular feature that is actually useless, and Vendor A tells the buyer the truth and Vendor B tells the buyer about a product with that feature and sells it, the buyer loses again. Furthermore, because business leaders' egos will not allow them to admit they don't understand what a product or service does, it is easy for the vendors to use meaningless phrases as if the buyers understand, when in reality they don't.

Hype is also the source of vaporware—a term used to describe software with all the features we want and need at an affordable price advertised, sometimes heavily, by a technology vendor. The only problem is that the software doesn't exist yet. Someone has put together the requirements and specifications, but the programming to actually make it happen hasn't been completed yet, and may never be. Technology vendors such as Microsoft frequently use vaporware to scare off rivals from developing competing products.

More recently another term, *marketecture*, has been introduced to describe early marketing methods for nebulous products like .NET (pronounced "dot-net") or SOA (for Service Oriented Architecture). Not quite content to simply advertise software products that don't exist, IT vendors moved on to describe an entire computer networking architecture that didn't yet exist (though some components are finally working and able to be purchased). In descriptions these new architectures sound wonderful: secure, easy, convenient, cheap, connecting to the world seamlessly through the desktop. They might even, someday, exist. Even when they do, however, I very much doubt that either will solve all the problems that they purport to. Chances are they may create so many new problems that buyers give up on them. As of this writing .NET encompasses a few components that don't quite work together or with other products—yet. SOA does not really have any real products. Descriptions of remarkably integrated systems abound, whereas actual examples of integration are few and far between.

I've always thought that the technology industry was uniquely filled to the brim with hype. In 2007 I carried out a research study to confirm this fact, and instead discovered that there is nothing unique about IT products and services. All advertising is filled with hype. But we don't have as much of a problem with other hyped products. I finally decided that the difference must be that everyone recognizes, without thinking, the hype surrounding normal products. Do we really believe that if a young man wears a certain aftershave the girls will have trouble keeping their hands off him? Do we really think that if we start using this brand of color copier, our customers will flock to us because of our wonderful color brochures, no matter what is inside? Of course not. And yet, when a vendor tells us that this piece of network management software will "allow us to relax on the beach while the system heals itself" we believe it. When a technology vendor tells us that installing this CRM program will "increase our sales," we believe it. Because IT is not as well understood, it is more difficult to separate actual capability from hype.

One of the major problems is that IT seems to have some amazing capabilities. When you think about what computer systems have accomplished, it is sometimes hard to believe. How fast can they compute formulas? Billions of computations per second! Huge complex formulas—in nanoseconds. They work 24 hours a day, seven days a week, 365 days a year. Tirelessly. They remember word for word trillions of documents and can recall a single requested phrase within seconds. These are things even genius human beings have a hard time doing. Information technology systems can do all of these things quickly and easily. They have achieved amazing results.

Given the unbelievable capabilities of computer systems, it is sometimes difficult to understand how and why they can't do certain things. In the late 1980s, expert systems, artificial intelligence, and natural language processing were all the rage. Scientists and engineers were convinced that within a very short time frame we would have computers that could understand simple spoken commands just as they do on *Star Trek*. This misconception is now laughable. The funniest moment in the movie *Star Trek VI: The Undiscovered Country* occurred when engineer Scotty, who had gone back in time, became frustrated at the senseless computer that didn't respond when he asked it a question. Upon being directed to use the mouse, he picked up the mouse and talked into it.

People who have worked with computers for a while understand intuitively what computers can, and cannot, do. They understand that computers can follow simple step-by-step logical instructions. But they cannot handle directions that are incomplete or ambiguous in any way.

Which is why they can't handle natural language yet, not even in the written form. A two year old has better language capability than the most sophisticated computer in the world. Why? Well, the easiest way for me to explain is to share the sentence provided by my artificial intelligence professor at Lehigh University when I was working on my doctorate. Dr. Hill asked us to consider the following sentence:

The boy hit the other boy with the girl with the blond hair with the hammer.

Picture it. What vision does this sentence conjure in your mind?

Now try to diagram this sentence grammatically. How do you know the hammer is in the hand of the first boy and was the instrument used to hit the other boy? How do you know why the boy hit the boy? How do you know the blond hair is on the girl?

Logically this sentence makes absolutely no sense. It says that one boy picked up the girl and hit the other boy with her. We know that's not what happened and we know why. The boy was jealous of the other boy because he was with the girl with blond hair. We know this because we read the sentence in the context of the human condition where girls with blond hair and boys might mix with jealousy and end up with violence perpetrated by hammers. There is no computer in the world that could figure out the meaning of the sentence without the human context.

Business data have the same problem without context. Take the following inventory list:

- 4 tires
- 2 windshield wiper blades
- 5 quarts of oil
- 1 oil filter
- 6 spark plugs
- 2 headlight lamps
- 4 petunias

Anyone reading will immediately recognize six of the items as normal automobile maintenance supplies. A 10-year-old child could probably tell you the seventh item doesn't belong. But how would a computer know? It wouldn't. There is no way to program a computer so that it would immediately recognize that flowers don't belong with automobile accessories without explicitly telling it so.

No computer in the world can identify the relationship between two items meaningfully. Computers can store billions of facts and figures—but not in context. Computers can sort and organize information, but they cannot turn that information into knowledge. Computers cannot analyze. Computers cannot make judgment calls. If you cannot clearly and unambiguously describe the rules that are accurate 100 percent of the time, the computer cannot follow the rules. That means they cannot follow common rules of thumb. There still are no computers that can predict the weather as well as a human being can. There still are no computers that can read human language. Despite millions of dollars spent on studying what seemed to be a very simple problem, computers still cannot recognize human emotions from subtle body language.

The volume and quality of relationships surrounding nouns and verbs that can be stored by the human brain is exorbitant. The brain is much more capable in this regard than a computer. A human brain has over 100 billion neurons, and even more glial cells that support and nurture each neuron. In comparison, there are only a little more than 500 million computers on the public Internet. Even if you factor in each integrated circuit chip, there is still more processing power in the brain of a six-month-old baby than there is in all the computers of the world combined.

Unless it is crystal clear to us what computers can and cannot do, we might develop unrealistic expectations for what they can accomplish for us.

Take cleaning up dirty data.

Cleaning up dirty data has got to be one of the most difficult, laborious, and thankless jobs in all the world. (Well, okay, maybe cleaning up latrines beats it, but not by much.) I've already mentioned the old saw GIGO (Garbage In, Garbage Out). One would think that given its importance, all data stored by computers by now would be clean and pristine—but they are not. Most of the information stored is contaminated in some way: duplicate records, inaccurate entries, incomplete information, and so on. Dirty data are the scourge of every computer system.

Computers cannot clean up dirty data. Only a human being can do that. Expecting the computer to do so is unrealistic, although a common misconception. Often decision makers think that a new technology implementation will magically solve the problems caused by dirty data. I have seen highly intelligent leaders choose, purchase, and implement a new system—while at the same time claiming that there isn't time to clean up the data from the old system. Somehow they think the computer itself will do the cleanup. Months later they are shocked (shocked!) to find out that the new system wasn't any better than the old system, since the problem wasn't the system, but the dirty data all along! What they obviously didn't realize is that they could have had all the benefits touted by the vendor simply by cleaning up their data and saving themselves a bundle by continuing to use the perfectly adequate existing system.

Whole businesses have been built on unrealistic expectations. Remember Jan, the client who tried to get me to identify a system that would allow her to provide transcription services to doctors and lawyers without using people typing into word processors? She had seen a demonstration at a conference of Dragon's Naturally Speaking system. She actually saw people who talked into a computer while the system typed their words into the document. She figured she could set up a telephone system and have doctors and lawyers call up on the phone and dictate into it. On the other end would be a computer that would transcribe their words. What is so scary is that she'd already gone to a bank and gotten funding for this new business, and now she just had to choose the hardware and software to do it!

Expectations of technology are clearly out of whack with reality. The devil is in the details. Yes, voice recognition really works—in a very limited way. A system can recognize a myriad of voices but only a few select words (such as numbers or a limited list of known phrases). Or a system can recognize many different words, but only if a single person spends dozens of hours training it specifically to his or her voice. Additionally, the system is only about 80 percent effective on a good day—and having a human being going back and cleaning up the 20 percent that is wrong takes more time than if you had simply hired someone to do the typing to begin with. Truth be told—businesses today are wasting money on voice recognition systems to replace operators and receptionists; people are cheaper and more accurate.

Vendors often take advantage of the tendency toward unrealistic expectations. Why else would enterprise network management systems sell at all? Buyers of these $100,000 systems expect the system to warn them before a network device fails. Occasionally, when the situation is just right and people who know the network very well have tuned the configuration for months and months, the system will provide the right people with the right warning at the right time to avoid a problem before it happens. More often, the system will let them know that the network has gone down after the fact (big whup!). But if the buyer asks the vendor, "Will this system warn me before the network goes down?" The vendor will answer, truthfully, "yes."

How can vendors obfuscate this way? Remember asking road builders if blue cars would drive on the road? The road builders said "yes" even though they have nothing whatsoever to do with the color of the car. They just knew that it was possible.

Let's take another analogy. We want to get to Africa, but we're a bit ignorant about exactly where that is. We go to a dealership selling Mercedes Benz vehicles. We ask the dealer, "Can this car get me to Africa?" The dealer says "Sure!" Obviously, a Mercedes can get us to Africa as well as any other car can get us to Africa. We buy the car and drive toward Africa. But we have to stop suddenly when we run into the Atlantic Ocean.

The Mercedes Benz dealer hasn't lied; the dealer just took advantage of the fact that when we heard "yes," we assumed that the Mercedes was all we needed to get to Africa. Because the dealer knows that no car can get us to Africa, the dealer is not worried we will buy from someone else. Besides, we still need a car to get to the airport, don't we? Is it the dealer's fault we thought a car could get us all the way to Africa?

I have been a victim of unrealistic expectations quite a few times—even after I thought I knew better. A few years ago, I was considering a decision to join a new start-up. The high-powered references of the CEO checked out. But when he told me that he wanted to develop and sell live video customer service across the public Internet, I initially told him flat out he was nuts. The infrastructure did not yet exist, I said. High-quality live video could not be done over the public Internet, I said. I explained that the public Internet was not stable enough and did not have enough bandwidth for the kind of traffic video generated. It would be like trying to take a train through the intertwining streets of your neighborhood.

The CEO insisted that it could be done and was already being done. He flew me to the West Coast to meet with people from the telecommunications company, and they demonstrated high-quality video over the Internet (they said). Perhaps the technology had improved more than I had realized, I thought. After all, I'd been a bank VP for seven years and out of the networking game. When the telecommunications company promised to provide circuits to any of our customers for $300 a month, no matter where they were in the country, I crunched the numbers and I realized that at that price, the CEO was right—the service could be cost effective. I joined up and became CTO of Commercelinks.net. I invested quite a lot of time and money on the venture, led the team to develop the top-end live video customer technology that would utilize the Internet protocols, and applied for the preliminary patents. We were all ready to go.

Our unrealistic expectations came falling down on us just as the same was happening to everyone else involved in dot-coms. The telecommunications company reneged on the $300 per month connection promise. During my investigation into why, I got one of the technologists to admit that the demonstration they showed us was sort of rigged. They had not demonstrated the technology over the public Internet, but rather over a private Internet (their own private network using Internet protocols, something that's easy for a telephone company to do since they own the public lines). The cost to provide the kind of quality we required far outstripped the $300 per month quote unless every customer we worked with was already a customer of that particular telecommunications company.

There are plenty of technologies that will work fine over a private Internet, but not work well at all over the public Internet. On a private Internet, the network traffic pattern can be controlled from end to end. On the public Internet, no one controls the traffic, jams are frequent, and there are no guarantees. The difference is like traveling to China via a charter plane or taking an unreliable, slow boat (not even a cruise liner) with 400 other people squeezed into tiny cubicles all around you. With private lines (i.e., the charter jet) live video customer service is a viable alternative. But at $30,000 a month, it is not feasible.

Failing to differentiate between the public Internet and a private Internet is still a common misunderstanding among technology businesses everywhere today. In the second chapter I spoke of trying to find a simple 10-gigabyte storage area for my files that would be accessible from any machine on the public Internet. I tried three different companies that promised on-line storage. After several months, I finally had to give up. Certainly, if I could afford a leased line directly to their data center, the on-line storage would work fine. But over the public Internet? No matter how many times the vendor promised that it would work, it simply doesn't work. Here is the conversation I had with their tech support (several times actually).

Me: I'm trying to upload my files and the connection hangs after a few hundred megabytes.

Tech support: Have you tried rebooting your machine?

Me: Yes, several times. This is the fourth day in a row I've worked on the problem. The upload starts, works for about an hour or two, and then quits. I can't get all 10 gigabytes of files up to your site.

Tech support: Hold on a minute while I test it.

(Pause for 15 minutes or so.)

Tech support: I've just uploaded 10 gigabytes of information to the server, so there's no problem on our end.

Me: Did you upload the information over the Internet?

Tech support: Yes, I did. I'm in Canada, and the server is in Houston.

Me: What kind of connection do you have?

Tech support: I don't know. I'm not a networking person.

The tech support people kept testing the service in-house on a (admittedly huge) local area network with tons of bandwidth. Of course downloading and uploading worked fine on that network. When it wouldn't work for me, across the public Internet on a DSL line, they told me it was my system's fault. It wasn't. The idea was doomed because the infrastructure of the public Internet isn't stable enough yet. It would be like having a job that required you to be on the East Coast half the week and on the West Coast the other half of each week when there were no airplanes. The expectation that it can be done is unrealistic at the present time. But since even the technical support people could not distinguish between the public Internet and their private Internet, I could not get even them to understand why the service they were selling did not do what it promised to do.

Unrealistic expectations can really do damage when naive buyers presume information technology vendors and consultants are giving them unbiased information. In the early 1990s, in my role as a consultant for the company that bought my first business, I was often paid to do a study to identify the best option for systems management or network management for customers. It was always understood by them that my time would be spent identifying which of the many options offered by my company would best meet the needs of the customer. Referring them to a competitor's products or services was not an option. Neither was not doing anything; there would always be a technological solution to their request. Although I always made this clear to my clients, I am aware that many consultants do not.

Let's again look to an analogy. Upon arriving at the lot of the Porsche dealer, would you would expect the salesperson to answer that the Cadillac dealer down the street was a better choice when asked "Which car is the best for me?" Of course not! However, in the immature technology world, it may take weeks of interviewing and learning current processes in order to determine which service or system would work for the business—and someone has to pay for that time. Vendors cannot afford to spend time to make recommendations without charging for them—but that doesn't mean that they are looking at all options—usually just the ones that will make them money.

It is possible, but rare, to find unbiased consultants whose income doesn't depend upon vendors' projects. Even independent consultants who evaluate several systems usually get a referral fee from the vendor of the winning bid. Even third-party consultants like Gartner Group indirectly make money on technology solutions, so there are few unbiased reliable sources to whom a decision maker can turn when they want to know whether or not to do something.

The final place where obfuscation raises its ugly head is a popular solution touted by many consultants and vendors: the service level agreement (SLA). Putting in place an SLA was supposed to solve typical problems between buyers and sellers of technology. The idea sounds convincing. An SLA puts in writing exactly what the seller is going to do and what the consequences are if the promises aren't delivered. Huge outsourcing contracts where big technology vendors took over all the technology needs of Big Business use SLAs.

Here's the problem: Because technology is immature, both the vendors and the buyers are in the same bind. Neither can understand the challenges they face as they try to implement new technology. IT projects are not like construction projects. The construction industry has thousands of years of history to let them know what works and what doesn't. IT projects are more like promises to build a bridge for a price without knowing how wide the river is or whether the banks are sand or rock. No one can estimate the time involved, or the costs, or even the long-term risks in most IT projects, although we keep pretending we can.

An example: One of my clients had a five-year contract with a company to manage the company-wide help desk for 8,000 employees. The agreement was almost a hundred pages long, with financial penalties for every month that the quality standards were not met. The quality standards? That every help desk call had a response within 24 hours, and that every new PC was deployed within three days of delivery. The agreement also required that 10 help desk people be available round the clock, 24 hours a day. Sounds reasonable, doesn't it? Just what we want, right?

In this case, the help desk vendor usually met a 10-minute response time instead of a 24-hour response time. Every time people called the help desk, they received an immediate response saying that someone was looking into the problem. The vendor also deployed every new PC within two days of delivery instead of three, and they averaged 12 help desk people every day. The client should love them, right?

Wrong. Within months, employees stopped calling the help desk because, despite the immediate e-mail response, they were rarely actually helped. The tech support people staffing the phones seemed to be high school dropouts who didn't know very much about the systems implemented at the customer's site. And that quick response time for new PCs was really helpful—until the employee tried to actually use the PC and discovered that the mouse drivers had never been installed and the wrong printer driver had been. It usually took four or five calls to the help desk to actually fix all the problems so that the PC was usable. I was called in to help document the hundreds of costly problems so that the lawyers had a case to nullify the contract without paying the huge penalty for early termination.

Armed with my documentation, my client finally cancelled the agreement after two years and said good riddance to the vendor. Unfortunately, they didn't learn the lesson. Instead of taking my advice, they chose to replace the vendor with another one, getting more lawyers involved in negotiating yet another multi-year deal with another SLA. They wouldn't admit that the attempt to codify technical support was a losers' game.

The nature of IT people can also contribute to the failure of SLAs. When there is a shortage, and there usually is, vendors put the technologists with people skills on the sales end of the process, and put the more heavy duty, and often more technically knowledgeable, engineers on the implementation side. For buyers, what sounded great when described by the sales engineer turns out to be not so great when implemented by a different, more recalcitrant, technical engineer. This problem is worse when the sales engineer is both good with people and good at technology. Technically proficient sales engineers describe a great system that could be great if they were the ones implementing it, but because they spend all their time in sales, they don't really have any hand in making it happen and the technical engineer may not be as good as they are, or simply unwilling to go the extra mile.

The bottom line is that most SLAs are worthless. SLAs either have to be written so vaguely that they actually mean nothing (and it comes down to whether you can trust the vendor—in which case you can save yourself the lawyers' fees), or they are so specific that they are unworkable in real life, or obsolete before the signature dries on the page.

SPEED OF CHANGE

Two suited business colleagues walking into their office together: "I knew we shouldn't have gone to lunch. Now our technology is obsolete!"

You don't have to be a marketing guru to recognize that in recent years the product lifespan for technology has gotten shorter and shorter. For just

Figure 6.1
Length of Product Life

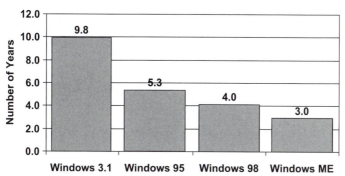

a sample, look at the life cycle of the most popular operating system in the world, Windows, in Figure 6.1.

In the 1970s and 1980s, technology was expected to last for 25 or 30 years. Nowadays, a company is lucky to have the same technology for five years in a row.

You may notice that Figure 6.1 does not include Windows XP. There's a reason for that. After Windows ME, Microsoft changed their method of updating and renaming products and services, as many other vendors had already done. Windows XP was more like a subscription service than a one-time installed product. In other words, Windows XP was on a continuous update cycle so that the product only lasts for a few weeks, until the next update, at which time our systems might get more secure and have earlier problems fixed, or (unfortunately frequently the case) become less secure and break our previously working system. In either case, we can no longer measure the life of our operating system in years, because now the life cycle is weeks, and we are paying for a subscription rather than a product.

Companies that develop and sell technology products (hardware, software, even consulting concepts like Six Sigma or Reengineering) know and understand this product life cycle very well. Success for these vendors generally rests on their ability to introduce new products at the exact right moment, usually in the death throes of declining products. The shorter the life cycle, the more money the vendor can make.

Vendors might argue that customers demand new features, that a public outcry for improvement has shortened the life cycle. However, I would argue that more often than not customers would prefer simply to have software that works, and works well, 100 percent of the time.

I would argue that most new features of products are unnecessary, unneeded, and unwanted. Unfortunately, it is very difficult for any individual company or consumer to fight the trend and stick with the same hardware or software for long. Vendors typically stop supporting declining products and share horror stories about how much it will cost if there are problems later down the road. Vendors like to lead customers to believe that they would be up a creek without a paddle without upgrades, and that they shouldn't take that chance. Many technologists echo this sentiment. It's hard to fight (though in the next chapter we will share how we can and why we should).

The short product cycle would be bad enough if the products all fit together modularly, but they don't. There is no technology independent of the technology to which it is connected. So when one component changes, all the other components must change as well.

One of my CEO clients, Kim, wanted to install an optical wireless mouse. She ordered the mouse that she wanted—much as she would order a new knob for the credenza cabinet of her desk. Kim didn't want to bother her technical people when it arrived, so she sat down early one morning and followed the directions to plug it in.

Fourteen hours later Kim called me to come and fix the system since nothing she had tried would get the new mouse to work, and now her old mouse wouldn't work either. She was stuck. Of course, being a CEO she preferred to pay big bucks for me to come and fix the problem rather than let her technical employees know what she'd done. She said that she didn't need their "sneers."

As soon as I started working on it, what happened became obvious. It is a simple example of what happens when you want to make one tiny change in any working computer system.

In order for a wireless mouse to work, there have to be connections in five places:

- The mouse hardware must be able to talk to the interface software.
- The interface software of the mouse must talk over the wireless connection of the mouse to the wireless receiver.
- The wireless receiver of the computer hardware must talk to the USB connection.
- The USB connection must talk to the interface software of the mouse on the computer.
- The interface software of the mouse must then communicate with the operating system.

When her particular computer system was installed, wireless optical mice were not very common. Since the mouse, the hardware, and the operating system were developed and sold by three different, unrelated manufacturers during different generations, the chances were astronomically small that all the details would have been worked out between the three vendors on an uncommon peripheral like a wireless mouse. In this case, the breakdown apparently occurred at the wireless connection of the computer hardware, which wasn't talking with the interface software of the mouse. Bottom line: To install an optical mouse, she would have to install an entirely new system.

The speed of change in information technology does not necessarily mean that other fields such as finance and accounting have kept up. I used to think that the rules of capitalization were an accountant's exercise—highly boring, pretty useless in the real world, and certainly not of any interest to the manager of a technology project. You wouldn't find me under green eyeshades and cuff protectors poring over columns of numbers to determine the depreciation of an item, no sir!

But then a strange thing happened. As a VP for a Fortune 500 financial services firm, I had to create a spreadsheet template that would calculate the return on investment (ROI) to be used by the budget analysts when requesting funds for projects. So in 1996, there I was, poring over columns of formulas in a spreadsheet (sans eyeshades and cuff protectors) grunting my surprise at a new accounting discovery: The rules of capitalization could make the difference between a positive ROI and a negative ROI.

We're not talking pocket change, either. Using a different option for capitalization rules on one of the projects I analyzed, for example, switched the payback period from eight months to eight years.

I became very concerned about the consequences of this finding. I knew the top decision makers in the company didn't know—and certainly didn't care—which rules of capitalization were used in assessing the value of the project. I'd probably drop from shock if I ever heard the CEO of a $4 billion company ask, "Did you capitalize or expense the programming on that project?" At the same time, my experience showed how centrally important the question is to information technology projects.

Here's how it works. If we pay a flat amount for the hardware and software, an amount that includes the consultants to customize and install the system and train the employees, we are allowed to capitalize the entire purchase price. In other words, if we spent $15 million, only $1 million had to be charged to expenses that first year. Only the depreciation, based on 15 years for an enterprise-wide system, affected the current year's profit.

On the other hand, if we used hardware we already had, and had our employees or even outside consultants, but not as part of the purchase price, write the software, implement the system, and train the employees, we had to expense the entire project. While the project itself would probably be cheaper (say, perhaps, only $10 million instead of $15 million), the entire amount had to be charged to expenses, and therefore would impact the profit in a major way. Instead of $1 million cost, we faced a $10 million cost even though we just saved the company $5 million!

Keep in mind that we are talking about two different ways to accomplish the same goal. Nothing in the hardware, software, programming, training, or project implementation was different except how it was billed. The operational outcome for these two choices would be exactly the same, but one would show a positive ROI, and the other would show a negative ROI.

The accountants I talked with didn't seem concerned about this issue. They declared that the rules of capitalization had been well established, were used consistently, and made perfect sense. But I could see a mile-wide gap in their knowledge about technology projects that led to their indifference: The exact same system could be described as either off the shelf and configured or customized to the client's needs, or developed by programmers. The difference was only semantics, not an inherent difference in the technology itself.

This is why technology vendors sell customized programming and development as if it were an off-the- shelf product. Most ERP systems, for example, are actually custom development projects although they are talked about as if they are packages of software. When I worked for a system integrator, we carefully shrink-wrapped and shipped boxes containing nothing more than a piece of paper with a license number on it. The software (worth $25,000) was actually being delivered dynamically by our programmers, but the customer needed to receive the shipment, so we sent them the license number (without which the system wouldn't work). I now see that the capitalization rules were probably to blame for this bit of idiocy as well.

Outdated rules of capitalization is just one of the problems with generally accepted accounting principles that causes the ROI calculation to lead entrepreneurs and business owners to make the exact wrong decision on technology projects. ROI calculations have difficulty accounting for concepts such as ongoing maintenance, residual value, infrastructure separation, and the risk of unproven capabilities. Projects using new technology are much riskier than projects using stable technology. Projects requiring new infrastructure are more expensive (but often have higher residual value) than projects using existing infrastructure. Project using common technologies will have much lower ongoing maintenance costs than projects using less common technologies. Until ROI algorithms have been modified to take into account these issues so that we can separate a technology project from a building (where none of these concepts apply), a positive ROI calculation will lead to approval for the projects most likely to fail, and rejection for projects most likely to succeed.

When I discovered this in 1996, I lobbied hard to get a text field included in the ROI results stating whether the technology in the project proposed was obsolete, stable, new, or leading edge. I couldn't imagine a senior leader making an informed decision without that basic information. Unfortunately, although I was successful in getting the information into the presentation, I was not successful in communicating its importance. The senior leaders continued to make decisions without looking at that information.

These problems are further complicated by the inability of buyers of new technologies to get accurate technical documentation. In the 1980s and 1990s, vendors would make available technical descriptions of their products in documents called white papers. A white paper usually described exactly what the new technologies were under the covers: how they worked, how they differed from previous technologies, and so on. They were written in technical jargon, and were meant for IT people, but at least they were available.

When the speed of change accelerated drastically, due, in part, to the public Internet, and as leaders with less IT knowledge started making technology decisions, the marketing department took over. White papers lost their technical edge. Instead, they evolved into the same type of marketing fluff that one might find in a product brochure. Even if buyers are relatively knowledgeable in the world of IT, they cannot get access to the underlying structure of new technologies in order to assess their stability and "fit" into an organization's existing technologies without purchasing and installing it to see.

GETTING THE MOST FROM VENDORS

By now you must be thinking, "Whoa! Those are a lot of obstacles. How can anyone ever get around them? Given the problems, how can we ever know if technology will help us reach our goals? How can we ever get a good partnership with hardware and software vendors?"

There are solutions to each and every one of these obstacles. It is possible to have good relationships between buyers and sellers of technology. Step one is to recognize the difficulties involved in each one. Step two is to neutralize the problem with knowledge, attitude, and behavior. And that's just what we'll cover in the next chapter.

SUMMARY

Purchasing technology is fraught with difficulty because:

- ☑ The field of information technology is immature.
- ☑ The specialized terminology has not yet entered general domains of knowledge.
- ☑ The public infrastructure for IT is still in its infancy.
- ☑ The components are not yet integrated and must be purchased separately.
- ☑ The vendors of IT products and services are often subject to volatile finances.
- ☑ Capabilities of IT products and services are often not recognized as hype.
- ☑ IT products and services have amazing capabilities but strange limitations.
- ☑ IT products cannot make judgments or meaningfully relate two items.
- ☑ IT products cannot speak natural language or follow rules of thumb.
- ☑ IT products cannot clean up dirty data or fix process problems.
- ☑ IT buyers often have unrealistic expectations about IT products.
- ☑ Lack of understanding (sometimes even from the vendors themselves) of IT concepts makes communication about products and services difficult.
- ☑ Accounting rules and standards have not kept up with IT project realities.
- ☑ IT products and services have a very short life cycle, getting even shorter.
- ☑ Getting technical information about IT products and services has become more and more difficult.

7

The Inside Secrets of Software and Hardware Vendors

Now that Chapter 6 has us thoroughly discouraged, allow me to identify a ray of hope. It is quite possible to mitigate all the challenges and come out with great decisions about information technology and good relationships with vendors regardless of the obstacles. All we need to do is keep the following rules in mind:

- Become technically literate.
- Recognize the immaturity.
- Define your own standards.
- Maximize periods of stability, minimize periods of instability.
- Cultivate long-term vendor partnerships.
- Ignore hype.
- Get off the bleeding edge.

Let's look at each of these in detail.

BECOMING TECHNICALLY LITERATE

Please grant me the knowledge to understand the technology I do;
the courage to ask about the technology I don't;
and the wisdom to know the difference.

> (Just in case you didn't catch it, this is a parody of
> "The Serenity Prayer.")

Just as the first step on the road to recovery for an alcoholic is recognizing the problem, the first step on the road to better technology decision making is recognizing that having the necessary knowledge is a prerequisite to make the decision. Since we know that the gap between those who understand IT and those who don't is costing us money, we are faced with the difficult task of learning what we need to know. There is no alternative.

There are several ways to learn so we can recognize the best deal when we see it. First, we start, as suggested in Chapter 1, by creating an internal technology map that places, in relationship to each other, all the current technologies our organization is using. Second, we gather additional information from IT vendors, making sure that we understand which layer of the technology map each one is on. Third, we need to find people in whom we can place our trust who understand IT. We can't abdicate our decisions to them; we must spend the necessary time to pull from them their knowledge so that we can make the decisions ourselves.

As discussed in the first chapter, an accurate technology map of the different technologies used within the business is essential. Developing this map may initially require us to tamp down our egos a bit. First we have to admit what we don't know. Then we have to ask technology vendors and staff to explain every buzzword, clarify every glossy phrase. We may have to put up with an occasional rolled eye and impatient sigh. The result, however, often means the difference between a good decision and a bad decision. The temporary condition of not understanding will shortly be replaced with easily keeping up with the ever-changing technology landscape. Eventually we will understand the technology better than the salespeople, which is a good position to be in.

Knowing as much or more than salespeople do can help us evaluate the information they give us. Remember that IT salespeople often don't have a very deep understanding of IT, either; they defer to IT engineers. Often it is very difficult to get technical information from IT vendors. If we can get an IT vendor to provide us with detailed technical information without purchasing, we should do so. If not, one way to get the information (albeit a bit sneaky) is to ask for detailed proposals from many different vendors as if you are ready to purchase. A well-done proposal can teach us many things about the hardware, software, and services—facts you cannot get in any other way. (Apologies to all technology vendors for this advice. You can avoid spending hours on proposals that won't necessarily lead to commitment by providing information in technical white papers devoid of marketing gibberish.)

Sometimes vendors are willing to do a pilot project to resolve any technical issues before the buyer commits to purchasing the technology. If it costs absolutely nothing, go for it. Be aware, however, that many vendors use doing a pilot as a ploy. In many cases, the actual hardware and software are extremely cheap, and the real cost for the system is in the customization and development, for which you are charged even in the pilot. Be careful. Make sure that your commitment of time and money is low, and that you won't end up with a big bill if the pilot is successful. Make sure you have an out.

Another way to get information is to ask vendors for references and talk with other users of the products and services. When discussing it, however, keep in mind the differences between their businesses and yours. One size does not fit all.

Additionally, it is up to us to be sure, before we ask a question, that we are asking the right vendor the question. It doesn't make any sense to ask the person filling the potholes which car is the most reliable, and the car dealer won't be able to tell us which type of material makes the best roads. So why would we ask an application vendor which server to purchase, or rely upon the advice of the networking salesperson about which financial system to purchase?

Remember that mystification question discussed in Chapter 3?

> *VP of IT:* Can this software check the entry of the clerk so that the transfer always goes through?
> *Sales engineer:* Absolutely—yes. Every time a packet gets sent, an acknowledgment is returned so that the sending computer knows if it was successful. The transfer always goes through.

The mystification was caused because the VP was on the application layer and the sales engineer was on the network layer. If we have a technology map we would know better than to ask a network engineer a question applicable only to the application program.

When we hire consultants, we want to sop up all their knowledge like a sponge rather than allow them to keep their expertise to themselves. Another way to ensure that money paid to a consultant is not wasted is to pay them for more permanent knowledge in the form of documentation and formal training. Penny-pinching managers often skimp on documentation hours, and technology staff who hate to document are only too happy to comply with a lack of emphasis on the documentation. But documentation often can save multiples of its cost by providing the exact right information necessary at a critical decision-making time.

One of the projects I managed as VP for a Fortune 500 financial firm required reconnecting our new systems with all three credit reporting agencies. Three years earlier, a consultant had done the original connection for our existing systems. This time, the entire project was put on hold for days because none of the people on the team knew what needed to be done to update this connection or whom to contact at the credit reporting agencies to make the change. The team estimated the time needed to reconstruct the missing information: two weeks. This would cost the project well over $300,000 in lost opportunity and team time. This would have been an unexpected expense we couldn't afford on a project already behind.

In the midst of this crisis, however, almost by accident I happened to be talking with someone who had previously worked in the department. He told me exactly where to find the documentation the previous consultant left, along with the names and phone numbers of the people to contact at the credit reporting agencies. Within 24 hours the connection was done. I whispered my thanks to the heavens for the unknown manager who had insisted on that documentation. (Now if they had only insisted on making sure the next manager knew where the documentation was so there wouldn't have been any delay!)

It always behooves senior leaders spending money on IT to understand it. When I was working as an enterprise network management consultant,

I would facilitate a series of concept of operation meetings with the business leaders of the company during the first few weeks of the project. I can tell you from experience that the business leaders often did not understand their role. Even the rare occasion when we did get the right people in the room (the CEO, COO, CFO, and CIO), they were not patient enough to become knowledgeable enough so they could see how their decisions connected to the concept of operations or the software implementation.

Despite my attempts to explain, they were limited by their own misunderstanding. They thought that we were simply installing a piece of software like Microsoft Word or Excel, and didn't understand the decisions they were making. Normally, I ended up making many of the concept of operation decisions based upon my best guess as to what they needed from our discussions. But the value of the system to their business would have increased dramatically if they'd simply understood how they could align the way the software worked with their business. That understanding would also enable them to make adjustments in the future as the business changed. As it was, I suspect that after the engineers implemented the concept of operations requirements that I defined, the senior leaders never thought about the system again. They missed an incredible opportunity to achieve commensurate value for the hundreds of thousands they had paid for the system.

RECOGNIZING THE IMMATURITY

The first step to mitigating the immaturity of the information technology industry is to accept that it is not going to respond like a mature field. I like to watch for signs that it is maturing—such as that you can now get a computer, operating system, monitor, storage drives, and printer from the same manufacturer, (although there are still problems in getting them all to play nicely together). However, we shouldn't be surprised when IT falls down once in a while and fails. IT is still at the teenage stage rather than the adult stage, and we should expect mistakes.

It is because of the immaturity that we can't expect the same from technology vendors as we do from car dealerships or appliance stores. We must remember that, more often than not, the vendor is in new territory and doesn't have the answers any more than we do.

We also need to recognize which technologies are easily purchased commodities and which are not. We've come a long way over the years toward not needing consultants for every little technology decision. Think about word processing. Over 20 years ago, I was teaching for a local school district, and it had hired a consultant's two-person firm to do a six-month study that would determine the clerical staff's word processing needs. The outcome was a Wang word processing system costing tens of thousands of dollars, which was used in the district for the next 10 years.Word processing was a complex topic back then. There were typewriters with storage capabilities. There were huge systems like Wang that could handle 20 or 30 word processors (secretaries) at the same time. There were PC-based systems like WordStar and MultiMate. The features available in these different solutions were leapfrogging each other, with capabilities changing month to month. Most people had experience only with a simple electric typewriter. They were confused by all the choices. They needed an expert consultant to do a study and indicate the best choice. Purchasing a word processor was an expensive multi-month proposition.

Can you imagine spending six months today to identify whether you want to use Microsoft Word or WordPerfect? Of course not! Today we might give the decision five minutes' consideration before choosing Microsoft Word because of its ubiquity. Word processing decisions no longer require the expertise of a consultant.

A decade ago, Internet technologies were at the same level as those old word-processing systems were in 1984. During the Internet bubble, businesses hired e-strategy consultants to help them get on-line, and often spent millions of dollars doing so. Today, the public Internet is cheap and ubiquitous. Today, a company can get on the Web within hours. There are thousands of public Internet sites that can register domain names, provide us with a Web site template, and take us through an easy-to-use wizard to build Web pages. One fast-growing company that burst on the scene in 1997 delivering this service for the princely sum of $3.95 a month is Go Daddy. By 2004 Go Daddy had ranked number eight on the 2004 Inc. 500 list; and number 20 on the 2005 Deloitte Technology Fast 500. While its pace has slowed (they ranked only 632 on the Inc. list in 2007), and their prices have increased ($6.95 a month now) they are still the largest domain registrar on the Internet.

At the height of the Internet boom, getting a simple Web site on the public Internet might have cost hundreds of thousands of dollars. It is hard to believe that what was once an expensive undertaking can now be had for pennies a day. But this is a standard path for technology. (More details about how entrepreneurs can get on the public Internet are found in Chapter 8.)

Some companies, however, are still paying big bucks for simple public Internet Web sites. The problem occurs when big-spending decision makers don't learn anything new about the technologies they've funded. I know one business owner who is still paying $200 a month for a simple brochureware Web site. A consultant recommended it in 1999, and he hasn't changed anything since. This business owner won't believe me when I tell him that he can port his whole Web site somewhere else and stop paying such huge amounts. Unfortunately, my free advice didn't seem to trump the incorrect but expensive advice he got years ago. (This is one of the reasons why I have stopped giving out free advice. It's amazing how much more people listen when they are paying thousands of dollars.)

It is not easy to figure out exactly when the expensive new technology becomes cheap old technology. Think about the consultants and staff people at the school district that implemented the Wang word processing system. Five years after it had been installed, were they going to share with the school district decision makers how cheap WordPerfect had become? The employees who ran the system weren't about to let their bosses know that the whole thing could be replaced for a fraction of the annual maintenance cost. The staff who had struggled to figure out how to use the difficult-to-learn system weren't about to change even if the new system was easier. The school district continued to pay whopping fees for five more years after the cheaper alternative was available because it didn't know any better. It would have been better for them to have waited for a few more years, after the tipping point, (a phrase made famous by Malcolm Gladwell[28]) to even look at the decision.

The *tipping point* is the moment when a previously expensive and customized solution becomes a cheap-and-easy commodity. We can tell when that point occurs in a product life cycle by watching for the following signs:

- The majority of businesses already use it successfully.
- It can be purchased off the shelf in office-supply stores.
- Dozens (or hundreds) of smaller software firms have consolidated into two or three large competing publishers.
- We do not see articles or success stories about the technology in industry magazines anymore.
- Salespeople stop calling on us to sell the technology.
- Consultants don't recommend the technology anymore because its use is a given.

In most cases, we want to wait until technology moves from innovative product to commodity before investing in it. When we purchase commodity items, we should not need the help of a consultant.

When faced with highly complex and unintegrated technologies, however, entrepreneurs and business owners do need to rely upon unbiased consultants to help them make the right decision. As noted in the previous section, the first step is to recognize the difference between the easy commodity stuff and the newer innovative stuff. Security, streaming video, voice-over-data lines, databases over the public Internet, wireless implementations, radio-frequency ID codes, customized handheld applications—there are still plenty of technologies for which there is no other choice but to hire a consultant.

These, too, will become commodities within five years of their tipping point, but for now, if we need them, we should hire a consultant to ensure that we understand what we are getting, how much it should cost, and how to implement it. Of course, when we do that we want to pay very close attention to ensure that there are no behind-the-scenes partnerships or deals that would bias the consultant. If we look, we can find consultants whose income doesn't depend upon vendors' projects and who don't get a referral fee from vendors. It makes sense, if we can, to only work with consultants who will not profit from the choices we make. Most important of all, we want to make sure that "none of the above right now" is one of the options considered. There's nothing worse than spending money on a new technology that we actually don't need.

DEFINING COMPANY-WIDE IT STANDARDS

Technology leaders are known for lauding the cost savings of standards. It has been shown again and again that simplifying the technical environment can save a company a great deal of money in the future. But how standards help organizations save money is still a mystery to many.

First, let's differentiate what we mean by the word *standards*. Earlier we introduced the term in conjunction with standards bodies. That is not what we mean here. Nor do we mean implementing a similar-looking desktop on all the PCs (e.g., the same screen saver and the same menu choices on all PCs). At a recent workshop I heard one manager brag about how his company's computers were completely standardized because they locked down all the desktops with the same screen and application programs. Yet later I found out that their technical environment included DB2, Oracle, Sybase, SQL, and Access (all different databases) as well as Solaris, HPUX, Linux, Windows NT, Windows 2000, and AIX (all different operating systems). I wouldn't exactly call that standardized.

In this case, standards refers to the list of hardware and software, including models and versions, in use in our organizations. Within our business, it is important that we define what is current, what is stable, and what is future. *Current* is the brand and version of each component we are purchasing today. *Stable* is the component we are no longer purchasing, nor replacing, but just leaving in place to work effectively. *Future* is a component that may be selling currently, but which we are not purchasing yet—though we probably plan to switch at some point in the future. Once we've defined current, stable, and future, we have documented what we have and what we want, as well as what we are not ready for yet.

The secret for saving money is not to push. We don't get rid of what we have just because it is not our standard. But the next time a purchase decision comes up, we simply look in the current column and purchase that.

The only hardware and software we push to replace with current is anything not listed as stable. In Chapter 5 we introduced the formula: $P = (PE * A * E) + (PR * T) + (HSC * I)$. The longer our current technology remains stable, the better value the system provides. Our standards chart, which becomes part of our technology map, is the tool we use to implement those guidelines. Examples can be seen in Appendix A. The best value is obtained when the current, stable, and future are all the same, which is only possible in already mature technologies like wiring. Nonetheless, this is the goal for all levels.

There is no such thing as the best standard for all businesses—each will be unique and can only be determined after carefully reviewing the existing environment. Undoubtedly, the first time the standards are documented, there will be multiple answers in the Stable and Current columns. For each multiple in each column, the cost to support it increases exponentially because we need technical support people in multiple domains. Take the previous example. To pay for technical expertise in DB2, Oracle, Sybase, SQL, Access, Solaris, HPUX, Linux, Windows NT, Windows 2000, and AIX, we need a cadres of people, at least a dozen. If we have 1,000 employees, the cost per employee would be $600 per year just for ongoing support. If all 1,000 employees were supported by simply Oracle, HPUX, we would drop down to $100 per employee for support.

The goal, then, is to slowly move toward simplification. We cannot push it because existing applications don't always port to other environments. Eventually, however, our environment will mature. We will have only one answer in each category and we will save scads of money on maintenance and support.

MAXIMIZING PERIODS OF STABILITY, MINIMIZING PERIODS OF INSTABILITY

We can't do anything about the fact that the IT industry itself is unstable and constantly changing. But we don't have to give in to that method ourselves. One of the best ways to ensure smooth computing is to hold on to our existing information technology configuration without making changes—neither people nor process nor hardware and software—as long as possible.

Holding on to existing configurations without changes is not easy. One problem could be that the vendor goes out of business or gets acquired. When considering a new technology, we'll want to know where the market currently resides in this cycle of technology innovation, capitalism, and financing in order to prevent this problem. We want to stick with established profitable companies—companies with financial stability that aren't dependent upon a constant influx of venture capital dollars even when the market for some new technology is just beginning. Additionally, funding often depends upon the amount of buzz surrounding the new technology. Since the amount of buzz often depends upon hype rather than actual revolutionary change, we need to be careful of products in the growth phase of a new market cycle. So we want to stay away from whatever everybody is writing about and talking about.

We want to pay attention to the life cycle. Within the overall market cycle, each component of technology has a life cycle. In general, we can say every product goes through four stages from birth to death. The phases of a product life cycle are the following:

1. Development
   - Introduction of idea
   - Developing, testing (alpha and beta), feasibility

2. Growth
   - Commercial introduction (piloting)
   - Commercial acceptance
   - Expansion
3. Maturity
   - Stability (longest phase for successful products)
   - Decline
4. Obsolescence
   - Gasping
   - Completely dead

During the development and growth stages, expect quite a bit of hype about the product. After maturity, the hype will fall away, leaving only the actual capabilities of the product. After maturity, the vendor will stop issuing bug releases and start encouraging customers to upgrade to the replacement product. After a while, the vendor won't even help with problems. The vendor will eventually charge you more and more money to upgrade (to encourage people to upgrade earlier in the new product life cycle). Finally, at the gasping stage, the vendor will not even give you credit for having purchased earlier versions. When all customers have given up using the product, it is completely dead.

The following guidelines will help us to recognize when in the product cycle to purchase and how to fight the pressure to constantly change your IT.

- Buy in the expansion phase.
- Follow the crowd.
- Buy only in generations.
- Skip generations between purchases.
- Avoid patches and upgrades.
- Avoid maintenance contracts.

Buy in the Expansion Phase

The best time to purchase technology is near the end of the expansion period, but before maturity has set in. While the terminology below may seem to fit software best, it also applies to hardware (operating systems or firmware releases) and process methodologies (TQM, Six Sigma, Reengineering, etc.).

It is not easy to identify when a product is in expansion. We cannot rely upon the vendor of the technology. A vendor will always tell us that a product is already mature before it is, or that the technology is obsolete before it actually is. Remember, the shorter the product life cycle, the more money vendors make.

I've already discussed one of my clients who purchased a highly touted Data General system in 1999. I noted that all the industry magazines at the time spouted in glowing terms how wonderful this new technology was. And, indeed, it had far surpassed any other system I'd seen in terms of reliability, speed, and flexibility. But a few months after my client bought the system, EMC purchased Data General. Within a very short time, all other vendors stopped supporting the hardware. It was very difficult to find administrators who understood it. New programs wouldn't run on it. Parts could not be found for it. My client was forced to purchase an entirely new system within three years.

If my client had waited until the expansion phase to purchase the hardware, the system wouldn't even have been in the running because it never made it to that phase. They bought it at the commercial acceptance phase, when a relatively small number of customers had installed it and the industry was beginning to notice how good it was (as noted earlier, a prime moment for buyout in a venture-capital-based company). My client simply bought it too early.

Unless we are already an expert in the technology, we are faced with browsing existing clues to find out which phase a technology product is in. Here are some general signs to recognize that a product has matured:

- There are many companies similar to ours who are already using it.
- New releases and updates have slowed.
- Replacement products are not actually on the market yet, though they may have been announced. (Remember also that replacement products might be vaporware, announced but never produced.)

We can find out this information by searching the vendors' sites on the Internet and by asking a few questions of the account manager:

- How often do new releases come out?
- What comes after this version? Is there another major revision on the drawing board?
- How financially stable is the vendor? Is it capitalized with venture capital?

We must be careful not to share with vendors what our hoped-for answers are prior to the questioning or they will tell us just what we want to hear. The answers should be as close as possible to the following optimum answers:

- About half of our competitors and other companies similar to ours are already using it.
- Last year, there were five minor releases (for example, three in the first quarter and two in the second quarter). This year, there might be one in the first quarter, but no more are expected.
- The developers are working on the next major version—expected to be released more than a year from now.
- The vendor companies are profitable and have not spent beyond their means recently in advertising or non-direct capital investments.

Here are the danger-point, too-soon, still-in-early-growth stage answers:

- Less than 10 percent of our competitors or similar companies have installed the technology.
- The vendors released two minor upgrades within the last quarter and expect another one soon.
- The vendor is putting all of its efforts into improving the existing product.
- The vendor has plenty of cash, and it is backed by some successful venture capital companies.
- The vendor has been written up recently in some industry magazines.
- The vendor expects to be profitable soon.

Here are the danger-point, too-late, almost-obsolete answers:

- Almost all of our competitors or similar companies installed the technology years ago.
- The products are very stable. There have been no minor releases (except year-end updates if payroll-oriented) within the past 18 months.
- The next major versions are due to hit the market next quarter.
- The companies have been profitably in business for more than 20 years. Except during the Internet bubble when the whole industry took a hit, they had been growing each year. They recently began a new expansion with the release of major revisions of their products—the first in the last 10 years.

Why is it so important to purchase at the expansion time of the product life cycle? There are several reasons:

- Purchasing after bugs have been fixed decreases time we spend being frustrated by products that don't work as promised.
- Purchasing after market acceptance ensures that there are plenty of other people who purchased it—which increases the chances for a long life.
- Purchasing before maturity ensures a stable product for the longest time.
- Purchasing from financially secure companies ensures that we don't get surprised by an unexpectedly short product life often caused by acquisitions.

For example, the new operating system by Microsoft, Vista, came out about three months prior to my writing this. But Vista had been announced years before when Windows XP had just been hitting its expansion phase, about two years after XP was introduced. At that point, Microsoft engineers stopped working on Windows XP, which meant that XP became more stable. Therefore, 2004 was the perfect time to purchase a new computer with Windows XP. If you purchased Windows XP in January 2007, you purchased it too late—after XP had started its decline. At the same time, if you purchased Vista during the year 2007, you were purchasing it long before it was stable. Within the first year of release most IT products are little better than beta versions; full of bugs and problems. The year 2007, therefore, would have been the wrong year to purchase computers. I advised my clients to wait a year or two. If they can't wait, then I advise them to purchase used computers with Windows XP on them.

Following the Crowd

We've all heard the truism of the 1980s: No one ever got fired for buying IBM. These days, it might as well be replaced with: No one ever got fired for buying WinDell. You might have heard this as Wintel, referring to Windows Operating System on a PC using an Intel processor. Due to the proliferation of non-Intel processors and the elephant's share of market going to Dell, I've taken the liberty of updating the saying.

This is not just a truism, it is sound advice.

In an immature industry, a technology with a huge installed base is as close as we can get to a guarantee that the technology will not become obsolete in a matter of months. When we are using the same hardware and software as most people, the vendor cannot afford to simply drop support. They are forced, by the sheer volume of past customers, to continue to invest in the future of the product. Nothing will prevent the obsolescence of the product, but the life cycle can be stretched significantly when there is a huge installed base.

An easily demonstrable example is Microsoft Windows 3.1 versus IBM OS/2. OS/2 was a superior operating system in every way to Microsoft Windows (as well as all the other choices at the time including Mac, DOS, and Unix). But the better mousetrap does not necessarily bring market share. Due to the sheer number of installations, applications were developed for Windows and not for the other operating systems.

The sheer number and variety of applications have made Windows the most common desktop operating system in the world. If we had purchased OS/2 in 1992, we received the last release of it in 1994. If we had purchased Windows 3.1 in 1992, we would have used it until 1998 or 1999. And we would still be using a version of Windows today. Some of those applications we purchased in 1992 would still be running on Windows.

Another example discussed in Chapter 2 is Ethernet versus Token Ring. Token Ring was more controlled, could handle many more computers, and was more reliable than Ethernet. Despite being of superior quality and based on an industry standard, Token Ring simply never had the installed base to compete. If we invested in Token Ring in 1985, we would have had to replace it around 1992 or suffer spiraling costs for network hardware. If we invested in Ethernet in 1985, we would still be using the same network today. Ethernet was less reliable, but cheaper, and before you could blink an eye, there were 50 Ethernet networks for every Token Ring network. The volume of sales caused the price to drop even further until there was a huge differential in the price. Ethernet's installed base was the competitive advantage.

Historically in technology purchasing, if we bet on what was popular, we bet wisely.

Vendors know this, of course. Many will not reveal what their actual installed base is, or they exaggerate how many companies are using their technology. Some will only publish the number of packages out there, not the number of packages installed. Since many applications come prepackaged with certain hardware, the delivered number is never equal to the number of systems that are using the software. Others will use faulty sampling to provide incorrect or misleading data.

I noticed this problem in 2004 when I signed up for a Webcast. This particular Webcast promised to reveal which infrastructure standards were in use. I wanted to know how much had changed since I last looked at this sort of information, so I registered to watch it.

The Webcast was sponsored by an industry publication and presented by a well-reputed research company, so I had expected unbiased statistics on what businesses today were using in their networks. I was disappointed. The presenter's statistics made it look as if the majority of networks were using Gigabit Ethernet, a very fast, and very new, version of the Ethernet, which I knew was ridiculous. I knew from experience that among the billions of networking devices out there in the world, Gigabit Ethernet was barely a blip—about on the ratio of Rolls Royce vehicles to common cars. This fact is still true three years later, so you can bet that in 2004 Gigabit Ethernet was not as prolific as the numbers in this Webcast seemed to represent.

It took me a while to figure out how the presenter got his numbers (proving Mark Twain's comments about "liars, damn liars, and statistics"). The presenter had taken statistics from a vendor who specialized in Gigabit Ethernet devices and extrapolated those numbers as if the average network reflected only what was being sold today by that vendor. That would be like looking at sales of a Mercedes Benz dealer, seeing that SUVs were selling the best, and announcing that 8 out of 10 cars on the road today were SUVs. (I know it may seem like they are everywhere, but count the cars in the parking lot. SUVs are not the majority of cars on the road—and now with the price of gas, may never be.)

A *Webcast* is like a television show over the public Internet. While a commercial or infomercial may cost thousands or millions to show on television, a Webcast can be done much more inexpensively—making it a viable alternative for smaller audiences. Webcasts are often used by technology vendors.

Imagine someone without any real experience or knowledge attending this Webcast and thinking, "Oh no! Our network is only slow Ethernet and our competitors' networks are faster—we'd better get moving on those RFPs!" Not good.

Because there are still competing standards, purchasing GigaEthernet right now to replace Ethernet would be a big mistake. Furthermore, most local area networks don't even use the 10 megabytes of bandwidth available to them with Ethernet. Replacing a dirt road with a four lane highway does not speed up the horse and buggy traveling on it. For most businesses, as of this writing, GigaEthernet to the desktop is not (yet) a good idea.

The lesson is this: We can't depend upon vendors (and sometimes not even supposedly unbiased research firms) to tell us the real installed base for any particular technology. Instead, we should rely upon our own eyes and ears. We should ask other businesspeople around us what technologies they are using and plan accordingly.

Buy Only in Generations

We generally want to buy technology in bunches. If we are smart, we buy new hardware, software, peripherals, and connectivity methods all at the same time. We want to answer the questions regarding phases presented earlier for all the interrelated components of technology. If the answer from the software application vendor is optimum (i.e., expansion phase), but the answer from the hardware vendor is subpar (i.e., growth phase or obsolescence phase), we have to weigh the value of each piece of the technology before committing. The technology chain is only as strong as its weakest link.

Consider the decision to replace an operating system such as Windows XP. The hardware that the operating system originally came on was optimized for Windows XP, and may not have the necessary firmware upgrades or hard drive space necessary for Windows Vista. The applications written for Windows XP may not work on Windows Vista. The peripherals will not have drivers for Vista. As noted in Chapter 5, all the components of a technology are interrelated (even though they are still manufactured or published by different vendors). Trying to replace just one part will lead to an endless stream of bugs and fixes and problems and diagnoses.

We will never find a perfect solution with optimum everything. The objective is to strive for as close to optimum for as many of the layers of technology as we can. If we follow this simple advice, we can maximize the technology life cycle for our own company in real time—extending the normal three to five years into 10 to 15 years. The key is to get IT running smoothly and then *leave it alone*.

Skip Generations between Purchases

Think about the whole product cycle. It often takes three to five years for a new component to be fully debugged and stable. And it takes even longer for the rest of the interrelated hardware and software to adjust to a new technology so that we can upgrade our systems to the new generation.

Notice that this plan means that we will be skipping generations—sometimes several generations. Purchasing every version of a component would mean an ever-changing system since upgrades are so frequent, which ensures that we would eventually lose a prime benefit: a stable system. Therefore, it's best to ignore major upgrades until all the components in the generation of technology we purchased are almost all obsolete.

As explained in Chapter 5, if we can stretch the time of stability, when the hardware, software, people, and process do not change, and shrink the time of instability, when they are switching to new technology, then productivity has a chance to reach its peak before taking the inevitable productivity hit when the technology changes. If, on the other hand, we are constantly changing one thing or another, we are constantly experiencing the productivity dip of new technology. The opportunity for peak productivity is never reached. This commonly happens under three circumstances:

- When companies try to change just one component of a technology at a time.
- When they choose technology either too early or too late in the product life cycle.
- When they try to implement every new upgrade for a component.

How long we can keep mature technology going depends solely upon the success of the expansion phase and the number of other customers who are still using the technology. The more customers who use the technology, the longer the maturity phase and the slower the decline phase. With the right combination, it can be years and years, perhaps even as long as 15 or so.

Until 2005, I still had a small business client who was using 386 systems with Novell 3.12 networks and WordPerfect 5.0 that we implemented in 1989. They were poised to replace it within two days when it failed. They had already chosen its replacement system and documented the process to transfer the data. For those years (and the previous 15 years as well) their technology costs were zero. They have saved thousands each year by not upgrading, and have had extremely reliable stable systems all those years. Every year they revised their replacement plan, but they didn't actually spend any money until the existing system failed in 2005.

That is not to say that this plan would be good for anyone else—often businesses themselves change and need new systems. Larger businesses could not afford to wait until the system fails to replace it. But even in a large business, there should be an element of "If it ain't broke, don't fix it." This attitude can be very profitable under the right circumstances.

One requirement for following through on this plan is to ignore the pressure to upgrade put on us by vendors and techies. If we listened to them, we might get very nervous using technology after the vendor announces that it will not be supported anymore.

But what, really, is support? The vendor certainly does not help us if our systems go down. They aren't concerned with error messages or problems we have getting their software to work. To a vendor, support means sending out patches that need to be fully tested before they are installed—which we don't want to do any more than necessary anyway. As long as we are not changing our configuration (i.e., installing new software or hardware), our systems will continue to chug along without problems (barring a hardware failure, of course), so it is economically beneficial to stretch out the life cycle as long as we can. When we replace it, we replace it all with a completely different generation of technology.

Let's take another specific example. Microsoft announced in 2005 that it will support Windows NT, introduced in 1996, only until the end of the year. (Incidentally, this was two years short of the originally promised life cycle. You can't always trust IT vendors!)

Many of my clients have Windows NT. They are not alone. Windows NT has been very popular. Even nine years after it was introduced, at the time of the "no more support" announcement, market research firm IDC estimated that 17 percent of all Windows servers still used Windows NT. NT's popularity was due to two main reasons: (1) Windows NT was much easier to learn than Novell or Unix (the two alternatives at the time), and (2) Windows NT servers opened up the possibility of LAN-based applications for small offices because non-techies could manage the servers without specialized network training.

Some of my clients, however, thought that Microsoft's announcement was a big problem. They wanted to replace all their Windows NT systems immediately. My response was to advise my clients to wait. I didn't view the announcement as a problem. Yes, Windows NT servers had (and have) many problems. It is well known, for example, that NT servers must be flushed or rebooted on a periodic basis or they simply stop working. But for the most part, NT users have learned to live with the bugs (e.g., most system administrators schedule reboots every week or so). Hastily switching to a new system without proper planning would cause huge headaches—and the switch would be the problem, not the older operating system.

In other words, we cannot allow a vendor's lack of support to change our well-planned migration strategy to the next generation of technology. As long as we don't try to make any other changes on those particular systems, they will hum along without any problems—perhaps even for years. And since we have already planned the next phase, we can take our time and follow our plan. The trick is to avoid panic at the thought of no support from the original vendor.

That doesn't mean that we fly without a net. Whenever a major vendor stops supporting a product, an after-market of smaller consulting or integrator companies generally picks up the slack. When Data General was purchased by EMC, for example, one of Data General's partners purchased the entire inventory of parts and documentation from the new owners.

Purchasing parts to keep obsolete technology going while waiting for the next generation to reach the expansion phase is the one exception to the admonition to stay away from cheap technology. In this case, as long as the technology remains cheap and the systems haven't broken, we can keep the components going as long as we need to so that we can maintain our plan to replace all the generations of technology at one time. (Be aware, though, that as the parts become scarcer and scarcer, there will come a time when they will become more and more expensive. Plan the replacement before that time comes to avoid that problem.)

In brief, for most companies and for most technologies, maximizing stability and minimizing instability will enable employees to gain peak productivity before the next generation of technology is forced upon them.

Don't Patch or Upgrade

Imagine that we have purchased a washing machine from a well-known vendor. About a month after we purchased it, we receive in the mail a hose, with directions to open up the case of the machine and install the hose. A month later, we get a new dial to install. A few months later we receive a new lid. A few months later, in a large box, we receive a replacement for the entire rotating assembly. After about a year, we get a letter in the mail saying that the washing machine we purchased is now obsolete, and that we can't get it fixed if it breaks—we have to purchase an entirely new one.

Would we buy from that washing machine vendor again?

Of course not. And yet, we have no choice when purchasing technology. We can, however, choose whether to get on the endless upgrade wheel. I advocate not patching and upgrading software and hardware unless absolutely essential. With the exception of security issues and bug fixes for problems that we actually have, it makes much more sense to leave a working system alone than to constantly subject it to ever-changing code. And remember, if we waited until the expansion phase to purchase the software, the most egregious bugs will already have been fixed.

Many technologists and vendors find this advice controversial. In their minds, software is not something that we purchase and implement so much as we buy into the existing state of code and a subscription to any new code the vendor may develop in the future. Software is an ever-changing dynamic product that is never done. Like the early buyers of automobiles, the non-techie users of millions of PCs are being told that they must become mechanics, understanding just how and when to apply a patch to fix software.

The problem with that view of software is that, more often than not, patches and upgrades crash more systems than they fix. Since the year 2001, when Windows XP came out, most users have gotten weekly (sometimes daily) updates for the operating system, with occasional requests to be sure to apply the update because of some major security threat. Like old fishermen telling tales of the big storm, many technology folks will relate what happened to them on August 13, 2004, the day Service Pack 2 upgrade of Windows XP was released. This major upgrade was the worst ever. Because it had major security fixes, the upgrade ripped the guts out of the XP operating system and replaced it with new (untested) features. In the month following that release, Microsoft listed on its tech support site over 450 common programs that the upgrade broke. We've had a repeat of that scenario with Vista, with many people uninstalling it and returning to XP. I always advise my clients to turn off automatic updating so that they can fully test updates *before* they are installed.

The key lesson is that, while recognizing that it is not always possible to follow the path of leaving a working system alone, we should always strive to do so. Avoiding patches and upgrades (and the changes that go along with them) can extend the life of the system.

Avoid Maintenance Contracts

Many vendors force a maintenance charge onto customers (usually about 20 percent of the cost of the hardware or software) with the promise that buying the maintenance will provide the customer with all the upgrades to a product. Whenever possible, we should avoid paying this amount if we can. Remember—we don't want to install unnecessary patches or upgrades anyway. Why should we pay for something we don't plan on using? While there are a few circumstances in which we do want to pay for the extra attention of the vendor, it behooves us to be sure of what we are getting for the fee.

Again: I've been on the vendor side of this equation. The maintenance manager at the system integrator vendor where I worked conscientiously sent a tape with any modifications of the system code to customers three or four times a year, knowing full well that very few of them ever actually installed it. For most customers, the whole maintenance process is a waste of their money and a waste of the vendors' time.

Unfortunately, more and more vendors are requiring this maintenance fee. Vendors often view the maintenance fees as gravy—income with no costs—so they make it required and you have no choice but to pay it. Even worse, many software vendors are switching over to a subscription service model where, instead of paying for a piece of software, you pay monthly in order to use the software from the servers of the vendor. Great for vendors. Bad for buyers. While it may be impossible to avoid in the coming years, it would behoove you to stay away, as long as possible, from renting software instead of buying it.

LONG-TERM VENDOR PARTNERSHIPS

There are several guidelines to keep in mind as you work on creating long-term vendor partnerships. First, you should stop haggling. You don't want to buy solely on price. You want to avoid cheap technology, because it may end up being the worse value. As explained earlier, the only exception is when you are purposefully keeping an older system going with cheap parts until it either fails completely or our planned next generation of IT is being installed.

Though many a purchasing manager would like to deny it, there is a difference between toilet paper and computer systems. Trying to get the best deal on information technology will almost always cost you more than you bargained for.

I'm not saying that you can't save money. But there is an art to spending bottom dollar on technology. Haggling over the component prices of each item is not the way. Neither is using hard-line negotiating tactics with software or hardware vendors. I've seen it a thousand times: A purchasing manager feels good about saving $1,000 on a $10,000 invoice because she doesn't see the $3,000 cost that follows up on the savings. I once talked to a CEO who was bragging about getting a 30 percent discount on software licenses—only to discover that he had negotiated for named seat licensing instead of concurrent seat licensing because he hadn't realized that there was a difference. A named-seat license means that you pay for each individual named person who uses the software. Concurrent-seat licensing is when you pay for a certain number of people to use the software at the same time. For this reporting software, the company had about 30 people who needed to use it, but every day only five different people needed to use it at the same time. What would have cost them $3,218 for concurrent seat licensing was now going to cost them, with his remarkable discount for named seats, $14,850!

Someday, the industry will mature. Someday, we won't have to read the fine print in every software licensing agreement. Someday, it won't make a difference if we purchase the software from Vendor A or Vendor B. Someday, we will have more power to negotiate a better deal.

But today is not someday. Hard-line negotiating tactics will only force the good vendors to flee the table in search of buyers who understand the costs and are willing to pay them. Believe me when I tell you that for every dollar you get the vendors to cut, they will find a way to cut services that will cost you twice as much to mitigate.

In 1999 the Data General system was an expensive system costing well over $200,000. In 2001 the same system could be purchased for less than $50,000 because EMC had purchased Data General. But if you purchase the cheaper system in 2001, the cost of keeping that technology going would skyrocket within a few years. If you added the $70,000 a year that it would cost to find someone who understood the system, or the $20,000 it would cost to replace a single burned-out card, you can see that even at a quarter of the price, you are not getting a bargain. The cheaper price was great for those who had already purchased the system and wanted to keep it going as long as possible, but being cheap should not be the reason for the purchase.

Another important factor to which we should pay attention is financial stability of the vendor. Fast increasing growth in sales may be a danger sign. Venture capitalists love successful new companies, but they tend to pull out at the peak when the returns are largest, and to hell with the ongoing technology support needs of the customers. Therefore, look beyond growth and success. Buy from the vendors who have the wherewithal to go for the long haul.

There are thousands of services and products that were, at one time, the top of the heap, but are now broken and bleeding or simply gone. Once again I use as an example Data General being bought by EMC at its peak, leading to Data General's chief product becoming obsolete within a year. If anyone had looked at the balance sheet of Data General at the time, it would have been obvious that the company was going to be sold, and soon. DEC, Netscape, Ashton-Tate's, Foxbase, Compaq—all these companies had great technology that fell by the wayside after they were acquired.

Companies funded by venture capital are not necessarily bad. But an important prerequisite to financial stability is a healthy amount of cash and financial control by those who are interested in building the company rather than obtaining a financial return. We might want to avoid vendors who have had several rounds of funding without the assets to continue on in the foreseeable future.

Even more important than financial stability is integrity. In a world where the CEO of a charity steals the money for himself, where CEOs of major corporations lie about sales and go to jail because they stole money from their shareholders, it is difficult to believe that there are honest people in the world, much less at the top of a technology vendor. I'll admit that I've seen more of the former type than the latter. But people of integrity do exist. There are companies that try to put the needs of their clients and customers above their own needs whenever possible. In the words of Warren Buffett, regarding the characteristics he looks for in his people: "Integrity, intelligence, and energy. Hire someone without the first, and the other two will kill you."

We want to look for vendors who know what they are doing, who have the intelligence to understand our goals, and who have the energy to accomplish them. But none of that means anything without integrity. As I noted earlier, because of the immaturity of the industry and the number of unknown issues that typically arise in every technology project, even formally drawn up agreements such as service level agreements (SLAs) can't safeguard your interests. With vendors of integrity, we don't need SLAs.

When I had another client in the same position as the failed help desk contract discussed in Chapter 5, instead of one huge contract outsourcing their help desk, I suggested that they have smaller contracts with different local fix-it shops—each near one of their remote office locations. They had staff people on-site for the main office. This is how we arranged it: The local fix-it shops got paid a fixed amount each month that all problems reported were successfully solved. It was a great rate when the problems were few and far between, and when they could be fixed within minutes on the phone. It was a horrible rate (for them) when the problems took multiple visits or hours to solve. Only the caller at my client company could "close" the ticket as successfully solved. No long-term contract. No paperwork.

Within a few months, the fix-it shop staffs had gotten to know the customer systems like the back of their collective hands. They spent quite a bit of time in the early months figuring out how to prevent future problems so that in the later months they could get paid without having to spend much time. They focused all their energy on making every person who called a happy customer, usually by fixing reported problems within minutes. In only one case did a vendor have to be replaced because it grew too big and began to ignore calls. The client used this method of partnering for years and is still going strong with it.

Instead of spending months negotiating a multimillion dollar deal with legions of lawyers, it makes much more sense to put our efforts into developing long-term partnerships with knowledgeable vendors of integrity. We need to know who will be responding in times of need and how experienced and knowledgeable they are. We want to pay enough so that our vendors stay in business and don't seek alternative sources of income. Our dollars are better spent investing in vendors with integrity rather than constantly negotiating and searching for a better deal.

IGNORING HYPE

As discussed in Chapter 5, hype is so rampant that we've come to expect it. Technology vendors usually tell us what we want to hear instead of the truth. Knowing this, I am always surprised when people actually believe what a vendor tells them, but it happens frequently. It's easy to recognize hype once we know to look for it. To see it, we need to understand market cycles and product cycles. That will help us recognize marketecture and vaporware, and differentiate between what's possible and what's not. Finally, we can use a Hypometer (my own little invention) to measure the amount of hype.

One key to recognize hype is to understand the market cycle, which is intertwined with the nature of technology innovations and capitalist financing. Whenever a new technology hits the market, there is a predictable flurry of new companies exploiting and selling the technology. This is a period of fast-track growth with much public adulation, followed by a shark-fest of mergers and acquisitions. These finally unmask the two or three winners who will dominate the market for another decade.

To see the impact of hype, I use an imaginary machine I call a Hypometer to dissect ads and claims so I can distinguish the hype from the real information. I took one of the ads from the hype section in Chapter 5 and put it through the Hypometer so that we could see the fact from the fiction.

What if you had someone to watch your back?

Pure hype. No one is going to watch your back, and no software or hardware can do it either.

Someone to *integrate* your back-end logistics with deadly efficiency.

There's no such thing as deadly efficiency. But there is a factual clue here—this company has something to do with integration. They have no product of their own, but they integrate other products.

Someone to manage your warehousing, delivery, and financial settlements.

Some examples of the products or services of their clients, obviously, but it says nothing about the integrator, except that it doesn't specialize.

Someone to protect your entire *e-commerce* operation.

Again—a dream. No one will protect your operation but you. They also seem to specialize in e-commerce rather than typical technologies.

What if one company could handle your entire *back-end operation?*

They meant to say that their company can handle all your software integration needs—they don't want you using their competitors also. But this phrase feeds the dream that you can just hire someone else and all your problems will go away. Hype.

That's the idea behind Product A. Built around an *open* and *extensible transaction* network, our *integrated approach* enables you to outsource any or all of the logistics behind your buy button.

An "open and extensible transaction network" could mean anything. I don't think it means software. I think they're referring to their network of vendors with whom they've worked on projects. This means that they give you the opportunity to pay them for the approach and to pay an outsourcer or vendor for the actual work.

A partner to *plan* it, *implement* it, and stand by it.

Here's a real clue: They don't program, they plan. Sounds like a company that does project management for integration projects using other vendors' software and hardware. The "stand by it" is hype—I've yet to see a vendor provide a full money-back guarantee if the client is not satisfied for any reason.

In short, someone to make sure it pays off.

Here's the question for the contract reviewer: Are they willing to return our money if one of the vendors doesn't live up to its promise? In writing? I'll believe it when I see it.

Well, the Hypometer gives this a 12.5 on a scale of 100 (12 factual words out of 96 altogether).

Here's an exercise for you. Take a look through a magazine, pick a product at random, and count the words that give you meaningful information and the words that are just marketing fluff. What's the Hypometer score? Try it again for an advertisement for an IT product or service you've just recently purchased.

Hype is fueled by unrealistic expectations about what IT can do. We use the terms *vaporware* and *marketecture* to describe solutions for which there is a deep need, but for which there are no shrink-wrapped products. Sometimes vaporware and marketecture are announced by technology vendors to dissuade other vendors from attempting to develop a solution to fulfill a gap between available products and the needs of business. Other times vaporware and marketecture are simply ways for vendors to describe what could be in the future.

Strictly speaking, many ERP systems would actually fall under the definition of marketecture or vaporware. Most ERP systems aren't actually commercial products at all, but rather a defined way for developers to custom-develop whatever code the business needs, while still getting the benefits of capital funding. This is one of the reasons there have been some spectacular failures amidst the smattering of successes for ERP systems; the quality is entirely dependent upon the skills and talents of the developer rather than the software itself—which doesn't really exist outside of the mind of the developers. When a company purchases a seat for these enterprise products, they are actually purchasing the future right to use custom-developed code using the programming language and the tool set developed by the vendor company.

How does vaporware and marketecture hurt us? It doesn't—as long as we recognize what it is and what it isn't. I remember one time in particular when I was at odds with my boss because he wanted me to implement a project management software. After an initial analysis, I suspected that the software was vaporware. My boss didn't agree. He waved away my concerns, saying that the consultant recommending the software was highly regarded.

The system my boss was pitching was an application from a small firm in Scotland. They had implemented this so-called package at exactly one location, a bank. When I asked them to send us a CD so I could install it, they had to send the developer from Scotland, on our dime, to install it. I watched as he wrote hundreds of lines in programming code in order to customize the software. When he first installed it, all of the screen forms and reports still had the name of the Scottish bank on them—obviously hard-coded from the previous client.

> **Hard-coded** means that instead of using a variable that can be changed, the programming code contains the actual contents. When developing a program for one company, it is quicker to hard-code everything. When multiple companies will be using a program, such as in a shrink-wrapped commercially produced software package, soft-coded variables are set up for each customer to fill in. The cost differential between writing a program for one company and writing a program for many companies to use is dramatic. One way to tell if a particular program is off the shelf or custom programming is to ask to see the screen where the user configures the variables. Custom programming won't have such a screen, instead relying upon the programmer to code the variables.

When I talked to my boss again about my misgivings, he again minimized my concerns. He claimed that when the consultant came to do the best-practice training, I would see the value of the application. Furthermore, I was expressly forbidden from sharing my misgivings with the CIO, the final decision maker.

The highly regarded consultant came to do the best-practice training, and I tried my best to keep an open mind. However, after the first half-day session, the project managers came just short of booing him out of the room due to his contemptuous treatment of their current project-management methods. All refused to attend another session. Privately I was still lobbying to drop the entire project which I had concluded was a bad project with a capital B. My boss ignored my advice, and instead mandated the use of the software by all project managers in the company.

I still remember that decisive meeting when my boss and I presented "our" views to the CIO using the materials provided by the vendor. Publicly I was still doing my boss's bidding and supporting the software, though privately I harbored the tender hope that the CIO was sensitive enough to read between the slides. "Please," I silently directed him, "ask these questions":

- How many other companies have implemented this system?
- What do potential business users think of the software?
- How will this system help the business meet the needs of the customer?
- What do the project managers who have met him think of the consultant recommending this software?

The result? My ability to predict a poor decision outstripped my ability at telepathy. The CIO asked no such questions. My hope had been dashed against the rocks of my boss's enthusiasm. I'll bet you can guess who got the blame when the project publicly failed.

Once we understand how prevalent vaporware and marketecture are, it is easy to recognize one or more of the signs of software not-yet-ready for commercial package status:

- Described only in terms of benefits and features, and priced by the installation and/or seat.
- Doesn't fit into technology maps of existing hardware and software layers.
- Difficult to get pricing breakouts. One price for a nebulous list of items, or many prices for modules of unexplained roles.
- Tiny installed base (i.e., only a few companies have actually implemented it).
- Software has no installation modules.
- Hard-coded variables instead of soft-coded variables.
- Comes with a requirement for customization.
- Difficult to answer the question, "Exactly what does it do?"
- Coupled with "methods" and "training" and "best practices."

The bottom line is: Vendors do both themselves and their customers a favor when they try, as much as possible, to eliminate wishful thinking and generic benefit lists. The entire industry and all the customers of information technology would benefit from a lot less hype.

GETTING OFF THE BLEEDING EDGE

Haven't you heard since the dawn of the first microchip that you don't want to be left behind? That you want to be competitive? That you need the best and the newest to do that? Isn't the leading edge where you should be?

In a word, **no**. We use the term *bleeding edge* instead of leading edge for a reason. Even though some vendors will proclaim this advice as scandalous, you should be behind in technology, not ahead (with the noted exception when dealing with your hedgehog concept as explained in Chapter 2, of course). Many entrepreneurs discovered this truth when they surfed dangerously out in front of the wave during the Internet bubble. They found themselves dashed against the rocks and sands of reality when the bubble burst.

Paddling behind the wave where it is quiet and the surfboard bobs gently may be boring, but it is much more profitable. For the most part we are better off watching other companies do all the surfing, falling, and wiping out. For most technology, we should wait at least a year, sometimes two, after any component has hit the market before purchasing.

First, if you buy too early in the growth stage, other interconnected technology products will not work with the new technology (as discussed in the buy in generations section). Second, vendors always release products before all the bugs have been worked out. Early users can count on spending many frustrating hours with software and hardware that does not work as promised (as discussed in the recognizing immaturity section). Third, many products never get past the growth phase (as discussed in the buy in expansion phase).

In brief, except for some very specific situations, and in the research labs of our top technology gurus, our operational technology should be older than everyone else's technology.

SUMMARY

We can made good decisions and develop good relationships with IT vendors by:

- ☑ Becoming technically literate.
- ☑ Recognizing the immaturity of the IT industry.
- ☑ Defining enterprise-wide standards for hardware, software, and processes.
- ☑ Maximizing periods of stability, and minimizing periods of instability.
- ☑ Buying hardware and software during the expansion phase of the product life cycle.
- ☑ Buying hardware and software that has been popular and stable.
- ☑ Buying in generations; all components manufactured or developed around the same core components (chip and operating system).
- ☑ Avoiding maintenance contracts, updating or upgrading.
- ☑ Skipping generations and keeping the same hardware and software going as long as possible.
- ☑ Developing long-term partnerships with vendors of integrity.
- ☑ Ignoring hype and staying off the bleeding edge (except for the test lab where you investigate new technologies aligned with your hedgehog concept).

8

Getting the Most from Networking

A *network* is an interconnection of three or more communicating entities.[29] Never has a term been so utterly confusing to everyone who uses it. In business, when people boast about their networks, they are usually referring to the number and level of people they know. Entrepreneurs and business leaders use their network or hone their network or build their network, usually one node at a time.

In the world of IT, however, the term network has a very different meaning. It refers to how computers are connected together. There are personal area networks and local area networks and campus area networks and metropolitan area networks and wide area networks and global area networks. There is the public Internet as well as private Internets and intranets and extranets. Networks can be wireless through the air, or directly connected through copper wires or fiber optics (and usually a combination of all three). While knowing more about how networks work is essential to making good decisions, it is beyond the scope of this book to explain the underlying technology. (Again, for a complete description of these terms and a clear easy-to-understand description of how networking and the Internet works, read the Introduction to IT Concepts on the Web site http://ETMAssociates. com/ITConcepts. Just enter the password INeedATechMap when asked.)

Remember that the power is not in the technology of networking. The power is in the connective ability (yes, the other kind of networking). E-mail and the World Wide Web together enable salespeople to connect to customers with much less time and effort (and yet with increased attention!). They enable team members to collaborate virtually. They enable employees to be anywhere and still work. They enable whole functions to be outsourced to other parts of the country or even other countries. In his book *The World Is Flat*, Thomas Friedman laid out the entire case as he saw it from a nontechnical point of view, so I won't revisit it here. But the key element is that there are business capabilities available today that were not available 10 years ago[30]. There are very few businesspeople who can afford to ignore the revolution that is taking place right under their noses. Information technology is neither good nor bad, but using it properly is essential.

What we will do here is focus on just what entrepreneurs should know about the applications that sit on top of the network: e-mail and the World Wide Web. Additionally, this chapter will delve a bit deeper than the other chapters into simple but practical instructions on using e-mail and the World Wide Web.

THE POWER OF THE WORLD WIDE WEB

The public Internet is a worldwide network of computers. It was developed through the efforts of hundreds of people, but primarily Bob Kahn at Bolt Beranek and Newman (a consulting firm) and Vint Cerf at Stanford University. It was funded by the Department of Defense during the Vietnam War in quest of a reliable networking method that would not fail in the event of a nuclear attack. The answer was an Internet protocol named TCP/IP (Transmission Control Protocol/Internet Protocol). In the early 1990s, the United States government handed over management of TCP/IP to a private company and opened it up to commercial venture, mainly due to the influence of Al Gore. Many people fault Al Gore, thinking that he boasted imaginary credit for the public Internet, but the fact is that Al Gore helped create the public Internet by opening up the management so that it could be used by everyone, not just the government.[31]

At the same time, Timothy Berners-Lee and Robert Cailliau developed an easy-to-use interface (a system of hyperlinks) that sat on top of the public Internet. The system of hyperlinking is called the World Wide Web. Suddenly, someone with no technical training at all could connect to any other computer on the public Internet network, and could retrieve information from any of those computers. (To be accurate, it felt like suddenly, but actually it took many years. The Internet started functioning in 1982, and the World Wide Web was invented in 1990.)

All we have to do to connect to any computer on the World Wide Web anywhere in the world is *click a mouse.*

This capability can't help but change the way we do business. For our organizations to take advantage of the Web, we want to ask these questions:

- What are we losing as we rely more and more on technology? What are we gaining? How must our businesses change?
- Have we expanded our footprint through the use of a Web page?
- Do our employees have access to the information they need to get their jobs done? Should we have an intranet?
- Can our customers, vendor partners, and/or potential investors get what they need from our Web pages? Should we have an extranet?

Google Paradigm Shift

Sometimes it takes a while to think through all the different aspects of the power of the public Internet and the World Wide Web. Six years ago,

I was working on a technical glitch on my computer. My system kept telling me it was out of memory, though I knew for a fact it had plenty of memory. I spent hours reading through my system documentation, looking at the virtual memory settings in my control panel, trying one thing, then another, then another. I was getting frustrated and beginning to make noises of exasperation when my husband wandered into my office to find out what all the pounding and swearing was about.

"I can't figure out this %$&✳ problem," I said with a tone of disgust. "I've been working on it for hours."

"Did you Google it?" my level-headed, practical, but computer-illiterate husband asked.

"What do you mean?" I responded, not quite understanding, and a bit annoyed that he thought he could help me. I'd been on the public Internet since 1992! Of course I'd been on all my technical resource sites, the Microsoft support site, and read everything I could about memory problems. What did he think I was, an idiot?

He ignored my patronizing tone and calmly sat down at my computer, wrote down the exact wording of the error message on a piece of paper, switched over to Google.com, typed in the wording exactly as it appeared on screen, and got a whole list of troubleshooting sites that gave the exact right diagnosis and fix for my problem. I felt like an idiot. It wasn't the memory at all, of course, it was a virus for which my anti-virus software did not yet have a fix. I downloaded a file that deleted the virus and my system was fine 10 minutes later.

Although I didn't grow up with the capability of going to a single source to get, within seconds, any type of information that I needed, I have since taken to it like a duck to water. I can't imagine writing anything without my ever-present-all-knowing adviser at my beck and call.

The weird blindness that affected me until that fateful day when my husband flattened my inflated ego happens to us all. I was riding down to a speaking engagement the other day with a group of fellow businesspeople. One of them complained that her business was decreasing every year. "I don't know what the problem is," she said. "We're in the Yellow Pages, but no one seems to be calling anymore." I didn't say it out loud because I didn't want to offend her, but I thought, "Who uses the Yellow Pages anymore?"

When computer savvy people want to find a business, they Google it. "Dry Cleaners, Carson City, NJ" will undoubtedly get them to some Web page somewhere that lists all the dry cleaners in Carson City, New Jersey. If our businesses don't appear on the Web site list when Googled, and several others do, why would anyone waste time trying to find ours?

Now, it is still the case that there may be a city or town where none of the dry cleaners have a Web page. In that case, it may still be important to have a business listing in the Yellow Pages. But as our competitors switch from Yellow Page ads to Web sites, we can switch from expensive full Yellow-Page ads to Web sites. We can simply put our Web site name in a smaller ad in the Yellow Pages. Prospective customers can get all the information they need from that.

If you are not the sort to have your computer on, up, and running most of the time day and night, then this paradigm shift may not have hit you yet. But for most of today's generation of purchasers, at one point in the last five years they had that "aha" moment when the Google paradigm shift hit them. The bottom line is that slowly but surely everyone is going to discover how much easier it is to research and shop on the Web. It won't eliminate shopping-as-recreation, of course. But for people who hate to shop (like me) and for businesses who just want to purchase the item as quickly and cheaply as possible, nothing can beat the combination of Google and the World Wide Web.

Okay, none of this is news for most of you. But the fact is, there are still a ton of businesses out there that haven't yet understood that they have to change their marketing to start taking advantage of the Google world. This is why every business, even small local businesses, is best served by considering their Web channel as carefully as they consider the rest of their marketing strategy. In other words, every business should have an Internet strategy.

INTERNET STRATEGY

Now that we can count on most people being able to get to the public Internet, every business needs a strategy for taking advantage of it. But what is not well established is just exactly what that means.

P. K. Agarwal, the director of California's Department of Technology Services[32] has identified five stages of e-strategy for government entities: (1) Publish, (2) Interact, (3) Transact, (4) Integrate, and (5) Transform. Forrester's John Hagelian has identified three: (1) Deconstruct, (2) Reinvent, and (3) Breakaway. Gartner Group has also identified three: (1) using the Web as a marketing channel, (2) creation of a virtual organization, and (3) e-commerce and on-line customer service.

From a conceptual point of view, these stages are wonderful—but they do little to help a company that is not yet on the Web figure out what to do. Jeff Duffell of IC Solutions has a simplified list that is helpful: (1) Product Communication, (2) Simple Product Selling, and (3) Customized Product/ Full Integration. But from my point of view, this list is too unadorned. There seem to be stages missing.

The click and mortar companies which have gone through a series of phases, in a certain order, seem to have been the most successful. The first step for a company looking to formulate (or improve) its Internet strategy is to establish in which phase it is in currently.

Click and mortar refers to traditional companies with buildings that also do significant business over the Internet.

There are six phases:

- Corporate presence
- Product/service information
- E-commerce
- Advanced e-commerce
- Intranet and extranet
- Community

Corporate Presence

No matter how big or small a company is, it should have a corporate Web site. A corporate site is often known as the *business card Web site*. Some companies spend millions designing just the right look and feel of their sites; others get a high school kid to put their company logo on a welcome page and link another page with a list of their products and services. But in both cases the Web site contains static information about a company.

In the early days, Web sites cost hundreds of thousands of dollars. The World Wide Web has matured enough now, however, that anyone can put up a corporate Web site in a matter of hours for less than $100. That means that there is no excuse for not having one. Your Web presence should roughly match your size. A small mom-and-pop shop or single-consultant practice Web site should be relatively small, between eight and 10 pages, and needs only a single domain name. A large corporation or well-established firm should spend some time and effort, hiring media or graphic specialists, to ensure that the site looks ultraprofessional. The cost of the actual Web hosting part doesn't really change much—only the cost and professionalism of the logo, text, and placement. An established corporation can afford to hire an advertising agency or media specialists, and they all do Web sites as well these days, but entrepreneurs may not want to spend their money needlessly that way. Just as in the past when business owners had their kids or a handy neighbor's kid create a logo and design their own brochures, smaller organizations can make do with their own efforts.

A corporate presence Web site project has several steps:

- Choosing a domain name.
- Designing the Web page content.
- Choosing a Web hosting service and registrar.
- Making the site findable.

Choosing a Domain Name

When creating your first Web presence site for your business, the first and most important decision is the domain name. The domain name should be the company name, if at all possible. For example, if your business is called Pete's Hardware you might want to get the domain name PetesHardware.com.

The letters that follow the period at the end of a domain name are known as the *top level domain*. There are many top level domains, 13 of which were added after 2000. Nonetheless, most people are only familiar with the first three: *com* for businesses, *org* for nonprofit organizations, and *edu* for educational institutions. There is no formal restriction on the top level domains, however, so when you purchase a domain name, it is generally a good idea to purchase both the *com* and the *org* versions, and maybe the new *biz* domain, to avoid confusion on the part of your customers. The idea is not so much to use the second version as to prevent someone else from using it. Someone who owns the business MarshasFashions.com (a clothing store) does not want to be confused with MarshasFashions.org (a porn site).

Unfortunately, with all the existing Web sites, the domain name for your company may already be taken. PetesHardware.com, for example, is already the Web site for Pete's Hardware in California. When I started worked for MBNA (a Fortune 500 financial firm), I looked up the domain name MBNA.com and it was owned by a plumber in Texas. Later Mercedes Benz acquired it. Eventually MBNA paid Mercedes Benz for it, and by 2001 the MBNA.com domain was working for MBNA. Until then they used the domain MBNAon-line.com.

I originally wanted my own company name to be Enterprise, Technology, and Management, but ETM.com and ETAM.com domains were already taken. So I changed the name to Enterprise, Technology, Management Associates and purchased the domain name ETMAssociates.com. I kept hoping for ETMA.com, which was owned by a defunct company called Entertainment and Music Associates, but a domain squatter beat me to it, and I won't pay the inflated price. Domain squatters are people who purchase domain names that someone else might want so that they can resell the right to use them for a higher price—like a ticket scalper. My advice is to stay away. Just figure out a different domain name that works.

Obviously, if the company already exists with a certain name, you may have to become creative and add a word like *on-line* or *inc* or *group* or *company* or something of that sort to the domain name. If you haven't yet named your company, then it makes sense to review available domain names before naming the company so that you can get a domain name that is the company name. Anyone can go to any domain registration site and type in a bunch of domain names to see what is, and is not, available. Just don't actually purchase it yet—there's lots more to do.

Designing the Web Page Content

Once you've found a domain name that is available, you can start planning your Web site. Obviously, an established company would hire a media designer or specialist to design a highly professional Web site that meshes well with the print brochures and advertising. Entrepreneurs, of course, generally don't have the kind of cash necessary for that kind of expense.

Ask your friends and neighbors who designed the Web site of their business. It also might help to look at the Web sites of several of your competitors. Many Web site hosters provide templates, which are almost always much less expensive than hiring a designer, and probably quite adequate for a beginning entrepreneur.

At the very least, a corporate presence site would have pages containing information about:

- The company.
- The people.
- The products or services.
- Contact information, including phone number, e-mail address, physical address, and directions.

While it is beyond the scope of this chapter to give a whole course on Web design, a few important points may facilitate your planning.

The first important point is to have easy-to-understand menus. It helps to make the navigation as simple as possible, and always enable people to get back to where they were on the previous page without using their "back" button on their browser. Keep it simple.

While you might want to insert a picture or two to break up the text, make sure the pictures have been optimized for the Web. You don't want bloated graphics to slow down the time it takes for people to read what's on your site. Line drawings take much less time than pictures, and pictures take much less time than photos. Larger graphics take more time than smaller graphics. You can modify any pictures or photos to make them faster to download by opening them up in a graphics program and saving them as JPEG file. There is usually a choice to optimize the file so that you can decrease the dots per inch. Since the Web can only show 72 dots per inch anyway, you can use that number to make the file smaller.

JPG or **JPEG** is pronounced "jay peg" and stands for Joint Photographic Experts Group, which is the industry group that developed the compression standards for electronic photographs. Note that once you have optimized a JPEG file , the picture will look good on the screen but will not print well. A picture needs a minimum of 200 dots per inch to look good when printed. In other words, don't overwrite the original file.

You can purchase a $68 DVD that shows you, step by step, how to do a paper prototype from Nielsen Norman Group's Web site, www.nngroup.com/reports/prototyping/video_stills.html. Jakob Nielsen and Donald Norman are the top gurus when it comes to designing a Web site that is usable.

Placement of the graphic is also important. In the underlying code on the page, you want the graphic to come after the text so that people don't have to wait for the graphic to load in order to read the text on the page.

Avoid writing a book; it's best if everything can be read on one screen without scrolling. Make sure that if people click their printer icon, the whole screen prints. Typically, the last inch on the right side of a Web page gets cut off. This happens because most people have a wide screen, and the printer margin setting is usually 1 inch on both sides, leaving just 6 1/2 inches for the Web page.

If you're not using a template, your initial designs should be hand drawn on paper and shown to several people for their input before any coding is done.

What might make perfect sense to you might not make sense to half the people who look at it, so showing people several drafts of the design and making sure they like it is important. It's very easy to change the paper and do another draft. It is not easy to change the Web site. A foundational change in the menus or placement of graphics and text will cost mucho bucks once the Web site is coded.

In the end, remember that this initial site is read-only. Don't use forms; they look hokey, are rarely used, and often don't work well. Furthermore, they can be used by spammers to get access to the server in order to send out spam that annoys everyone. For the same reason, you probably don't want to put your e-mail address on your Web site directly as a link or as text. The best thing to do is to write your e-mail address in a graphics program and save it as a JPEG picture. That way, people will be able to read it, but spam-generating programs will not be able to decipher it. Once you've finished designing the Web site, and have shown it to at least a half dozen people to get their input before finalizing it, you're ready to choose a Web hosting service.

Choosing a Web Hosting Service and Registrar

Once you've decided on a domain name, the next decision is to find a Web hosting company and domain registrar. A Web hosting company provides your business space on a server it has attached to the public Internet. The space can be either shared with many other customers (cheap) or on a dedicated server that you can completely own and control (expensive).

A domain registrar is a different function. For an annual fee, the domain registrar can register the domain name for you. Since every domain name in the world must be unique, there is a centralized organization that manages all the domain names. However, that centralized organization works with thousands of registrars—companies that can get the domain names from them and "rent" them to us, the buyers. It is important to note that we can't ever permanently own a domain name. The license to use a domain name must be renewed every year (though many registrars will do the renewing for us for a period of 10 or more years).

While often the Web hosting company and the domain registrar are the same, they don't have to be. For example, my domain registrar is an Internet site in Australia. Until this year my Web hoster was a tiny company in Conshohocken, Pennsylvania, who rented space on a few servers in a data center in New Jersey. When my needs grew beyond what that Web hosting service could handle, I moved my site to a new hosting service in Rhode Island. This move pointed out one of the technical advantages to having the registrar separate from the Web hosting service, similar to not having all of your money in the same bank. I could control the move myself and didn't have to rely upon the old hoster and the new hoster to coordinate with each other.

Nonetheless, for the most part these days, it's far easier to let the Web hoster deal with the hassles of registering your domain name. These days, most of them don't even charge for the service. Just be very sure about the Web hosting service, because it may be difficult to move from one hosting company to another if the hoster is also your registrar.

In any case, there are thousands of Web hosting companies out there. They tend to fall into one of five categories:

- Shared or regional Web site using content management templates.
- Bare-bones hosting-service only.
- Hosting service with open source applications and database.
- Hosting and Web development services—simple.
- Hosting and full-service Web development including database integration.

Shared or regional Web sites are generally more expensive than all but the full-service Web development services. They are generally run by local newspapers, or chambers of commerce, or a trade association. In my neighborhood, a business can sign up for www.berkscountycorner.com/ and take part in the local marketing efforts of the site, have their customers log on and download coupons or check inventory. Because they use already developed templates in a content management framework, they are the easiest to use. You don't need to learn a single word of coding. Instead they will provide you with a series of forms where you fill out your business name, contact information, products and services, and so on. The cost for these types of sites ranges from $30 or $40 a month to $100 to $200 a month. Usually there is an initial setup fee (probably less than $1,000). The templates are usually inflexible; you can easily change the information, but not where it is located on the screen. They are a good way to get started if you are not willing to learn anything about creating a Web page, but they are an expensive way to go.

Bare-bones hosting services are on shared servers, similar to the regional sites, except that they aren't as expensive. They may have a Web-building template, but it won't have sophisticated tools like mailing lists, coupons, or user log-ins. The price ranges from $2.99 a month to $20 a month for these types of sites.

When building their own site using a bare-bones hoster and not taking advantage of templates provided, buyers are expected to have a smattering of technical expertise so that they can use one of the many Web development programs such as Microsoft's FrontPage (or its soon-to-be replacement Expressions), Adobe's Dreamweaver or Adobe's original GoLive. These programs are easy enough to use if you are already technically adept and take a workshop or two, but they are not as simple as word processing or e-mail. Most experienced Web developers who do brochureware sites forgo these tools and just do hand coding in HTML, the base language used by all Web sites.

> **HTML** stands for HyperText Markup Language. HTML files are simple text files that use beginning and ending tags to identify where items should go on the page and what format they should take. For example, if the heading of a page contained the words "About the company," the HTML code would look like *<H1>About the company</H1>*. <H1>is the beginning tag for Heading 1 and </H1> is the ending tag for Heading 1. Someone who knows how to code in HTML knows what all the tags are and how to use them.

The next step up is a hosting service with a few additional features that can be used by a Web developer. There are dozens of open source applications available for experienced Web developers. Open source, if you remember, is the movement of technical folks who preferred to work on huge joint projects for free—just for the benefit of using the results of the efforts of other technical folk for free. In other words, many different developers around the world have collaborated to make some tools freely available to each other. One of those is a database called MySQL. There are also many content management tools, blogging tools, list management tools, and so on. Anyone with the technical expertise can go to a Web hosting service that provides access to these tools in order to develop a full-fledged complete Web site including all the advanced features of the next phases in the Internet strategy. If you plan to stop at the brochureware site, then you don't need to worry about these capabilities. However, if you plan on moving through the ladder of phases, you might want to consider getting a Web hosting service that includes these tools. Keep in mind that a common use of these tools is for an enterprising, technically adept person to set up a Web hosting service using content management templates. In other words, the Web hosters you choose in category one might just be people who are reselling the Web hosting services they purchased from category three. Alternatively, many of the Web developers in the category four also use Web hosters who provide advanced Web development tools.

The final category is the full-service Web development company. Instead of a single independent Web developer, this company will have a staff of

Web developers. Although they can do the simple brochureware site, it would be a waste of their talents (not to mention a waste of their fees) to just have them do a simple site of text and graphics. Most of these types of companies can't even start a project that doesn't cost over $10,000 or so. This final category is the one we need as we move up the phases into providing detailed product and service information, e-commerce, and community-oriented tools. Before we discuss those advanced issues, however, we should discuss a few more items regarding our simple brochureware site, like making sure people can find it.

Making the Site Findable

An aggregating site is a Web site that lists other Web sites. It is a simple but necessary task to identify any aggregating sites, and make sure that the business information is listed there. They are often hosted by trade organizations, chambers of commerce, local newspapers, or geographically based community sites. Often, these aggregating sites have a form for businesses to enter their information on the lists.

In addition to getting listed on aggregating sites, it is important to ensure that there are title and description meta tags embedded (hidden) on the Web pages of our site. If we have hired Web developers, we just tell them to make sure they do it (although a good developer would do it without being told). If we are doing the site ourselves, we just make sure we do this important task. By entering on each page of the Web site a meaningful title and description, we ensure that people looking for the Web site will have an easier time finding it.

Which brings us to search engines.

A *search engine* is a site where people go to find other sites (a more generic form of an aggregating site). The most popular search engine site today is Google.com (unless you are Chinese, in which case Baidu.com is the most popular), but in past years Ask.com, Yahoo.com, MSN.com and AltaVista.com have all made a run for top status, although none have attained the popularity of Google. How do search engines list their sites? Well, the answer is constantly changing. Years ago, when there were many search engines, they all used keyword meta tags to index pages. It took a lot of time and effort to get listed on the search engine sites. The work involved in getting a high profile on the search engine listings led to a whole new industry—search engine optimization. Anyone considering putting a new Web site up may get inundated with sales pitches from search engine optimization (SEO) consultants.

My advice? Stay away from all of them.

They often do more harm than good. For example, in the past, the more keyword meta tags embedded in a site, the higher the chance that the site would appear in the search list. The people doing search engine optimization focused on loading up on keywords, throwing everything but the kitchen sink into the keyword meta tags. But search engines took notice of this method of getting listed, and took umbrage. As a result they changed the rules so that sites that had too many keywords on each page became disqualified. (This does not apply to all meta tags, just *keyword* meta tags. The title meta tag and the description meta tag are well supported by search engines and should definitely be entered on every page on your site.) The abuse by those early search engine optimization consultants made keyword meta tags useless.

Another early abuse that led to search engine algorithm change was the number of links. A friend of mine, Charles, spent $60,000 on a supposedly sure-fire search optimization scheme proposed by a consultant. At the time, the search engines counted how many times each Web page on a site linked to each other Web page. Through special coding, Charles managed to get his site listed first on all the search engines every time someone entered any of the words on his site—until one day when suddenly his site didn't show up at all. The search engine rules disqualified sites that had too many internal links.

So how do you get listed higher on the page in the search engines? Currently, the following items influence the placement:[33]

- Search term use in title tag, headings, and body text.
- Relationship of body text content to search terms (topic analysis).
- Global link popularity of site (how many other sites link to yours).
- Age of site and document (the older the better).
- Amount of indexable text content (more text, less graphics).
- Frequency of updates to page (the more frequent the better).
- Documents not too deep (less than four folders in the path).
- Accuracy of spelling and grammar (no misspellings or errors).
- Well-designed code (no coding errors).

As noted, as time goes on this list will constantly change. What doesn't change is the intent of the search engines—providing the person searching with a list of high-quality sites matching the keywords for which they are looking. If we just concentrate on providing high-quality content on our site and don't worry about search engine optimization, we will tend to get a higher and higher profile over time.

Even so, showing up high on the list with generic terms is actually a minor issue. Of course, you will never hear a Google salesperson admit that. It is on the promise that people will find us and buy from us that has made Google the economic success it has been so far. We can purchase a sponsored link—and pay Google every time someone clicks on our Web site. Only you can determine if your business is of the type where doing this makes financial sense. In my experience, for many businesses, the click-through rate greatly exceeds the actually-buy-something rate.

While the World Wide Web is a great channel for our customers to be able to get information about your company, it is much more likely that someone will already know your company name and be looking specifically for it than that someone will type in a generic product or service and decide to buy from you based on your being in a list of 20,000 companies offering the same product or service. So you just want to make sure your business appears on the list when someone types in your specific name and/or address or some other unique piece of information (like a trademark phrase). For example, if you Google "hedgehog concept" a dozen links to various pages on Jim Collins's Web site appears.

Therefore, it is essential that when people are already specifically looking for your site, they should be able to find it. The test is to go to the search engines and type in your company name or your own name and see if your site appears somewhere in the first list (don't agonize over how high on the list it is). If you've put in title and description meta tags, your site should appear. If you have proper titles and descriptions, and your site still doesn't appear on the search engine lists, you can submit your information to ensure that your site is being indexed. More often, the automated indexing programs eventually find and index your site without any effort on your part—no submission necessary.

Product Information

Once businesses master the brochureware site, depending upon the businesses, they may be ready to start providing detailed product information on their Web sites.

In order to put dynamic information about products on the Web we must think about databases, middleware, links to inventory systems and full-service Web service companies. The costs of our Web site will increase dramatically—into thousands of dollars, (although nowhere near the costs from years ago). Nowadays, many financial systems have a Web module already built in and ready to install on the Web site, fully integrated with the inventory. This was very different years ago. In the early days, in order to avoid the high cost of integrating their Web inventory with physical or in-store inventory, many businesses simply set up their Web sites as a completely different storefront with separate inventory.

It didn't work well.

Customers complained bitterly. They couldn't return something to the store that they had purchased on-line. They don't want to buy something on the Web only to find out later that the item was actually out of stock because someone on the physical plane just purchased the last one, and the Web site doesn't get updated until the evening. They don't want to see something out of stock on the Web that they could have easily gotten in-stock at a local store had they only known it. Customers have the unreasonable view that the Web inventory should be a reflection of the actual, real-time inventory at every moment. Anyone who has tried to keep track of inventory knows how difficult it is to keep inventory accurate and up to date. Synchronizing inventory between a live store and a live Web site is a real challenge.

If there are so many problems in putting products and services on the Web, why would any company do it? It is an essential part of putting a catalog of items on the Web. But why is it listed as a separate phase then? I've placed it in a separate category because it is such a huge project. Non-technologists often don't realize the difference between an inventory control system that works just fine when there are people somewhere along the chain and an inventory control system that works when there are no live thinking human beings in the process. Any operational manager responsible for inventory control can describe the myriad of difficulties in keeping track of inventory. Let's discuss just a smattering of common problems, mostly surrounding the difficulty of granularity.

Granularity refers to the level at which a unique item exists. Imagine that we own a mom-and-pop knickknack store. We sell decorative candles. We can order a skid of candles from any one of three different vendors. We take the skid and break it apart into three levels of inventory: cases, boxes, and individual candles. The candles come in either small or large, and either red, blue, green, or white. For a small knickknack store none of this is any problem. When we sell the items, we know that the individual small candles are $2 (regardless of color) and the individual large candles are $4. A box of 12 small candles is $20, and a box of large candles is $40, a case of small is $240, and so on. When we want to reorder, we just take a look at the inventory that is left. If all the red candles are gone, we put them on the sheet to reorder.

What a non-technologist doesn't understand is how complex this process is for a blind and dumb computer system. In order to properly figure out what items are in stock, how much to sell each candle for, which vendor to purchase from, and which items need to be reordered, we actually need the number of vendors times the number of sizes times the number of unit types times the number of colors. This results in 72 ($3 \times 2 \times 3 \times 4$) unique identifying numbers for a single item, in our simple example. Furthermore, we would also need some system for converting one type of inventory into another type of inventory (as happens when we open up a box to sell individual candles).

Most inventory systems in use today don't work at that level of granularity, choosing to ignore color, for example, when identifying the SKU (stock keeping unit), resulting in only 18 unique identifying numbers instead of 72. These systems rely upon a human being who can easily recognize which color needs to be ordered. Unfortunately, that wouldn't work in an on-line system because people oddly enough generally don't want to be surprised by what color candle they ordered. Some on-line systems get around this by adding an "attribute" field and expecting the buyer to type in the color, or choose the color from the list. This, then, gets into a huge programming issue because each product would need a different attribute list.

This is just one example of the complexity involved when trying to provide an on-line purchasing experience. None of these obstacles is overwhelming, but they always take longer than we think they will take to resolve. Therefore, it is a good idea to put a live real-time inventory of the products on-line in a separate project before connecting them to the e-commerce portion of the Internet strategy: the shopping cart. To get around this complexity, many smaller businesses place the product information on-line and then provide a toll free number for people to call to order them.

E-Commerce

E-commerce occurs when people can order the products and services directly from your Web site. This typically involves putting a catalog of items on-line and providing screens for ordering and paying for the items.

Setting up e-commerce is a little more complex than it looks. One solution to eliminating the complexity is to simply place our products and services on someone else's Web site like Amazon.com or eBay.com—both of which are like distributors for on-line vendors. If you've ever shopped on Amazon.com or eBay.com or any other major on-line vendor, you have seen really advanced e-commerce that is way beyond the capabilities of most entrepreneurs. These systems are highly complex due to the billions of dollars of investment in their development over many years. Unique features like Lands' End virtual model that lets people try on clothes virtually, and one-click shopping pioneered by Amazon are major e-commerce advancements not easily duplicated. Many people do choose to use them, paying a percentage of each sale. For Amazon, the costs range from 6 percent to 15 percent plus per transaction charges (a few more bucks). For eBay, the costs range from 6 percent plus an insertion fee of up to $5. These charges are in addition to the normal 3 percent to 6 percent charges for a credit card or PayPal sale.

If you wish to do your own e-commerce site, then there is a lot to learn. E-commerce involves the coordination of several different aspects of the transaction. We would need information on the:

- Customer who is purchasing.
- Shopping cart software used on the hosting Web site.
- Security encryption level of the hosting Web site.
- Bank with which we ordinarily do business.
- Merchant account service that processes the credit cards.
- Credit card company that processes the transaction.
- Payment gateway that authorizes the on-line transaction.
- Inventory of the product (if a product) or record-keeping of the service.
- Shipping or delivery of the product or service.
- Financial record-keeping system.

Because e-commerce is still relatively new, how we get this information together on our Web site and available to our customers on a shopping cart is still in flux. It can be super simple and easy—as long as we are willing to pay a chunk of each sale in transaction costs to the various institutions that all want a piece of the pie (or to the one organization that coordinates and integrates all the different pieces of the pie). For a large corporation the chunk is minimal (and made much smaller by the volume involved). But for an entrepreneur, the decision of when to get a merchant account and take credit card payments is a big deal. A few hundred dollars for setup fees, and $20 or $30 more for account and transaction fees monthly are no big deal when you've already got an income stream, but it's a big chunk out of nothing when you haven't yet built up sufficient volume to afford it. Of course, it's easier to build up volume when customers can pay with credit cards. Once the decision is made, the next question is how much work to do ourselves, and how much we should pay others to do.

Smaller Web sites get around this problem by using eBay and its payment processing subsidiary, PayPal. Customers can pay with a credit card on the PayPal site, which can be hidden so that the customers don't even realize they left our site and went onto PayPal. We (as vendors) only have to pay a percentage to PayPal. There is no monthly fee, there are no setup charges. There is no terminal equipment to pay for. We don't need to have a merchant account because basically PayPal is acting as our pseudo–merchant account. Our PayPal account allows us to transfer the funds paid by our customers to our bank, minus the transaction fee to PayPal, of course.

We do have to give PayPal direct access to our bank account. In the early days there was a lot of grousing because if a customer didn't pay their credit card bill or used a stolen credit card, PayPal would freeze the vendors' bank account until they transferred the money back to PayPal. For the most part, however, the transaction processing has become much more of a well-known entity as many of the early issues were caused by people who just didn't understand the charge-back system. Nonetheless, I do recommend setting up a separate bank account just for the PayPal transfer. Otherwise we are putting our entire business at risk if PayPal chooses to freeze our bank account due to an unlawful transaction caused by someone else using a stolen credit card.

PayPal, of course, is only for on-line transactions. If we want to take credit cards in a storefront, we still need to get a regular merchant account. Many smaller businesses who already have off-line accounts don't wish to pay (again) for setting up an on-line account. They simply gather the information on-line and then manually put the transaction through their off-line merchant account. Having an off-line solution for credit cards is always cheaper than having an on-line solution because card-present fees are generally lower than card-not-present fees. Remember that in all cases you, the vendor, are responsible for fraudulent transactions, so there are also various fee-based security authentication schemes you can add to the basic processing chain. Some merchant services are also resellers of on-line payment gateways such as Authorize.Net or PayPal's Payflow (the back-end authorization gateway for PayPal merchant accounts), so it is possible to get both the on-line and the off-line accounts from the same merchant service.

The next consideration, of course, is the financial software being used. Most of the time, newer financial software provides a link between the accounting software and the merchant account and payment gateway. Older financial software only connected to your bank account. Since your bank account would be connected to your merchant account, you would have an indirect link. Having your financial software linked to your bank will only give you the total transferred, not the detail information for each credit card transaction. For that, you must link your financial software to the merchant account and payment gateway service. Of course, the oldest financial packages didn't link anywhere, and you had to enter deposits and checks manually. It is not uncommon for organizations to still be doing it that way.

Now, however, the vendors of most financial software packages have made a deal with one or more merchant accounts and one or more payment gateways. Intuit, the owner of QuickBooks, for example, purchased Innovative Process Solutions a number of years ago, so they host their own payment gateway that is connected directly to the more recent versions of QuickBooks. QuickBooks is the most common financial system used by small businesses today. With one exception: The on-line version of Quick-Books does not work with any on-line credit card transaction processing at the present time. Undoubtedly that will change over time.

QuickBooks, therefore, can be the vendor of our financial software, our merchant account, and our authorization gateway (for setup, monthly, and per-transaction fees, of course). QuickBooks also works with PayPal's Payflow and Authorize.net gateways as well. While it is beyond the scope of this chapter to review every financial package and whether it links with on-line credit card processing, the vendor of your financial package would be one of the first calls to make when considering doing credit card transactions. If they are already integrated, that would be the easiest option.

Advanced E-Commerce

There's e-commerce, and then there's e-commerce. After the first few attempts at putting products and services on-line, most companies realize that it is harder than it looks to get right. It's not just the look and feel of the screens that's important, it's the usability of the site. How easy is it to order? How quickly does the screen download? Does the site remember what customers ordered before, or do they have to enter their name and address every time they get on? Can they configure complex items when they order them? How easily can they find what they want? Can others comment on the quality of each of the products or services? We should always work to improve the usability of our Web site.

The key to this is to have a few people, on a regular basis, go onto the Web site and go through the steps a customer might go through and report on their experience. Fresh new eyes are especially helpful in working out little kinks in the process that you didn't even know were there. We should also talk regularly with our customers and ask them whether they use the Web site, what more they would like to see on it, and so on. Keep in mind that large sites like Amazon and eBay are usually well-known and used by many, so if we choose not to use them for our e-commerce, we should at least try to provide as much similar functionality as possible.

Intranet and Extranet

Strictly speaking, an intranet does not belong on this list because it has nothing to do with the public Internet. An intranet is when we use Internet technologies (such as TCP/IP, HTML, and Web sites) to provide our own employees with access to needed information. For example, if we put our absence request forms on a Web site for our employees to download and fill out when they want a day off, we are providing an intranet. If an organization already has a well-defined process for distributing forms and information to employees using a central server or local area network, there is no need to provide an additional intranet. However, if an organization has not already gone to the trouble of setting up a central server for that information, using Internet technologies to do so only makes sense. It would be cheaper and easier than doing it the old way (setting up a Windows or Novell NetWare server). It works best to set up a central theme and style, and then appoint people in each department to place information needed by other departments on the Web page. Just make absolutely sure that only employees can access the intranet Web site; you wouldn't want competitors to be able to get to your intranet through your public Web page. It's best to keep the two completely separate.

An extranet allows us to utilize the power of the public Internet for a select group of people—a company's sales force, representatives, or partners. Extranets can often deliver productivity gains far in excess of the cost. Virtual teams can be enabled to share information in ways they've never been able to before. The actual hardware and software is the same as an intranet. An extranet is using public Internet hardware, software, and protocols for making resources available to partners (such as vendors and representatives) outside of the internal network.

To some extent, this is already happening every time our employees e-mail someone outside of our companies. Remember, it has been less than 15 years since we were limited to sending e-mail to just the people within our own company! But some companies have not yet embraced exchanging information electronically because of the inherent security issues with e-mail. This is where an extranet can come in. By providing passwords and a secure encryption protocol (provided by most Web hosting services) and an encryption transfer method (often called a VPN or virtual private network), we can allow select people to use the public Internet to access private data that stays private.

The productive uses are infinite: allow your employees to work from home, provide literature to your representatives, deliver promotional material to your resellers, share project milestones with your partners, share inventory needs with your vendors, conduct on-line focus groups about

your products and services, and so on. For example, when I was responsible for application security at a large Northeastern bank, I set up a Web
page for all of our vendors to submit their information regarding their
disaster recovery readiness so that we could report that information to the
OTS (Office of Thrift Supervision, the federal government agency that regu-
lates banks). Similarly, they could download the change management plans
so that if their systems interlinked with any of ours, they would know
when a change was coming.

Both intranets and extranets are more complex than typical Web pages,
so they require the use of a full-service hosting service or an internal team
of IT support people or both. But the value can be tremendous.

Community

One step further than an extranet is a real virtual community. For an on-
line community, there must be a two-way dynamic purpose. A community
is made up of people who associate with each other on the Web. The people
in the community develop a relationship that is only peripherally related to
the products and services they buy within the virtual walls of the community. They converse with each other (i.e., chat, e-mail, and post), know each
other, trust each other, and generally provide for each other's needs.

According to those in the industry, on-line communities are becoming
the new strategic business mandate. They cite statistics about how many
millions of people are members of popular on-line communities such as
Facebook (for youth) and LinkedIn (for business professionals). MySpace.
com, a popular on-line community, was actually started by a band that
wanted more fans to come hear them play.

Some products have sold due entirely to the virtual buzz surrounding
them created by vendor-supported communities. One of the earliest on-
line community marketing success stories was the Big Green Egg, which
is a high-priced ceramic grill. Devoted fans post frequently on www.
biggreenegg.com and that attracts others who purchase one.

Knowing what the customer wants and understanding current and
future needs is paramount to increasing revenue and exceeding customer
expectations. On-line Communities provide a prime opportunity for companies to get to know their customers more intimately and keep a finger
on the pulse of their needs and behaviors. On-line communities offer a
chance for companies to break down geographical barriers by connecting
people globally in many different ways through on-line interaction. They
allow for more detailed and sustained conversations and deepen customer
relationships. They offer on-line interactive access for people, marketing
collateral, information, and products. Ultimately, when effectively created,
on-line communities can build trust relationships by providing better communication channels. Vanessa DiMauro, president of Leader Networks, a
consulting company specializing in building on-line communities, is an
advocate:

The basics about business success are not changing—it is and has always been about strength of relationships, it is the expectations that are changing about what it means to be a customer. The time is now for companies to embrace communities to help them serve their clients better, faster, and in more cost-efficient ways. Through the use of on-line communities, companies now have an opportunity to forge a dialogue with their customers actively throughout the life cycle—not just at the point of sale. On-line communities also offer opportunities to make heroes out of users, enabling them to share best practice stories and to connect with other clients. The companies that venture into these new types of on-line relationships will see amazing competitive advantage.

For the most part I agree. As a veteran on-line networker and former member of the advisory board for several professional on-line communities, I know the power of developing on-line relationships. Several of my closest friends live in other parts of the world, but I converse with them frequently through chats and e-mail.

In February 2006 I was invited to be part of a panel at Wharton on social networking. I'm sure they expected me to jump wholeheartedly into the fray. It was at this point, however, that I placed a caution on the exuberance for developing on-line communities. At the current time, on-line communities have not yet proven to be a money maker for anyone. For teens who spend a great deal of time on-line, they started with Friendster, and then abandoned it for MySpace, and then abandoned it for Facebook. LinkedIn, for professionals, is a highly useful tool for keeping in touch with people you already know. It enables you to expand your network (yes, that kind of network) by being able to see who are the friends of your friends so that you can mine your own network more deeply. But if people begin to say ''yes'' when invited to become part of the LinkedIn network for people they don't actually know personally, the value of the network diminishes. And if a better tool comes along or if LinkedIn starts charging money, people will abandon it for the next community Web site.

My advice to businesses wishing to dip their toe in the on-line network is to simply have their sales and marketing people start to spend a limited amount of time on-line: talking to people, reading blogs, and commenting on them. Use on-line communities as you would a local chamber of commerce networking event. Don't make a hard sell, but see what people are saying. Ask customers what they think. If there is a good reason to do so, set up forums for customers to talk with each other and with others within your organization. Use on-line communities as a focus group and a way to contact customers directly. But don't expect to monetize it or make money. I've found that on-line communities with the following characteristics endure:

- Don't cost the members any fees (i.e., are free) and don't have too much advertising.
- Are focused on hobbies and interests of people.

- Have long-term leaders who post frequently and keep everyone interested and civil.
- Focus on relationships, not information technology.
- Have enough of a base membership to maintain frequent postings of the 10 percent active readers and the 1 percent active posters.

Sequence Is Important

As noted earlier, the successful companies of the future will include all of the different stages or phases in their strategy. A business that utilizes the Internet for their internal needs (intranet) will have a competitive edge over companies who think the Web is only a sales channel or only a vehicle to attract investors. A business that adds a community aspect to their extranet will have a competitive edge over companies who don't.

But the sequence of the approach is important, too.

- Corporate presence.
- Product/service information.
- E-commerce.
- Advanced e-commerce.
- Intranet and extranet.
- Community.

Companies that go right for the latter phases are making a mistake. We can't build a community without a specific purpose in mind. And if we pay attention to internal processes and ignore the power of the Internet in increasing our sales, we will be missing the boat, and you can bet some hotshot start-up will catch it. We can't provide a way of ordering unless our products and services are described on-line. And if we put our catalog on-line and haven't even established a domain name and corporate presence, it will be difficult for users to find the site.

We can't do everything at once, so working through the list one step at a time should be an important part of our strategy. And finding the right partners (and they may be different at each phase) is the key to doing it right. Before we even consider any of that, however, we might want to first look at a lower tactical level: how we use e-mail.

THE POWER OF E-MAIL

Customers expect businesses to have e-mail. With e-mail, any individual person can send information to any other single person (as long as they know their e-mail address). This is a powerful and essential business tool. Everyone, from the janitor to the chair of the board, should be accessible through e-mail—even if that means having an assistant print out all our e-mails and respond appropriately in our name.

From a personal and business perspective, however, we are just now getting used to all this new technology. We are like toddlers with a new toy, and we don't always use it in the optimum manner. In the last section we asked ourselves some questions about our use of the Web. Now let's consider the use of e-mail. Consider these questions:

- Do we overuse or underuse e-mail?
- Do we put e-mail in its proper place, supplementing phone and live conversations (not replacing them)?
- Can our customers get a quick response to e-mail requests or complaints?
- Are our employees able to contact each other quickly through e-mail?

Professional E-mail Netiquette

Like many technology professionals, over the years I have picked up the unwritten rules of e-mail netiquette: good e-mail behavior. My clients, however, are often just learning to send professional e-mail. There is a large gap of knowledge between people who have been e-mailing for years and people who haven't been e-mailing for very long (or don't have the volume necessary). If you don't have years of experience, it is hard to know what the rules are because most of them are unwritten. While the simple stuff is pretty easy to pick up (don't use ALL CAPS; use a meaningful topic in the subject line; begin with a greeting and end with a signature, etc.), there are many others that seem to get missed.

Like an unzipped fly or bad breath, no one will say anything if we break the unwritten rules, though they may laugh at us behind our backs. In some cases, the problem stems from not realizing that rules for business-oriented e-mails are different from rules for informal social e-mails. When we use social e-mail rules for business communication, it's like showing up at a business mixer where everyone else is wearing a suit and we've come in jeans and a T-shirt. No one will complain, but neither will they take us very seriously. We will discuss 11 usually missed rules. See how many of them you already know.

- Use a professional e-mail address.
- Properly configure your e-mail program with your real name.
- Share your e-mail address; put it on your business card.
- Deal with spam professionally.
- Avoid emotionless e-mail escalation.
- Use CC or BC judiciously to copy others.
- Only turn on request receipts if you can restrict them to internal e-mail.
- Only configure out of office messages if you can restrict them to internal e-mail.
- Don't use an e-mail distribution list as a discussion board.
- Don't send jokes, virus warnings, or other extraneous information.
- Don't write anything in an e-mail you wouldn't want to see written on the first page of *The New York Times*.

No matter how small your business is, use a variant of your name for your e-mail address and a variant of your business name for your e-mail domain. The e-mail name is the part in front of the @. The domain is the part in back of the @ and usually ends with a .com or a .org or a .net. Do not confuse e-mail addresses with Web pages. Only e-mail uses the @ sign.

While it may be fun to use ChickInHeat@Hotmail.com or PhillyFan@aol.com, your business communication will not be seen as professional. The side benefit to owning your own domain name is that it allows you to separate your physical Internet service provider (ISP) from your e-mail address so that it doesn't change when you move from place to place. The Internet service provider is the company with whom you contract to give you access to the Internet. It could be your phone company, your cable company, MSN or AOL.

If you've never sent yourself an e-mail, you may not realize how it looks if you don't fill in the "Name" field of your e-mail program. If you are relying upon a technology professional to set up your e-mail, don't forget to specifically ask them to go the extra step and set up your real name.

Put your e-mail address on your business card. I'm amazed at the number of people who don't do this. Giving out your e-mail address to people does not increase spam, is not dangerous, and cannot hurt you. (As noted earlier, putting your e-mail address on your Web site is a different story, so don't do that.)

One of the downsides of e-mail is spam (unwanted bulk e-mail). Even worse, e-mails can be [gasp!] fraudulent and filled with lies. Phishing is the name given to an e-mail that is fraudulent and trying to elicit private information from you. If you haven't been offered a percentage of the $30 million that some expelled Nigerian king would like to transfer to your U.S. bank account, you haven't been doing e-mail very long.

But spam and phishing can be dealt with professionally. First, don't be a whiner. Don't complain about spam. Spam is not going to go away. Railing against it is like railing against the humidity. Just like junk mail, accept that every day you will have to quickly look through all your messages and delete most of them because they are unwanted bulk messages not addressed to you. Learn to use your spam filter and don't respond to spam or phishing.

Why is spam filtering so hard? Like junk mail, spam is in the eye of the beholder. The most common definition for spam is "unsolicited e-mail," but that definition doesn't work. If I send a "how are you doing" message to my sister in California, it was unsolicited, but no one would call it spam. "Unsolicited bulk e-mail" doesn't work either. If I send the same message to all my friends and family with e-mail addresses, the number is well over 200 (I have a very big family). But again—no one would call it spam (though many anti-spam programs would refuse it because it is addressed to more than 50 names at one time).

In business, if I send a newsletter to 300 people that I know and have met personally even if they didn't ask for it, I don't consider that spam. If I send the same newsletter to 30,000 people, most of whom I've never met, I would consider it spam. If I sent a "how are you doing" message to 300,000 people, it would definitely be spam no matter what the content. But if the IRS sends out 2 million e-mails to people to let them know some information they need to get their refunds, that would not be spam no matter how many people receive it.

Unwanted bulk e-mail is by definition based on human judgment. While a human being can look at any message and pretty much figure out immediately if it is unwanted, a computer cannot. When sending an important e-mail, always follow up with a phone call so that the recipient can get the message out of the spam bucket if it landed there. Never assume that someone has read your e-mail. And most important, don't send spam.

Also remember that e-mail has the tendency to come across very harsh and aggressive. Normally, over 90 percent of a message's intent comes from facial expression and tone of voice, which doesn't exist in e-mail. When receiving a negative-sounding e-mail, reply by phone or a personal visit, not a reply e-mail. If it is from someone you do not know, ignore it. It took me a long time to learn this rule; it always seemed so much easier to respond in e-mail. I finally realized how much time I was wasting—both by responding in e-mail and then having to respond to the response (not to mention unruffling the feathers I had ruffled in my previous messages).

Be judicious in copying others on your e-mail communications, and circumspect in the topics you choose to e-mail. Filling in the CC: (carbon copy—and yes it is an anachronism) seems like a quick and efficient way to copy third parties on an e-mail message. But copying can be a problem. Last week I upset someone because I copied his boss on an e-mail I wrote him. He read the e-mail negatively and thought I was criticizing his program, though in my mind I was extending praise and sharing information. He assumed I copied his boss to chastise him when just the opposite was the case!

Copying to the wrong list can also be a problem. A couple of years ago when I was a VP in a Fortune 500 financial firm, I was copied on an e-mail from a senior vice president (SVP) containing a thread discussing the promotion and salary of one of my VP coworkers. The e-mail contained the guy's salary as well as the opinions of three different SVP's on his progress toward promotion. (It was extremely interesting reading, and provided me with foundational insight into the promotion process in a Fortune 500 company of which I had been previously unaware.) It turned out that I was not the only one to get the misdirected message. A secretary had accidentally copied the thread to the entire company instead of just the senior leader list. (Needless to say, the secretary did not last long after that.)

Blind copy (Bcc:) can also get you in trouble. Blind copy hides the e-mail addresses of the people receiving the e-mail. One legitimate reason to use blind copy is to avoid annoying the reader with a long list of e-mail addresses (through which they must scroll) before they get to the message. Another legitimate reason to use blind copy is when you are sending to a confidential list of people. The Society for Information Management sends out a monthly e-mail to all their members—but they don't want any of the vendor members to use the list for promotional offers, so they properly send it out as a blind copy.

The problem occurs when you use blind copy to hide the fact that someone was copied on the message. That's risky by itself, but it is even riskier if you don't communicate with the person who was copied. They may very well forward (or reply all) to the message—letting the original target person know that you've been duplicitous. It's better not to use blind copy to hide the fact that the message has been copied, but if you do, ensure that the recipient knows why you sent it as a blind copy. Alternatively, if you receive a message without your e-mail address in the To: or CC: fields, treat the message as confidential, and do not forward or reply.

Only turn on request receipts if you can restrict them to internal e-mail. A receipt request is a request that goes out to the recipient of an e-mail that requests a return message to let the sender know that the recipient received or read the message. The problem is that receipt request does not work well if the recipient is on a different network, a different e-mail system, or if the sender sends the message to the recipient's internet e-mail account. Instead of being convenient and under the covers, the recipients would get a second e-mail that asks for a reply whether or not they've read the original message—redundant and annoying for the receiver of such a request. Being able to tell if someone has gotten your e-mail sounds like a good idea, but since it can't be implemented without annoying the recipient of the e-mail, it's better just to leave the feature turned off.

Only configure out of office messages if you can restrict them to internal e-mail. An out of office message is a response to every e-mail you receive that says something like "I'll be out of the office from July 3 to July 16 and will respond to your e-mail when I've returned." I've heard the arguments for using out of office messages: " I want people to know that I'm on vacation, that I'm not ignoring their e-mails." Unfortunately, the distribution nature of e-mail means that you often get e-mails that are directed at a group, not just you. An e-mail distribution list is a single e-mail address to which an e-mail can be sent once, but is received by dozens or hundreds or thousands of people. Out of office messages are even more annoying when the e-mail list is configured to reply back to all members of the list. One of my on-line communities has another member who keeps turning on her out of office message. Every time she goes on vacation (which seems to be pretty often) 600 people who don't know her (and even more important, don't care) find out she's going on vacation.

Furthermore, when your system replies to a message that's been sent by a spammer, they get confirmation that there's a real live person on the other end of that e-mail address, and the value of your e-mail address among spammers just quadrupled—as will the amount of spam that you get.

The fact is, e-mail (alone) is not appropriate for information of a time-sensitive nature. Since there is no guarantee that people will see your e-mail in time (or even at all) it makes more sense to use the phone for time-sensitive issues, and expect others to do the same. Therefore, in most industries the appropriate place for information about when you are on vacation is voice mail. The news only goes to the people who are actively trying to reach you, and doesn't go out to the hundreds of people who might not care.

Also remember that e-mail distribution lists are meant to foster communication among various people who need to communicate some important information. A problem occurs when people don't realize that they receive a message from a distribution list and they treat it as if it were a personal e-mail. Invariably, someone who is unfamiliar with e-mail distribution lists will hit the reply button and say something like "I missed you at the meeting last night. Give me a call and we can get together and talk about George." For example, at the university at which I teach, there is a distribution list called StaffAndFaculty@Kutztown.edu, and this happens all the time on that list. Clueless faculty members don't realize that all 400 faculty members received their message instead of the one person who originally e-mailed.

Not quite as bad image-wise, but sometimes even more annoying, is the tendency for people to send out their opinion to the whole distribution list (as if everyone else wants to know what they think). Of course, if the purpose of the e-mail distribution list is to be used as a discussion board, then this behavior is not only okay, it is encouraged. But if the e-mail distribution list is meant for important announcements, then for various people to use it as a sounding board will lower its value as an attention-getting device.

A sure sign that someone is inexperienced in e-mail is the sending of jokes, virus warnings, or other items that they have been urged to send to everyone they know. The reason this behavior shows their inexperience is because anyone who's been using e-mail professionally for more than a few years has already seen all of the jokes, virus warnings, and feel-good e-mails.

Finally, be careful what you write in e-mail. Some people have the idea that e-mail should be private. Perhaps this mistaken notion stems from the federal laws against tampering with U.S. postal mail. (In 1792 Congress imposed the death penalty for that crime!) But in this way e-mail is very different from postal mail. E-mail can be read in plain text by anyone with a particular network device as it travels over the public Internet. Furthermore, e-mail is possessed by the owners of several servers through which it passes on its journey from writer to recipient. Those servers may be backed up several times throughout the day, resulting in several permanent copies of any e-mail message. Instead of thinking of e-mail as a sealed letter, think of it like a postcard. There is literally no way to keep an e-mail private. By the way—the same is true for IMing (instant messaging or chatting). So think before you text and send.

FINAL ANALYSIS

While this chapter has delved a bit deeper into practical guidelines, do not let its depth dissuade us from paying attention to the major points of this book.

Information technology is an accelerator; it can propel your business to new heights, or it can hasten your crash over the cliffs. In order to ensure help instead of harm, invest in new technology only when it is clear how it aligns with your hedgehog concept—that one important thing that your company does better than anyone else.

Pay more attention to the people and the process than to the hardware and the software. Over time, develop a technology map so that you can identify the various IT vendors and develop long-term partnerships with them. But be sure to learn enough about the hardware and the software so that you understand what you are buying and can recognize when to pounce like a panther on new technology. Use the power of networking (like e-mail, the public Internet, and the World Wide Web) to enhance and expand your networking (personal relationships).

When entrepreneurs pay proper attention to information technology and develop the knowledge and experience they need (or find trusted advisers until they do), there is no limit to the value information technology can contribute to the bottom line.

SUMMARY

We can take advantage of networking by:

- ☑ Recognizing the paradigm shift that occurs when we can get any information about anything anytime from a single source.
- ☑ Developing an Internet strategy (no matter how large or small we are).
- ☑ Choosing a professional e-mail and domain name.
- ☑ Designing and posting a Web page about our business.
- ☑ If appropriate, using the Web to provide information about our products and services.
- ☑ If appropriate, using Internet technologies to make it easy for employees to get needed information on an intranet.
- ☑ If appropriate, using the Web to provide private information to vendors, customers, and partners through a password-protected extranet.
- ☑ Using the power of networking to develop a community of partners and customers.
- ☑ Going slowly and maintaining alignment with our hedgehog concept. Do the phases in sequence.
- ☑ Learning how to properly configure your e-mail for a professional image.
- ☑ Recognizing the lack of privacy in e-mail, and not complaining about spam and phishing.

Appendices

Technology Map Basic Categories

Major	Minor	Categories (examples)
People	Ability	High ability, low experience
		Low ability, high experience
	Experience	High ability, high experience
		Low ability, low experience
Process	Who (role)	Flow charts and process documentation, often obtained by watching people and what they do as well as asking them.
	What (task)	
	When (prompt or time)	
Software	Application	Word processing (Word, WordPerfect, Multi-Mate, Displaywriter)
		Spreadsheet (Excel, Lotus 123, Quattro Pro)
		Database (Oracle, DB2, Sybase, SQL, MySQL,. PostgreSQL, Progress, Access, dBase, Foxpro, Alpha4, Filemaker)
		Presentation/graphics (PowerPoint, Illustrator, Harvard Graphics, Corel Draw)
		Communication: e-mail (like Outlook/Exchange or Notes/Domino), chat (like Yahoo! Messenger, MSN Messenger, AOL IM, Windows Messenger, IRQ), discussion group (like ASP Playground, PhpBB, SharePoint), knowledge management, etc.
	Specialized	Financial: ERP, GL/AP/AR (PeopleSoft, JD Edwards, Oracle, SAP, Baan, MAS90, Quick-Books, Money, etc.)

(continued)

Technology Map Basic Categories (continued)

Major	Minor	Categories (examples)
		CAD/CAM (Computer Aided Design and Manufacturing, Autocad)
		Vertical market (medical, attorney, retail, etc.)
		Publishing (Quark, Publisher, Adobe Acrobat), Web publishing (Frontpage, Expressions, Dreamweaver, GoLive)
Software	Development	Languages (Java, C, Cobol, Pascal, Perl, Visual Basic, etc.)
		Workbenches & middleware (Cold Fusion, PHP, Websphere, CASE Tools, Javascript, VBS, ASP, etc.)
	Utilities	Enterprise management, backup, firewall (HP Openview, Norton's Antivirus, SMS, Checkpoint, PICS)
	Operating system	Single user (DOS, Windows 95, 98, ME, 2000, XP, Vista, Mac OS, Tiger, etc.)
		Multiuser (NT, Windows 2003, Novell, Unix [Linux, AIX, Solaris, HPUX], AS/400, MVS, VSE)
Hardware	CPU box	Hard drive, RAM, BIOS, Chip (Dell, Gateway, IBM, HP, Honeywell, Unisys, etc.)
	Peripherals	Mouse, keyboard, monitor, scanner, camera, printer, etc.
Network	Network applications	Client (SQL Client), Browser (Explorer, Netscape), LAN, Novell, etc.
		Application servers (Progress, Orion, Jboss, Sun One, Enhydra, etc.) Web servers (Apache, IIS, iPlanet)
	Internet communication protocols	TCP/IP, IPX/SPX, UPC, NetBIOS (Microsoft, open source, Novelle NetWare)
	Network interface	Hubs, routers, switches, and network interface cards (Ethernet, ATM, Token Ring) Connection type: point to point leased line, frame relay, DSL, cable modem, dialup

Example Standards List

Technology Component	Current	Stable	Future
Office	Microsoft Office 2003	Microsoft Office 97 SP-2	Microsoft Office 2007
Project management	Can Plan 8.3	Project 4.0	Primavera
Collaboration	ASP Playground	Exchange	SharePoint
E-mail	Outlook 97 SP2	Outlook 97 SP1	Outlook 2000
Finance	SAP 4.5b	Various	SAP Enterprise
Printer	HP Deskjet 970	HP 1200	HP Designjet 5000
Desktop	Dell Dimension 3700, Windows XP SP2, 1G RAM, 80G HD	Dell Dimension 3400, Windows XP SP1, 512Mg RAM, 40G HD	Dell, Microsoft Longhorn
Web servers	Enterprise Linux 2.1, Apache 2.0, Dell PowerEdge 2600, 8G RAM, 80G HD	Enterprise Linux 1, Apache 2.0 Compaq Proliant	Linux 3.3 Dell
Apps servers	Solaris SP8 Sun Fire 3800 Server, 24G RAM, 120G HD	Sun OS 4.1.4 Sun Sparc 5	Linux 3.3 Dell
Database servers	Windows 2000 SP 4: Dell PowerEdge 6600, Xeon, 4G RAM, 288G HD	Windows 2000 SP 4	Windows 2003 Dell
File/print servers	Windows NT 4.0, SP 6a: Dell PowerEdge 400 SC Server: P4, 512K RAM, 72G HD	Novell 4.11 SP9 Compaq Presario	Windows 2003 Dell
Network interface card	Dell 10/100 2R069	3COM 3C509B-TPC	3 COM 3C996B-T
Switches	BayStack 350 Agent v4.3.0	BayStack 350 Agent v4.2.0	BayStack 470
Hubs	D-Link DE-816TP	D-Link DE-809TP	BayStack 250 Agent Ver. 3.2.1
Horizontal wiring	Category 6 UTP	Category 5 UTP	Category 6 UTP
Backbone wiring	ONFR Multimode fiber type SC	Multimode fiber: various	ONFR Multimode fiber type FC

Technology Map Sample 1

Category	Subcategory	Quantity	Manufacturer	Model	Inventory Description	Vendor
Network	WAN Router/ Firewall	12	Cisco	1841	Firewall, Voice over IP Gateway (VoIP), WIC-1T WAN CARD	Cisco
Network	Switch	11	3Com	Superstack 3300	12 port Switch & TP 12 Hub & Patch	CDL Micro
Network	Switch	11	Cisco	1548M	8-port 10/100 External LAN Micro Switch	Cisco
Network	Server - Email	11	Gateway	E-9220TX	Intel Pentium D Processor 3.0GHz, 1GB RAM, 250GB Storage	Gateway
Network	Server - Quickbooks	11	Gateway	E-9220TX	Intel Pentium D Processor 3.0GHz, 1GB RAM, 250GB Storage	Gateway
Hardware	Desktop	12	Dell	Dimension	Intel Pentium 4 Processor, 200GB Storage, 2GB RAM	Dell
Hardware	Desktop	13	HP	Pavillion	Pentium M, 200GB, 1GB RAM	HP
Hardware	Monitor	13	Acer	AL1916AB	19″ LCD	Acer
Hardware	Monitor	12	Gateway	FPD1785	17″ LCD	Gateway
Hardware	Monitor	12	Dell	SE197FP	19″ LCD	Dell
Hardware	Keyboard	17	HP	Standard	Wired	HP
Hardware	Mouse	17	HP	Standard	Wired	HP
Hardware	Printer	15	HP	LaserJet 1022	8MB memory, 266MHz processor	HP
Hardware	Scanner	15	Xerox	Documate 252	Sheetfed	Office Depot

Software - System	Operating System	2	Windows	Windows Server 2003	Microsoft Windows Small Business Server 2003 Standard Edition	Microsoft
Software - System	Operating System	25	Windows	Window XP	Professional	Microsoft
Software - Utility	Security; Antivirus, Firewall, Antispyware	25	Norton	Norton Internet Security 2007	Antispyware, Antivirus, Firewall	Symantec
Software - Utility	Backup	2	IBM	Tivoli Storage Manager	Tivoli Storage Manager	IBM
Software - Application	Office	25	Microsoft	2003 Professional	Word, Excel, Acess, PowerPoint, InfoPath, Publisher	Microsoft
Software - Application	Accounting	25	Quickbooks	Professional	Professional	Intuit
Software - Application	Email	25	Microsoft		Outlook Express	Microsoft
Software - Application	Browner	25	Microsoft		Internet Explorer	Microsoft
Software - Application	Scanner Software	4	Xerox	Kofax VRS 2.1	Drivers ScanSoft PaperPort Pro 9 ScanSoft OmniPage Pro 12 Pixel Translations Pro 3.0 ArcSoft Photo	Office Depot

This map was done by Mariya Papazova, Kutztown University. Used with permission.

Technology Map Sample 1 (continued)

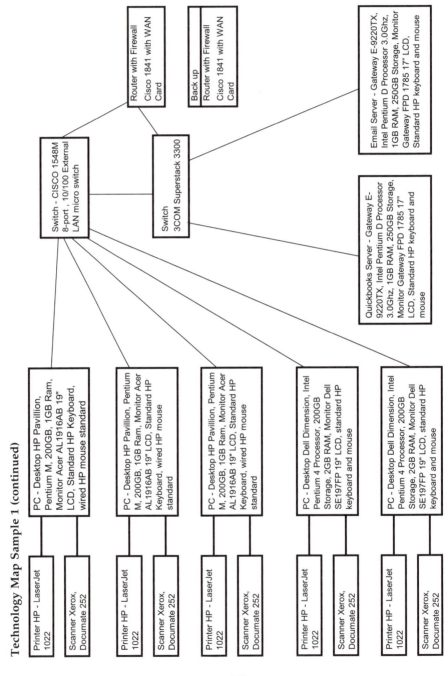

Technology Map Sample 2

Category	Subcategory	Inventory	Vendors
Network	WAN Telcom Vendor	Frame Relay: 1 T-1	D&E
Network	WAN Routers	Cisco 1841	Cisco
Network	WAN Communication Protocol	TCP/IP	
Network	Firewall	Cisco Pix 515e	Cisco
Network	Proxy Server	Blue Coat SG400	Blue Coat
Network	LAN Switches	(2) HP Procurve 2848,	Hewlett Packard
		(2) HP Procurve 2650,	
		(4) HP ProCurve 2824,	
		(2) HP Procurve 2324	
Network	Antivirus	Blue Coat AV400	Blue Coat
Network	Spam Filter	Barracuda Spam Firewall SF300	Barracuda
Network	LAN Wiring	Cat 5e Twisted Pair	Belkin
Network	LAN Wiring	Fiber Optic Cable	Corning
Network	Fiber Optic Connector Housing	LANscape Pretium	Corning
Network	LAN NICs	3Com 3C2000	Intel, 3COM
Network	LAN Communication Protocols	TCP/IP; Netbios	
Network	Telephone communications Vendor	T1 w / 6 digital POTS lines	D&E
Network	Telephones communications	4 Analog POTS lines	D&E over Verizon
Network	PBX	Iwatsu ADIX	Iwatsu
Hardware	Servers	(6) IBM xSeries 345	IBM/Hewlett Packard
		(2) IBM xSeries 346	
		(2) HP TC 4100	
		(1) HP LC2000	
Hardware	Network Attached Storage	Snap Server 4500	Adaptec
Hardware	Tape Backup	HP Ultrium 1-SCSI	Hewlett Packard
Hardware	Desktop CPU	15 IBM ThinkCentre S50	IBM

(continued)

Technology Map Sample 2 (continued)

Category	Subcategory	Inventory	Vendors
Hardware	Desktop CPU	3 Dell Dimension 2350, 1 Optiplex 160L, 1 Optiplex GX240 Minitower	Dell
Hardware	Desktop CPU	Brio BA410	Hewlett Packard
Hardware	Laptop CPU	(3) Latitude D600, (3) Latitude C840, (1) Inspiron 600m	Dell
Hardware	Laptop CPU	(3) Thinkpad R51, (4) Thinkpad Z60m, (5) Thinkpad Z61m, (1) Thinkpad T22	IBM
Hardware	Terminals	(18) Winterm S50	Wyse
Hardware	Monitors	Ultrasharp 2407WFP	Dell
Hardware	Monitors	(10) Planar PX1910M, (6) Planar PX191, (1) Planar S2031D	Planar
Hardware	Monitors	(6) Samsung 170N	Samsung
Hardware	Monitors	(9) KDS 17", (1) KDS RAD-7c	KDS
Hardware	Printers	(9) HP Laserjet 1320N (2) HP Deskjet 5550 (1) HP Deskjet 670C (1) HP Deskjet 932C (1) HP Laserjet 4345MFP	Hewlett Packard
Hardware	Printer	(1) Xerox Phaser Color Laserjet	Xerox
Hardware	Multifunction Printer/Copier/Scanner/Fax	(1) Canon Image Runner 2800	Canon
Hardware	LCD Projectors	(1) NEC LT240K	NEC

Category	Type	Details	Vendor
Software: System	Network OS	(6) Windows Server 2003 Standard Edition SP1, (1) Windows Server 2003, Enterprise Edition SP1	Microsoft
Software: System	System Software: OS	(26) Windows XP Professional SP2, (1) Windows 2000 Professional SP4, (1) Windows NT Workstation 4.0 SP6	Microsoft
Software: Utility	Security - Antivirus	Symantec Antivirus 10.0	Symantec
Software: Utility	Anti-spam:Web-based	MX Logic	MX Logic, Inc.
Software: Utility	Anti-spyware	Spysweeper	Webroot Software, Inc.
Software: Utility	Backup	Symantec Backup Exec Remote Agent for Windows Servers 10.1	Symantec
Software: Utility	Software patching	(35) Patchlink Update Agent 6.1.0	Patchlink
Software: Utility	Remote Access	(4) Cisco Systems VPN Client 4.6	Cisco
Software: Utility	PDF Printer	(21) CutePDF Writer 2.5, (2) CutePDF Professional 3.3	
Software: Application	Financial - ERP	(27) Syspro 6.0	Syspro
Software: Application	Email	(29) Microsoft Outlook 2002 SP3, (3) Microsoft Outlook 2000 SR1, (1) Microsoft Outlook Express 5	Microsoft
Software: Application	Document Scanning Archive software	(16) Ecopy Desktop, (13) Ecopy Viewer, (1) Ecopy Sharescan	Ecopy
Software: Application	Office Wordprocessing	(29) Microsoft Word 2002 SP3	Microsoft
Software: Application	Office Spreadsheet	(29) Microsoft Excel 2002 SP3	Microsoft
Software: Application	Office Database	(29) Microsoft Access 2002 SP3	Microsoft
Software: Application	Office Presentation	(29) Microsoft Powerpoint 2002 SP3	Microsoft
Software: Application	Office Publishing	(2) Microsoft Publisher 2002 SP3	Microsoft

(continued)

Technology Map Sample 2 (continued)

Category	Subcategory	Inventory	Vendors
Software: Application	Documentation	(1) Microsoft Visio Professional 2003 SP2	Microsoft
Software: Application	Publishing	(28) Adobe Acrobat Reader 7.0.01	Adobe
Software: Application	Publishing	(1) Adobe Acrobat Professional 7.0	Adobe
Software: Application	File Compression	(27) WinZip 9.0	Corel Corporation
Software: Application	Business process automation	(4) Automate	Network Automation
Software: Application	Payroll reporting	(15) Attendance Enterprise, (1) Attendance Enterprise Server	Infotronics
Software: Application	Drawing	(2) Autocad LT 2002	Autodesk
Software: Application	Label-making	(1) Labelview 7.0	Teklynx (Braton Groupe sarl)
Software: Application	Mapping	(1) Microsoft Streets and Trips 10.0	Microsoft

This map was done by Andrew Sims, Kutztown University. Used with permission.

People Technology Capability

	Hi-ability Hi-exper	Hi-ability Lo-exper	Lo-ability Hi-exper	Lo-ability Lo-exper
Receptionist				X
A/P Clerk	X			
Sales rep	X			
CSR1			X	
CSR2			X	
Payroll Clerk				X
A/R Clerk			X	
Customer Deduction Clerk			X	
Assistant Controller	X			
Controller	X			
Buyer			X	
Operations Manager			X	
Shipping/Receiving Manager			X	
Vice President				X
President		X		
Network Administrator	X			
IT Director	X			
Plant Supervisors (12)			X	
Outside salesperson 1				X
Outside salesperson 2				X
Outside salesperson 3			X	
Outside salesperson 4	X			
Outside salesperson 5			X	
Outside salesperson 6			X	
Total	7	1	11	5

Technology Map Sample 3

Type	Category	Vendor	Application Name	Version	Declining	Stable	New	Future
Application	Word Processing	Microsoft	Word	MS Office 2003		X		
	Spreadsheet	Microsoft	Excel	MS Office 2003		X		
	Database	Microsoft	Access	MS Office 2007		X	X	
		Microsoft	SQL Server	2000	X			
		Microsoft	SQL Server	2005		X		
	Presentation	Microsoft	PowerPoint	MS Office 2003		X		
		Adobe	Acrobat	6.0 Standard		X		
	Communications	Microsoft	Outlook	MS Office 2003		X		
	Graphic Design	Adobe	Photoshop	7.0		X		
		Adobe	ImageReady	7.0		X		
		Microsoft	Visio	MS 2006		X		
	Development Tools	Microsoft	Visual Studio	.NET (2003)	X			
		Microsoft	Visual Studio	2005			X	
		Sybase	PowerBuilder	9		X		
		Sybase	PowerBuilder	12				X
		SourceGear	Vault	3.5.1		X		
	Web Browsers	Microsoft	Internet Explorer	6.0		X		
		Microsoft	Internet Explorer	7.0			X	
		Mozilla	FireFox	5.0		X		
	Finance	Sage	MAS 500	7.0		X		
		Intuit	QuickBooks	2005 Premier		X		

Type	Category	Vendor	Application Name	Version	Declining	Stable	New	Future
System	Workstation	Microsoft	Windows	XP SP2		X		
		Microsoft	Windows	Vista				X
	Server	Microsoft	Windows	2000 Standard	X			
		Microsoft	Windows	2003 Standard		X		
		Microsoft	Windows	2003 Enterprise		X		
Utility	File Compression	Ipswitch Inc.	WS_FTP Pro	6.60		X		
	File Transfer	WinZip International LLC	WinZip	10.0		X		
	Anti-Virus	McAfee	VirusScan Enterprise	8.0i		X		
	Screen Capture	The Software Labs Inc.	ScreenPrint Gold	3.6		X		
		SOTI Inc.	PocketController Pro	5.02		X		

Asset Class	Subclass	Vendor	Model	Mfg Dt	Declining	Stable	New	Future
PC	Desktop	APEX	P4	6/25/2005			X	
PC	Desktop	Dell	DHM	9/30/2005			X	
PC	Desktop	Dell	Dimension 2400	6/26/2005			X	
PC	Desktop	Dell	Dimension E521	10/16/2006				X
PC	Desktop	Dell	Inspiron 1150	6/26/2005			X	
PC	Desktop	Dell	Inspiron 4150	9/13/2002	X			
PC	Desktop	Dell	Latitude C640	6/25/2005			X	
PC	Desktop	Dell	Optiplex	7/20/2005			X	
PC	Desktop	Gateway	450SX4	6/24/2005			X	
PC	Desktop	Gateway	600YGR	6/25/2005			X	
PC	Desktop	Gateway	ATXSTFFEDPRO933M	1/28/2001	X			
PC	Desktop	Gateway	E4200	5/31/2000	X			
PC	Desktop	Gateway	E4400	9/14/2000	X			
PC	Desktop	HP	d220 MT	4/1/2005			X	

(continued)

Technology Map Sample 3 (continued)

Asset Class	Subclass	Vendor	Model	Mfg Dt	Declining	Stable	New
PC	Desktop	Sony	Vaio PCVRX741	6/25/2005		X	
PC	Laptop	Acer	5002LMI	5/1/2005		X	
PC	Laptop	Dell	Inspiron 600m	9/1/2005		X	
PC	Laptop	Dell	Latitude D520	8/21/2006			X
PC	Laptop	Dell	Latitude D610	11/1/2005		X	
PC	Laptop	IBM	Thinkpad 32P44	4/1/2002	X		
PC	Laptop	IBM	Thinkpad A31 2652	8/1/2002	X		
PC	Notebook	FUJITSU	LifeBook P-series	6/25/2005		X	
Peripherals	Monitor	Acer	AL1515-1912series	4/1/2006			X
Peripherals	Monitor	Dell	1703FP-REVseries	8/1/2003	X		
Peripherals	Monitor	Gateway	DIAMONDTRONMFVX720	12/1/2000	X		
Peripherals	Monitor	NEC	ACCUSYNC120	10/1/2002	X		
Peripherals	Monitor	SHARP	L2-M17W1U	6/26/2005		X	
Peripherals	Monitor	SPETRE	1920B	6/26/2005		X	
Peripherals	Port Replicator	Dell	Port Replicator	9/13/2002	X		
Peripherals	Printer	HP	Business Inkjet 2200	8/28/2000	X		
Peripherals	Printer	HP	LaserJet 1320tn	8/1/2006			X
Peripherals	Printer	Lexmark	C750	8/1/2002	X		
Peripherals	Projector	Infocus	LP350	6/25/2005		X	
Peripherals	Scanner	HP	SCANJET 3970	6/26/2005		X	
Peripherals	Scanner	XEROX	DOCUMATE510	6/26/2005		X	
Peripherals	Tape Backup	CA	P4 2.8H	6/26/2005		X	
Peripherals	Tape Drive	Dell	CL1002	10/6/2006			X
Peripherals	Tape Drive	HP	E02010	10/1/2004		X	
Peripherals	UPS	APC	SHAREUPSAP9207	?		X	
Peripherals	UPS	APC	SMARTUPS700	6/24/2005		X	
Interface	Firewall	Cisco	ASA5520	3/1/2006			X
Interface	Firewall	Cisco	PIX 515E	8/1/2006			X
Interface	Hub	ATI	CENTRECOMFHT16SW	6/14/2005		X	

Category	Type	Manufacturer	Model	Date			
Interface	Hub	ATI	CENTRECOMFHT24SW	6/14/2005	X		
Interface	KVM	APC	COMPUSWITCH	6/26/2005	X		
Interface	Router	Cisco	1700	6/26/2005	X		
Interface	Router	Cisco	2500 SERIES	7/1/2005	X		
Interface	Security	Cisco	IDS-4215	6/26/2005	X		
Interface	Switch	3COM	3C16479	8/1/2006			
Interface	Switch	3COM	3C17302	6/26/2005	X		
Interface	Switch	3COM	SUPERSTACK3 3300XM	6/25/2005	X		
Interface	Switch	3COM	Superstack3 3870	2/6/2006			X
Interface	Switch	Dell	2161IDS	6/26/2005	X		
Interface	Switch	Dell	POWERCONNECT3324	6/26/2005	X		
Interface	Switch	XIRCOM	Net Station 8100	6/25/2005	X		
Interface	Switch (Core Switch)	3COM	Superstack3 3870	2/1/2005	X		
Interface	WAN Connector	ADTRAN	TSU ACE	?			
Server	Server	APEX	CELERON	6/21/2005	X		
Server	Server	APEX	P4	6/25/2005	X		
Server	Server	CA	P4 2.8H	6/26/2005	X		
Server	Server	CA	SEMPRON1.1	6/27/2005	X		
Server	Server	Dell	PowerEdge 1750	6/26/2005	X		
Server	Server	Gateway	ALR7200	11/10/1999		X	
Server	Server	Gateway	E4200	5/18/2000		X	
Server	Server	Gateway	GP7-500	8/31/1999		X	
Server	Server	HP	Proliant DL360	10/1/2004		X	
Server	Server	HP	Proliant DL380 G3	4/1/2004		X	
Server	Server	HP	Workstation xw6200	10/1/2004		X	
Server	Server	Speco	DVR16/IP	1/6/2006			X

Hardware and software list and standard assessment by Tammy Hein, Kutztown University. Used by permission.

Technology Map Sample 4

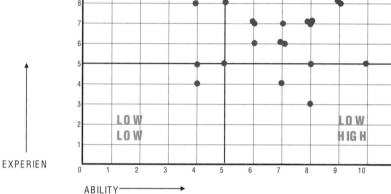

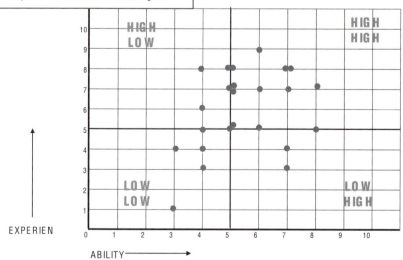

Sample 4 experience and ability assessments done by Michael Axman, Kutztown University. Used by permission.

APPENDIX B: COMMON TECHNOLOGY ISSUES MOST BUSINESS LEADERS EXPERIENCE

Do you have problems with ...	YES	NO	Cost
1. Tracking the time your programmers and technical engineers are working?	☐	☐	$
2. Projects going over budget, are underfeatured, or delivered late?	☐	☐	$
3. Tracking which projects are getting resources?	☐	☐	$
4. Properly prioritizing which projects should get resources?	☐	☐	$
5. Tracking requests for moves, adds, and changes to PCs and applications?	☐	☐	$
6. Balancing autonomy with cost-saving synergies such as standardization?	☐	☐	$
7. Setting expectations of people who use technology services at a reasonable level?	☐	☐	$
8. Measuring the performance of your people & systems?	☐	☐	$
9. Seeing the same problems come up again and again and again?	☐	☐	$
10. Making sure that you are not spending too much or too little on technology?	☐	☐	$
11. Implementing the most cost-effective solution to a technical problem?	☐	☐	$
12. Getting buy-in to a corporate technology initiative?	☐	☐	$
13. Getting users to actually USE the technology?	☐	☐	$
14. Matching skills of people to technologies & processes that they follow?	☐	☐	$
15. Approving technology projects in a timely manner?	☐	☐	$
16. Tracking the success of IT projects? Shutting down projects that are wasting time, money, and resources?	☐	☐	$
17. Comparing technology projects to determine which should get funded?	☐	☐	$
18. Quantifying the hard and soft dollar savings of projects?	☐	☐	$
19. Ensuring the safety and security of your systems?	☐	☐	$

Do you have problems with ...	YES	NO	Cost
20. Being confident in your disaster recovery plans? (Are you ready for another 9/11?)	☐	☐	$
21. Being confident in your business continuity plans? (Are you ready for another 9/11?)	☐	☐	$
22. Understanding government regulations regarding information within your systems?	☐	☐	$
23. Complying with GLBA or HIPAA?	☐	☐	$
24. Getting Line of Business (LOB) managers to understand and value technology?	☐	☐	$
25. Meeting the needs of the ultimate customer who uses the services or products?	☐	☐	$
26. Keeping up to date with new technologies?	☐	☐	$
27. Knowing which new technologies will help your business and when to invest in them?	☐	☐	$
28. Separating the vendor hype from the reality of what they can provide?	☐	☐	$
29. Taking advantage of globalization and standardization?	☐	☐	$
30. Optimizing your technology locally?	☐	☐	$
31. Understanding the needs of the business units?	☐	☐	$
32. Ensuring that your people are collaborating effectively?	☐	☐	$
33. Maintaining your Legacy Systems and planning for replacement systems?	☐	☐	$
34. Scoping and chunking projects or managing project milestones?	☐	☐	$
35. Communicating with others in the business?	☐	☐	$
36. Departments or technologies in use that are total messes?	☐	☐	$
37. Controlling technology experts and gurus?	☐	☐	$
38. Controlling technology "religious wars"?	☐	☐	$
39. Adopting bleeding edge technology?	☐	☐	$
40. Making sure all functions are covered when people leave (or are laid off)?	☐	☐	$

APPENDIX C: BASIC IT ABILITY AND EXPERIENCE SAMPLE ASSESSMENT

1. Can you start up, reboot, and shut down a computer?

2. Can you start and quit a program stored on the hard drive that is not on a menu?

3. Can you save and retrieve files to and from a floppy, USB, CD, or the hard drive?

4. Can you cut/copy text from one source and paste it into another?

5. Can you open, close and minimize menus and windows?

6. Can you move windows around on your desktop?

7. Can you resize windows on your desktop?

8. Can you create folders?

9. Can you navigate a directory structure to find files?

10. Can you rename files?

11. Can you delete files?

12. Do you have typing skills to produce at least 30-40 words per minute?

13. Can you create a word processing document using the various editing and formatting features?

14. Can you print a word processing document?

15. Can you use spell and grammar checking to revise your work?

16. Do you know how to log on to the Internet?

17. Do you know how to retrieve and delete e-mail messages?

18. Can you create, send, forward, reply and save e-mail messages?

19. Can you distinguish between an e-mail address and a Web address?

20. Can you send group mailings?

21. Do you know how to post messages to discussion lists?

22. Can you locate and access information using a WWW search engine?

23. Do you know how to save, modify, retrieve, and send an attachment to an e-mail?

24. Can you use talk or chat features for real-time communication?

25. Can you download and configure your Web browser with plug-ins such as Real Audio or Adobe Acrobat and use the bookmark features of your browser?

This assessment is a modification of the original (which can be found on: http://www.etech college.com/online/techskillsassess.htm). Used with permission.

References

1. Nordstrom, Bengt. 2004. Constructivism: A computing science perspective. Chalmers University of Technology and the University of Göteborg. http://www.cs.chalmers.se/~bengt/papers/vatican.pdf (accessed December 3, 2007).

2. DiMauro, Vanessa, and Ed Baum. 2003. PVN metrics and decision-making survey. Paper published by CXO Systems, Waltham, MA.

3. Collins, Jim. 2001. *Good to great: why some companies make the leap … and others don't.* New York: HarperCollins.

4. Carr, N. G. 2004. *Does IT matter? Information technology and the corrosion of competitive advantage.* Cambridge, MA: Harvard Business School Press.

5. Strassmann, P. A. 1997. *The squandered computer.* New Canaan, CT: The Information Economics Press.

6. Drucker, P. F. 2001. *The essential Drucker: Selections from the management works of Peter F. Drucker.* New York: HarperBusiness.

7. Drucker, P. F. 1987. *The frontiers of management: Where tomorrow's decisions are being shaped today.* New York: Perennial Library.

8. Peters, Thomas J., and Nancy Austin. 1986. *A passion for excellence: The leadership difference.* New York: Warner Books.

9. Aguayo, Rafael. 1990. *Dr. Deming: The American who taught the Japanese about quality.* Secaucus, NJ: Carol.

10. Covey, Stephen R. 2005. *The 8th habit: From effectiveness to greatness.* New York: Free Press.

11. Collins, James C., and William C. Lazier. 1992. *Beyond entrepreneurship: Turning your business into an enduring great company.* Englewood Cliffs, NJ: Prentice Hall.

12. Collins, James C., and Jerry I. Porras. 1994. *Built to last: Successful habits of visionary companies.* New York: HarperBusiness.

13. Hammer, Michael. 1996. *Beyond reengineering: How the process-centered organization is changing our work and our lives.* New York: HarperBusiness.

14. Weiss, Alan. 1995. *Our emperors have no clothes.* Franklin Lakes, NJ: Career Press.

15. Lane, D. 2004. *CIO wisdom: Best practices from Silicon Valley's leading IT experts.* Englewood Cliffs, NJ: Prentice Hall. Page 26 contains comments by Pat Anderson, CIO of Lockheed Martin's Space Systems.

16. Covey, S. R., A. R. Merrill, and R. R. Merrill. 1994. *First things first*. New York: Simon & Schuster.

17. Maloney, David. February 2004. Out the door in 7 minutes. *Modern Materials Handling*. 59:18–23.

18. Chad Dickerson. July 11, 2005. CTO connection. *Infoworld* 27, no. 2.

19. Soja, P., July 2006. Success factors in ERP systems implementations: Lessons from practice. *Journal of Enterprise Information Management*. 19:418–33.

20. Gattiker, Thomas F., and Dale L. Goodhue. 2005. "What happens after ERP implementation: Understanding the impact of inter-dependence and differentiation on plant-level outcomes." *MIS Quarterly*. 29:559–85.

21. Khosla, Vinod, and Murugan Pal. 2001. Real time enterprises: A continuous migration approach. *Information Knowledge Systems Management*. 3:53–80.

22. Grey, Vince. *Setting standards: A phenomenal success story*. http://www.iso.org/iso/en/aboutiso/introduction/fifty/pdf/settingen.pdf (accessed on July 3, 2007).

23. Taylor, Suzanne, Kathy Schroeder, and John Doerr. 2003. *Inside Intuit: How the makers of Quicken beat Microsoft and revolutionized an entire industry*. Cambridge, MA: Harvard Business School Press.

24. Erik Brynjolfsson, now a doctoral graduate from MIT Sloan School of Management, did a study on "Intangible Assets: How the Interaction of Computers and Organizational Structure Affects Stock Market Valuations." A paper based on his dissertation was published in *Brookings Papers on Economic Activity*, compiled by Laura Hitt Brynjolfsson from the Wharton School at the University of Pennsylvania, and Shinkyu Yang from Stern School at New York University.

25. Nay, Douglas L. 2003. An empirical study of the effects of enterprise solutions of profitability and internationalization. PhD diss., Lubin School of Business.

26. Drucker, Peter, Howard Raiffa, Alden M. Hayashi, Ralph L. Keeney, and John S. Hammond. 2001. *Harvard Business Review on executive decision making*. Cambridge, MA: Harvard Business School Press.

27. Kaplan, Robert S., and David P. Norton. 1996. *The balanced scorecard: Translating strategy into action*. Cambridge, MA: Harvard Business School Press, 1996.

28. Gladwell, Malcolm. 2002. *The tipping point: How little things can make a big difference*. Boston: Back Bay Books.

29. Institute for Telecommunication Sciences. *Glossary of telecommunication terms*. http://www.atis.org/tg2k/ (accessed January 14, 2007).

30. Friedman, T. 2005. *The world is flat: A brief history of the twenty-first century*. New York: Farrar, Straus and Giroux.

31. Cerf, V., and B. Kahn. September 30, 2000. IP: Al Gore's support of the Internet. http://www.interesting-people.org/archives/interesting-people/200009/msg00052.html (accessed June 7, 2007).

32. Sander, T., and P. Taylor. 2006. *Place matters: Geographically enabling government*. Folsom, CA: The Center for Digital Government. Available at http://www.centerdigitalgov.com/story.php?id=100608 (accessed December 3, 2007)

33. Fishkin, R., and J. Pollard. 2007. *Search engine ranking factors*. http://www.seomoz.org/article/search-ranking-factors#f3 (accessed June 8, 2007).

Index

Abdication (dangers of), 5–8, 45–48, 85–103, 104–7

Ability: assessment, 44–45; formula for, 80, 104–7; matching to, 51, 69; people, 22, 39–42, 56–60; related to process, 71–73; technical literacy, 6–10; trainer, 48–50; vendor, 85–89, 100, 116, 123–24; Web pages, 130–50

Accelerator, 34, 159. *See also* Collins, Jim

Access, 50, 112–13. *See also* Database; Microsoft

Adobe (Frontpage, GoLive), 141

Advance shipping notices, 19

Advice: from consultants, 2, 27–29, 53, 66–74, 89, 97, 108–11, 129, 130–50; how to use book, 18; on giving free, 108; on process, 66–72; pounce, 18–37. *See also* Vendors

Algorithm, 58, 80, 110

Amazon, 29, 144–48. *See also* E-commerce

Anti-virus, 30, 132

Apple (Macintosh), 27, 34, 36, 39

Applications. *See* Browsers, Contact management, Calendar, Databases, Spreadsheet, Word processing

Ashton-Tate, 125. *See also* Databases

Assessment, 2; people's ability, 43–44, 70; performance scorecard, 82; process, 67–75

Authorize.Net, 148. *See also* E-commerce

Bank: banking industry, 5, 17; connection to Web site, 140–48; example story, 5–6, 127, 148, 155; funding ideas, 94–95

Barrett, Edward (Hi-TECH Connections), 36

Bergman, Larry (Boscov's), 18

Berners-Lee, Timothy, 131. *See also* World Wide Web

Big Green Egg, 148. *See also* Virtual community

Bleeding edge, 18–20, 99–101, 126–32. *See also* Vaporware; Marketecture

BPM (business process management), 56; process example, 67–74

Breadcrumbs (using in communication), 81–83

Brochureware, 108, 134, 139–42. *See also* Web sites

Browsers (Explorer, Firefox, Safari, Netscape), 10, 31–32, 131–33

Business process engineer, 68, 75. *See also* Processes

Buzzwords, 1, 5, 55. *See also* Technology jargon

Cailliau, Robert, 131. *See also* World Wide Web

Calculating shipping costs, 29–31. *See also* ROI

Calendar (online), 32–35, 68
Capitalization, 7, 101–3; of standards, 23; venture capital, 27, 123. *See also* ROI
Carter, Rob (Federal Express), 17–19
Cerf, Vint, 131. *See also* TCP/IP
Colgate & Palmolive, impact of mergers, 87–88
Collins, Jim (*Good to Great*), 20–21, 36, 83, 142. *See also* Hedgehog concept
Commodity, 109–111. *See also* Product cycle
Commodore (personal computer), 87
Compaq, impact of acquisitions, 123
Competitive advantage, 18–37, 42, 110–21, 140–45. *See also* ROI
Computer: mainframe, 1, 6, 9–10, 27, 32, 39, 61–62; memory problems with, 30, 132; personal computer, 1, 22, 27, 30, 44, 115. *See also individual applications;* Operating System; Information Technology Map
Computer Educational Services, 36
Contact management, 13, 33, 44
Cost: how standards lower, 110–111; of competing standards, 23–29, 62–63, 117–18; of ignorance, 2, 42–46, 67; of inventory, 11–15; of replacing people, 52–54; of resistance, 47–48; of training, 49–51; of typing, 34,46; relationship to product cycle, 111–115. *See also* Calculating shipping costs; Natural language
Covey, Stephen, 18
CRM (Customer Relationship Management), 21, 35, 47, 56, 91
Culture (IT industry), 7, 42, 52–63
Customer service, 21, 31, 37, 155. *See also* CRM
Customized software, 23, 42, 61, 102, 111, 126–27. *See also* Vaporware; Web developers

Database, 8–10, 15, 51, 55, 109, 141–43; Access, 50, 112–13; DB2, 8–10, 112–13; MySQL, 142; Oracle, 8–10, 63, 88, 112–13; SQL, 8–10, 112–13; Sybase, 8–10, 112–13

Data General, 88, 113, 122–23
DB2, 8–10, 112–13. *See also* Database
DEC (mainframe), 87, 123
Decision maker: CEO (role as), 4, 11, 17, 35, 39, 47, 62, 78–89, 95, 100–102, 108, 124–26; CFO (role as), 12, 21, 79, 108; CIO (role as), 17, 21, 46, 53, 63, 78–89, 108, 129, 130, 162; Decision-making process, 11, 76, 131, 133
Dell, 22, 87–88, 117
Dickerson, Chad, 22
Dilbert, 43
Dirty data, 93–94
Disaster recovery, 3, 148
Distribution list, 13, 154–58
Documentation, importance of, 105–6
Domain: name, 138–59; registrar, 108, 137; top-level, 135
Driver (device instruction file), 7, 98; definition, 57

Ebay, 29, 144–47
E-commerce, 88–89, 125, 134, 142–47; credit card processing, 9, 32, 145–47
E-mail: 31, 133, 150–55; blind copy, 151, 153; request receipts, 151, 154; spam, 137, 151–56
EMC, 88, 113, 119, 122–23
Encryption, 147, 150
ENIAC, 85
ERP (enterprise resource planning system), 21–23, 48, 56, 88; impact of capitalization rules, 102, 126–27
Ethernet, 52, 63, 116–17; GigaEthernet, 25, 115–18; versus Token Ring, 23–25, 63, 115
Excel, 48, 65, 108. *See also* Microsoft; Spreadsheet
Expansion phase, 112–21, 129
Extranet, 134, 147–48, 150. *See also* Internet; Protocols

Feasibility, technological, 16, 19, 37; financial, 19, 25. *See also* ROI
Federal Express, 17–19, 31

First-mover advantage, 29
Flash drive (storage device), 56
Free advice, 108. *See also* Advice
Friedman, Thomas (*The World Is Flat*), 130
Frontpage (Adobe), 141

GAAP (Generally Accepted Accounting Principles) 49. *See also* Capitalization
Gap, 39–43, 47–48, 50–51, 126; communication gap, 81–82; exploited by IT, 60–62; financial accounting rule, 102; regarding vendors, 104–6. *See also* Commodity; E-mail; Hype; Immaturity
Generations, 81, 99, 112–21, 129–31
GigaEthernet (Gigabit ethernet), 26, 116–18
GIGO (garbage in garbage out), 65, 91
Gladwell, Malcolm (*Tipping Point*), 109
Go Daddy, 108; as Web hoster, 130–34
Google, 56, 133–36, 143–44
Granularity, 145
Graphic format (importance of optimizing), JPG (JPEG), 136
Guru, 51–57, 59–62, 88–89, 98

Hard-coded, 127. *See also* Reusability
Hedgehog concept, 14–24, 32, 35–36, 128–129; communication of, 80; definition of, 17–20; Internet strategy for, 144, 159; using with IT, 59–64. *See also* Collins, Jim
Help desk, 58, 98, 125
Hewlett-Packard (HP), 32, 56
Hi-TECH Connections, 36
Hole (missing feature), 16, 28–35
Hosting, 29–30, 133–50. *See also* Web, hosting; (World Wide Web)
HTML (HyperText Markup Language), 139, 147. *See also* Web site; World Wide Web
Hype, 102–3, 111, 129; examples of, 6, 33–34, 116; Hypometer, 124–26; why vendors hype, 89–94
Hypometer, 124–26

IBM (International Business Machines), 8, 18, 25–26, 87, 115
IEEE, 23–26. *See also* Standards bodies
Immaturity, 26–27, 85–89, 97–99, 104–17, 120–31
Incompatibility, 1, 47–48, 66–74
Information technology map, 1, 156; difficulty of sharing, 10; importance of, 5–15, 22, 29; used in decision making, 78, 90, 104–7; used to define standards, 110–12
Internet: private, 86, 96; protocols, 7, 25–26, 34, 53, 96, 150; public, 56, 79, 86, 93–97, 103–11, 133–59; strategy, 136, 142, 146, 156
Intranet, 134, 149–53, 156
Intuit, 29, 149, 162; Quickbooks, 29, 149
Inventory, 46, 89, 121, 141–46, 150; importance of, 11–15; linking to Web site, 31–32; phantom, 13

JD Edwards (Oracle), 88. *See also* ERP
JPG (JPEG, Graphic format), 88

Kahn, Bob, 131. *See also* TCP/IP
Kinesthetic (communication), 38, 79

Lands' End (E-commerce example), 145
Layers (of information technology map), 5, 8, 12, 118, 128
Leading edge. *See* bleeding edge

Macintosh computer (Apple), 27, 34, 36
Mainframe computer, 1, 6, 9–10, 27, 32, 39, 61–62
Maintenance, 48, 59, 93, 103, 110, 113–14, 124, 132; patches, 59, 114, 121; releases, 114–16; upgrades, 13, 59, 100, 114, 116, 119, 120–24
Map. *See* Information technology map
Marketecture, 91, 127–30
Matrixed staffing (dangers of), 58
Melcher, Raymond (Hi-TECH Connections), 36

Memory management (640K barrier), 30. *See also* Computer
Microsoft, 21, 25, 44, 53, 56; marketing practice of, 87, 91, 99, 109, 110–14, 121–23, 135, 141; Windows versus open source, 54, 62–63
Middleware (software), 88, 145
Mismatch. *See* incompatibility
Motivation of IT people, 56–63
Musser, Warren "Pete" (Safeguard Scientifics), 36. *See also* Novell
Mutual mystification, 61–62, 107–8
MySQL, 142. *See also* Database

Natural language, 35, 92, 104; costs of typing, 34; transcription of, 20, 35, 94
.Net (Microsoft, pronounced "dot net"), 90–91. *See also* Marketecture
Netscape, 30, 125. *See also* Browser
Network: definition, 133; relationships, 130–41. *See also* Ethernet; Internet; TCP/IP
NIH (not invented here) syndrome, 60
Novell (Netware), 25, 36, 62, 121, 150
NT. *See* Operating systems; Windows, NT

Obsfuscation, 85, 89. *See also* Technology jargon
Off-the-shelf software, 102. *See also* Customized software
OLAP (on-line analytical processing), 66–70
Operating systems, 5, 25, 29, 35, 53–63, 87, 99, 100–123, 132; NT, 10, 62, 112–3, 121–2; Unix, 10–12, 117, 121; Vista, 117, 120, 123; Windows, 9–12, 29, 32, 55–56, 62, 99, 150; XP, 10, 55, 99–100, 117–19, 120, 123
Oracle, 8–10, 63, 88, 112, 113. *See also* Database, ERP
Outsource, 90, 128

PayPal, 147–49. *See also* E-commerce
PDA (personal digital assistant), 32, 68
Peoplesoft (Oracle), 88. *See also* ERP

Recognition (of people), 34, 49, 57, 63–65, 94
Performance scorecard, 82
Processes, 1–2, 14–16, 32, 47, 66–67, 76, 87, 97; Internet strategy, 131, 147, 153; reengineering, 82–83
Process reengineering, 83
Product cycle (product life cycle), 111–14, 120, 131
Productivity, 39–54, 79–87, 120, 122, 150; formula for, 58, 80, 110
Protocols, 7, 25–26, 34, 53, 96, 150. *See also* Ethernet, TCP/IP, Token Ring

Quickbooks (Intuit), 29, 149
Quality Management (Total Quality Management, TQM), 83
Quality of Service (QoS), 56. *See also* TCP/IP; Videoconference

Requirements documents, 12
Resistance, 47–48, 51
Reusability, 60–61
ROI, 23; calculation of risk, 2–6; capitalization (rules of), 7, 101–3; cost of lost opportunity, 4, 12, 43, 82, 89, 108–9, 120, 128, 151; impact on decisions, 5, 6, 12, 21–22; impact on training, 44–47, 51; replacement of IT staff, 61; residual value, 101–3
Rules of thumb, 93, 104, 154

Safeguard Scientifics, 36. *See also* Novell
Search engines, 53, 125, 143, 144, 162; rules, 143
Security, 30–31, 111, 147
Simplification, 113
Six Sigma, 82, 100, 112
SLA (service level agreement), 97–98, 126
Smith, Fred (Federal Express), 17
Smooth-running system, 59–60, 117
SOA (Service Oriented Architecture), 91
Society for Information Management, 89, 157
Spam, 139, 152–55

Speed of change, 40, 101, 103. *See also* Immaturity; Productivity, formula for
Spreadsheet, 15, 41, 46, 60, 101
Spyware, 29. *See also* Anti-virus
SQL, 8–10, 112–13. *See also* Database; Microsoft
Standards bodies, 16, 23–26, 36–37, 59, 112
Star Trek example, 3, 92
Sybase, 8–10, 112–13. *See also* Database
Syntax (command line), 57

TCP/IP, 25, 60, 132, 147. *See also* Internet; Protocols
Technology jargon, 7; buzzwords, 1, 5, 55; obfuscation, 85, 89
Technology wars, 62–63
Tipping point, 109
Token Ring versus Ethernet, 23–25, 62, 118. *See also* Protocols
TQM (Total Quality Management), 83
Training (importance of), 3, 22, 35, 42–58, 70, 87, 94, 102, 108, 122, 129, 130, 134

Unbiased consultants, 97, 111
Unix, 8, 10–12, 115, 119. *See also* Operating system
Unrealistic expectations, 3, 89, 93–96, 104, 128
URL (Universal Resource Locator), 57

Vaporware, 90, 115, 127–30
Vendor, 5, 9, 86; Long-term partnership, 79, 106, 111, 124–26, 132, 159; negotiation, 99, 122–25; proposals, 107
VHS versus Beta, 23–24
Videoconference, 28–32, 35. *See also* Hype

Virtual, 11, 52, 56, 57, 134, 136, 147; storage, 28–30. *See also* Virtual community
Virtual community, 43, 148–56; Facebook, 148–49; LinkedIn, 43, 148–49; MySpace.com, 148–49
Vision, 16–21, 32–37, 76, 80–92. *See also* Covey, Stephen; Collins, Jim
VOIP (Voice over Internet Protocols), 27. *See also* Hype
VPN (virtual private network), 147

Webcast, 116–18
Web: developers, 61, 88, 139–43; hosting, 10, 29–30, 133–50; language (HTML), 142, 149; page, 130–52; server, 8; site, 130–52; Webcast, 116–18, World Wide Web, 22, 46, 133–59. *See also* Berners-Lee, Timothy; Cailliau, Robert; Guru
Web page, 130–52
Web server, 8, 29–30, 133–50
Web site, 130–52
Windell, 115. *See also* Dell; Microsoft; Windows
Windows, 9–12, 28, 30, 55–56, 62, 99, 150; NT, 10, 62, 112–13, 121–22; Vista, 115, 118–21; XP, 10, 55, 99–100, 115–17, 120, 123. *See also* Operating system
Word processing: Wang, 109, 110; Word, 44, 47, 50, 109, 110; Word-Perfect, 35, 110, 118
The World Is Flat (Friedman, Thomas), 130
World Wide Web, 22, 46, 133–59

Y2K (Year 2000), 12–13
Yellow pages, 135

About the Author

CJ RHOADS is a well-known guru, speaker, and author on making better decisions about business strategy and technology. Rhoads is the founder of ETM Associates, Inc., a consulting firm specializing in enterprise decision making, management, and technology. She's also an Associate Professor in the College of Business at Kutztown University, as well as the author of over a hundred published articles, dozens of manuals and whitepapers, and two books.